Book for
Present for

8:00

I am the

In Search of
the Loving God

In Search of the Loving God

Resolving the past traumas of Christianity,
and bringing to light its healing spirit

Mark Mason

Dwapara Press   *Eugene, Oregon*

In Search of the Loving God

First Printed November 1997

10 9 8 7 6 5 4 3 2 1

Printed in the United States of America

Publisher's Cataloging-in-Publication Data

Mason, Mark, 1953-
    In search of the loving God : resolving the past traumas of Christianity, and bringing to light its healing spirit / Mark Mason. — 1st ed.
    p. cm.
    Includes bibliographical references and index.
    ISBN 0-9658477-4-8
    1. God—Love. 2. Theology, Doctrinal—History.
  3. Christianity and other religions. 4. Church History.
  5. Salvation. I. Title.
BT140.M37 1997   231'.6
                    QBI97-40847

Library of Congress Catalog Card Number: 97-68386

Dwapara Press
5264 Overbrook Lane
Eugene, Oregon 97405

The author may be contacted by e-mail
at: mark_mason@compuserve.com

All Scripture quotations in this publication, unless otherwise noted, are from the Holy Bible, New International Version. Copyright © 1973, 1978, 1984 by International Bible Society.

Some Scripture quotations, where noted, are from THE JERUSALEM BIBLE, copyright © 1966 by Darton, Longman & Todd, Ltd. and Doubleday, a division of Bantam Doubleday Dell Publishing Group, Inc. Reprinted by permission.

Acknowledgment of all other quoted material is made on the Credits page, overleaf. I thank all these publishers for their kind permission.

Dedicated to a society come of age,
and to my wife Joanne, who has been so supportive and
helpful to me in the process of creating this book.

Credits:

Self-Realization Fellowship, for permission to use quotes from Paramahansa Yogananda and Sri Yukteswar from Paramahansa Yogananda's books *Autobiography of a Yogi*, *The Divine Romance*, *Songs of the Soul* and *Spiritual Diary*, and a quote from Sri Daya Mata from *Self-Realization Magazine*.

Colin Smythe Ltd, for permission to quote four lines from *Medieval Irish Lyrics* by James Carney (Dolmen Press, 1967).

Thames & Hudson Ltd, for a quote from *The Crucible of Christianity* by Arnold Toynbee. Copyright © 1969 by Arnold Toynbee.

Hodder & Staughton, for quotes from *Crack In the Wall* by Jackie Pullinger. Copyright © 1989 by Jackie Pullinger. Reproduced by permission of Hodder & Staughton Ltd./New English Library Ltd.

New Statesman Magazine for quotes from "God the Sod" by Jeanette Winterson, May 10, 1991.

Vedanta Society of Southern California, for quotes from *The Sermon on the Mount According to Vedanta*, by Swami Prabhavananda, and *Bhagavad-Gita, The song of God*, by Swami Prabhavananda and Christopher Isherwood.

Crystal Clarity Publications for a quote from *The Path* by Swami Kriyananda.

Lennard Publishing, for quotes from *Are These the Words of Jesus?* by Ian Wilson (1990).

The World Community for Christian Meditation, for quotes from their publicity material and the writings of Laurence Freeman.

Simon & Schuster, for quotes from *Why I am Not a Christian* by Bertrand Russell. Copyright 1957 by George Allen & Unwin Ltd. Reprinted by permission.

The Lost years of Jesus by Elizabeth Clare Prophet. Copyright © 1984, 1987 Summit University Press, P.O. Box 5000-5000, Corwin Springs, Montana U.S.A. All rights reserved. Used by permission of Summit University Press.

3 QUOTES from *The Religions of Man* by HUSTON SMITH. Copyright © 1958 by Huston Smith. Copyright renewed 1986 by Huston Smith. Reprinted by permission of HarperCollins Publishers, Inc.

A QUOTE from *A Return to Love* by Marianne Williamson. Copyright © 1992 by Marianne Williamson. Reprinted by permission of HarperCollins Publishers, Inc.

A quote from *The Dead Sea Scrolls in English* by Geza Vermes (Third Edition 1987) Copyright © Geza Vermes, 1962, 1965, 1968, 1975, 1987. Reproduced by permission of Penguin Books, Ltd., Harmondsworth, UK.

A quote from *Islam* by Alfred Guillaume (Second revised edition 1956) Copyright © the estate of Alfred Guillaume, 1954, 1956. Reproduced by permission of Penguin Books, Ltd., Harmondsworth, UK.

Quotes from *Christianity and Other Religions* edited by John Hick and Brian Hebblethwaite (Collins Fount, Glasgow, 1980). Reprinted by permission of HarperCollins Publishers Ltd.

Portion from *A Course in Miracles* ® © 1975 Reprinted by Permission of the Foundation for Inner Peace, Inc. P.O. Box 598 Mill Valley, California 94942.

Acknowledgments

When I started writing this book, I had the idea that writing is a solitary pursuit. Once I had finished it, revising it many times, and including into it suggestions made by people who kindly read it and encouraged me to persevere and make sure it was published, I realized writing is in many respects a cooperative effort. I could not have completed and published this book without the help I have obtained from many people. My thanks and appreciation go out to all of them.

Those whose help and encouragement have been crucial to this book are: my wife Joanne, my father, my mother, Bob Decker, John Lawrence, Kaya Stasch, Peter Stasch, Marcia Hildreth, Cynthia Blanche, Frank Steinke, Ian Baynes, Ron Ngata, and Kate Blanche.

Many others have helped me in important ways during the years I have been writing this book and endeavoring to get it published, either directly with the book, or in other ways which made it possible for me to continue with the project. I would also like to thank them. They include: Yvonne Baynes, Helen Blanche, Joseph Boehle, Jane Dillon, Bev Doak, Joan Evans, Cathy Fields, Paul Finkel, Marguretta Gannon, Barbara Ghem, Adam Handwerger, Marilyn Hartmann, Nick Hodgson, Marcia Jerath, Adam Kreindel, Karen Lawrence, Trish Lees, Amber Mailer, Rosalind Mailer, Isobel Morel, Julie Morrison, Adam Neidig, Kaethlyn Nimmick, Jeff Pasternack, Ian Potterton, Prema de Silva, Roxanne Purdy, Patty Sanders, Janelle Schaefer, Alan Smith, Margaret Smith, Annette Swanton, Terry Sweeney, Alicia Uteg, and Eve Woodward.

What has been passing for Christianity during these nineteen centuries is merely a beginning, full of weaknesses and mistakes, not a full-grown Christianity springing from the spirit of Jesus.

Albert Schweitzer

Contents

Part 1

Remembering—Ancient Inspiration and Medieval Abuse

Chapter 1

Seeking a Direction

There is a widespread and growing interest in the spiritual in the world today. Perhaps this is because so many people have known the pleasures affluence can bring, and have worked past an all-consuming desire for material things. And having lived through the sexual revolution, many people know how empty sensual satisfaction can be of itself, when divorced from deeper meaning in their lives. Experience of these things tells people that the pleasure they bring isn't the ultimate joy they are looking for — that there must be something more. So people everywhere are looking to add a spiritual dimension to their lives, sensing that this is where the ultimate in happiness, joy and meaning will be found.

In this situation one would think people would be flocking to churches in their millions to find that "peace of God which passeth all understanding." But most new spiritual seekers are not coming to the Christian church — they are going to Eastern religions or New Age organizations. Why? There is widespread concern about this in the churches. The question comes up again and again: "When are we going to have revival in the West? It's happening in Third World countries, but not here." One line of speculation is that our rationalistic education is a hindrance to the spirit, as it causes people to think too much, rather than having a simple "childlike" faith. Is it as simple as this, or are there more complex reasons?

This book will look at some of the reasons people who have chosen alternate spiritual paths give for why the church is unable to meet their needs. And it will analyze these criticisms in the light of the Bible, and of a study of church history, to see to what extent they are valid, and what can be learned from them. If the church could change in some ways to meet the objections of the disaffected, and at the same time become more like the original church of the Book of Acts, and be more in tune with Jesus' teachings, wouldn't this be beneficial? I believe there are areas of doctrine and attitude in the church which could be examined with this in mind. Many Christians may not immediately and wholeheartedly embrace this view, but I do hope this book will at least stimulate thought and discussion within the church. I also hope it will give some of those who have belonged to the church, but have become disillusioned and left it, some further insight into how the church has let them down, and into how a reformed church may once again meet their spiritual needs.

It will help to approach this book with an open mind, and not be too quick to judge it, because — I give warning in advance — many of the attitudes and beliefs discussed are ones we take for granted in the church, are comfortable with, and may even revere. I will not be sentimental about any of our hallowed "traditions of men," unless they can also be proven, from Biblical evidence, to be "commands of God." (Mark 7:8) If a traditional belief is obstructing the church and people's lives, and has no sound foundation in Scripture, what reason is there for keeping it? Should we continue to let such beliefs eat away at the church like cancers, pretending there's no problem with them? I am suggesting that if a lot of people are saying there is a problem, we should carefully and objectively examine what they have to say, and not just reject their suggestions out of hand. We can benefit by asking ourselves which of our beliefs are a part of our faith, and which are just prejudices. However, I believe the Bible should remain our touchstone throughout, and I will not be entertaining any ideas which are out of tune with it. I will feel free, though, to adopt new interpretations of the Bible, where they can be shown to be superior to the old. I don't accept the traditional criticism of Christianity that its shortcomings are a result of it being based on a flawed Bible. After much study of the Bible, and the scholarship surrounding it, I believe the Bible is an inspired Scripture, capable of being the basis for a truly vital religion, meeting the spiritual needs of our time. Rather, I will be proposing that the main problem with Christianity is that it is not, as it claims to be, properly based on the Bible at all, and that the time has come to rectify this.

I will not be concentrating on the policies and doctrines of particular denominations, though they may come up, but rather on attitudes and practices which are prevalent in many parts of the church. Churches are made up of individual people, and ultimately it is their attitudes, beliefs and actions which are important. My purpose is not to tear down the church, but to build it up. I love Christianity, and wish to see it prosper and become the life blood of Western nations.

Although much of this book is devoted to examining some of the beliefs and practices of the church which attract criticism, and proposing alternatives to them, it will start with a number of chapters of Bible and church history, in order to give an insight into how the church's modern body of doctrine was formed. This is important, as much of what has come into question in the church is doctrine, and the historical context of the introduction of a doctrine can be a significant factor in its validity. If it can be shown, for instance, that a particular doctrine was introduced in a climate where the church was seeking to expand its political power, that the doctrine would have helped this quest for power, and that it is a distortion of what the Bible actually says, this would seem to be good grounds for abandoning it.

Another reason for looking into the church's past is that it is much easier to understand the problems of the modern church if they can be seen in the light of its history. It also gives us an opportunity to examine the way the Bible relates history, and to learn from it something about how to validly interpret the Bible. Points of history could just have been mentioned within the chapters examining the church's current problems. History is, however, a chain of cause and effect, and cannot be convincing when presented in too piecemeal a way. As Arnold Toynbee said, "...like persons, events and movements and institutions have to be observed on the move through time in order to be comprehended."[1] This is why the first third of the book' is Bible and church history. It is there to provide a solid foundation for a new way of looking at Christianity. The reader is invited to look for the roots of modern problems, and the seeds of possible solutions to them, in this history, and anticipate some of the discussion in the second part of the book.

Chapter 2

Ancient Israel — the Seeds of Christianity

Formative influences on Christianity start right back in the most ancient history of Israel. This was a time of synthesis, when many influences molded Judaism. Cross-fertilization with other religions produced a strong hybrid Jewish religion.[1]

Archaeology catches up with the nation of Israel for the first time at the border line between the bronze and iron ages (about 1200 B.C.), just after Moses led his people to the Promised Land, and about the time Joshua is said to have sacked Jericho. At this time, just as the Bible says, the ancient nation of Canaan was destroyed. Archaeology shows it was not destroyed by the Israelites, though, but by marauders from the north, who went on to attack Egypt. In the end only Egypt's armies were strong enough to stop them. After their defeat, one of these tribes settled along the coast of Canaan. The Egyptians called them the Peleset. The Bible calls them the Philistines, the mortal enemies of ancient Israel. They were excellent artists, made fine pottery, and were good metal workers, not really "philistine" at all.[2]

At this time comes the first mention of the Israelites by an ancient source. In the Cairo museum is a large slab of engraved black granite, the "Israel Stela." It was inscribed in 1207 B.C., and contains a victory hymn telling about a war Pharaoh Merneptah's army fought in Canaan. It says in part:

> The fortress city of Askelon is taken,
> The fortress city of Gezer is captured,
> The fortress city of Yano'am is now non-existent,
> The people of Israel lie desolate, their seed is no more.

Israel is not called a fortress city, but rather "a people," signifying a nomadic community or tribe. The Bible talks about the Israelites of this time living in the hills, and mention is made of

mountain streams and caves. When archaeologists looked in
the hills of Palestine, back from the coastal plains the Philistines
occupied, they indeed found the remains of open, unfortified
settlements. Water must have been scarce, for they had large
storage tanks under their houses. It is clear that the occupants
were resourceful, intelligent, people living a hard life as
settlers.

Although this is the earliest picture archaeology gives, the
first five books of the Bible, the *Pentateuch*, detail a history of
the Israelites long before this, as a sub-group with its own
identity in Canaan, and then in Egypt. This earlier history isn't
directly backed up by any evidence outside the Bible, but it is
largely consistent with the Israelites' cultural links with Canaan, and the known history of the time. The Genesis accounts
of Creation, Adam and Eve, and the Flood are very similar to
Babylonian and many other legends from places as far away as
India, where these stories are recounted in the ancient Hindu
epic the *Mahabharata*. These accounts are a part of what seems
to be a common set of beliefs held by all Semitic (pre-Aryan)
peoples, and this suggests these peoples all had a common
origin in one area—around Babylon in Mesopotamia. Genesis
10 proposes this too. From this point on, though, with Abraham, a separate Israelite history emerges. Genesis 11 and 12
describe how, a number of generations after the flood, Abraham left Ur, in Lower Mesopotamia, and finally settled Canaan. Abraham's descendants continued to live in Canaan until
Jacob and his clan of about one hundred people followed his
son Joseph into Egypt. This pre-Egyptian period is quite possibly when the Israelites gained many of the Canaanite aspects
of their culture, including their early written language. For a
few generations the children of Israel lived in Egypt, and pros-
pered and multiplied. After Joseph's death they became enslaved and persecuted until Moses led them back into Canaan.
The war with the marauders from the north, which destroyed
the Canaanites and severely threatened Egypt, provided the
opportunity the Israelites needed to escape from Egypt and
claim part of what had been Canaan as their "Promised Land."

This story paints a picture of the early Israelites living in Canaan but not really seeing themselves as a part of it, and explains how they could have fought against Canaan for a homeland when their own written language and civilization had its roots there. It also explains why these tribes of escaped slaves were able to take land from the Canaanites: it was possible only because Canaan had been recently defeated and severely weakened by invaders from the north.

While this general reading of Genesis and Exodus lines up well with what is known of history and archaeology, certain specific statements do not. For instance, the book of Exodus claims the "sons of Israel" spent 430 years in Egypt, and that they were "about six hundred thousand on the march—all men —not counting their families" and that "people of various sorts joined them in great numbers." (Ex 12:37–40 JB)[3] This adds up to at least two million people, almost equal to the whole population of ancient Egypt at the time! If there had been such a preponderance of Jewish slaves in Egypt, there would certainly have been extensive mention of them in the numerous and detailed written records the Egyptians left. Yet there is no mention at all of the children of Israel in Egypt. Also, if that many people, and their "flocks...and herds in immense droves" (Ex 12:38 JB), had spent forty years wandering in the deserts of the Sinai, there would be archaeological evidence of their journey in abundance. This is an area where the extremely dry climate has preserved tiny traces of 6,000-year-old Bedouin winter camps, including flint tools and arrow heads, and ash and bones.[4] Two million people would have meant a caravan 600 miles long, yet there is no trace of the Exodus left in the desert.[5]

The Bible's statement of the size of the Exodus is not only challenged by lack of historical records and archaeological evidence, it is also brought into question by the Exodus story itself. On the basis of the story that the fall into slavery occurred not that long after Joseph died, "under a new king who did not know about Joseph" (Exodus 1:8), we can reasonably (though not certainly) estimate the length of the Israelites' stay in Egypt to be just a few generations. Even assuming, as there is some scholarly basis for doing, that they were there eight generations,[6] and that their numbers doubled each generation, the seventy or so descendants of Jacob who entered Egypt could only have grown to twenty thousand, at most, by the time of the Exodus. Another suggestion is that there were really just six hundred men and their families, not six hundred thousand. This would have meant about five or six thousand people, about what the land of Goshen, where the Israelites lived in Egypt, would have held.[7]

However, even if the numbers the Bible states are wrong, this is not to say the rest of the story is fictional, and the Israelites never were in Egypt — the intimate knowledge of Egypt revealed in the book of Exodus makes it virtually certain that some of the Israelites, at least, spent time there.[8] This is a Jewish history of the origin of their nation and their relationship with God, written many centuries later, and it seems likely that the number of people involved in the Exodus was exaggerated to mythical proportions to emphasize the vital importance to them of the event, and of the original tribes involved in it.[9] This sort of emphasis on the spirit of the truth about an event, at the expense of its letter, is a trend right through the Bible, and has to be taken into account if the Bible is to be properly understood.

Perhaps archaeology will one day provide specific evidence of the Israelites' stay in Egypt and their Exodus, but, in the meanwhile, careful analysis of the Bible, combined with archaeology and a study of surrounding civilizations, has revealed quite a lot about ancient Israel, its institutions and customs, and where they came from. What has been revealed is that, along with their knowledge of farming, most of the Israelites' religious practices were adopted from the civilizations around them — in particular, from the Canaanites. The Hebrew language evolved from the Canaanite, and circumcision and the two early forms of Israelite sacrifice, the "communion sacrifice" and the "holocaust," were all being practiced by the Canaanites

when the earliest Hebrews arrived in their midst.[10] When
Abraham (Abram) arrived in Canaan, his God even identified
himself as being one and the same God as the Canaanites' chief
god, El.

El was to the Canaanites the King Paramount, Father of the
Exalted Ones, Father of men, and the Creator of all, and one of
his titles was "the Kindly and Compassionate."[11] He is represented in surviving statues as an old man with a beard.
Melchizedek, king of Salem and priest of El-'Elyon, "God Most
High," came out with bread and wine and blessed Abram in the
name of El, "Creator of heaven and earth." Abram responded
by giving him a tenth of everything he had (Gen 14:17–20). A
little later in Genesis we hear that:

> When Abram was ninety-nine years old, Yahweh appeared to
> him and said, "I am El Shaddai. Bear yourself blameless in my
> presence, and I will make a Covenant between myself and you,
> and increase your numbers greatly."   (Gen 17:1–2 JB)

And in Exodus, God said to Moses,

> "I am Yahweh. To Abraham and Isaac and Jacob I appeared as
> El Shaddai; I did not make myself known to them by my name
> Yahweh."   (Ex 6:3 JB)

This makes it clear that God revealed himself to the patriarchs
as El, in identity with the chief Canaanite god, but that later, in
His dealings with the Israelites, He became known to them as
Yahweh (Translated as "LORD" in many bibles). There are also
many other passages in Genesis and Psalms which refer to
El.[12] The phrase "God Most High," when it occurs, is a
translation of the Hebrew *El-'Elyon*, and "God Almighty" is a
translation of *El Shaddai*.

A significant thing about these apparent adoptions of religious practice from the Canaanites is the devotion to God which
was shown by the way they went about it. Their adoption of
circumcision is a good example. Amongst the Canaanites, circumcision was an initiation rite before marriage, as it still is in

some African tribes.[13] Abraham adopted the practice only
after arriving in Canaan, when God said to him,

> "…This is my covenant with you and your descendants after you,
> the covenant you are to keep: Every male among you shall be
> circumcised…"   (Gen 17:10)

Early references to it in the Bible, such as the story of the
circumcision of the Shechemites in Genesis 34, suggest its significance as a required marriage initiation rite, as do certain
metaphorical uses of the word, as when Paul refers to hearts
and ears not prepared to receive the word of God as "uncir-
cumcised hearts and ears." (Acts 7:51)[14] Its religious significance soon became paramount, though, and it was performed
on the eighth day after birth, where possible, rather than on
reaching sexual maturity. The Israelites, in deference to their
God, gave circumcision a religious significance, and they kept
practicing it long after the Canaanites ceased to. They clearly
did more than just conform to the customs of the peoples
around them.

A similar discrimination was involved in the Israelites' use
of the "communion sacrifice" (where the fat was offered to
God but the meat was eaten) and the "holocaust" (a burnt
offering of the whole animal, other than its skin). They
performed these sacrifices in common with the Canaanites, but
drew the line there (where they perceived God wanted them
to), and didn't, except in deviation from their own law,
perform other Canaanite sacrifices, such as the sacrifice of
children. We know the Canaanites burnt children, from both
archaeology and history. Urns have been discovered in the
sanctuary of Tanit at Carthage, containing the burnt bones of
lambs and goats, and, more often, of children. And the ancient
author Diodorus Siculus recorded that when, in 310 B.C., a
disaster threatened Carthage, the people living there decided it
was being brought about by the anger of Kronos, to whom they
had previously sacrificed their finest children. They had begun
to offer sickly children, or ones they had bought. To make up
for this they sacrificed two hundred children from their noblest

families. Each child, in turn, was placed on the outstretched arms of a statue of Kronos, and rolled into the furnace.[15]

Two stories from the Old Testament show the struggle and anguish the ancient Israelites went through in deciding whether they should sacrifice children like the Canaanites did. The first is the story of Jephthah, from the book of Judges:

> ...Jephthah made a vow to the Lord: "If you give the Ammonites into my hands, whatever comes out of the door of my house to meet me when I return in triumph...will be the Lord's, and I will sacrifice it as a burnt offering."
>
> Then Jephthah went over to fight the Ammonites, and the Lord gave them into his hands. He devastated over twenty towns...
>
> When Jephthah returned to his home in Mizpah, who should come out to meet him but his daughter, dancing to the sound of tambourines! She was an only child. Except for her he had neither son nor daughter. When he saw her, he tore his clothes and cried, "Oh! My daughter! You have made me miserable and wretched, because I have made a vow to the Lord that I cannot break."
>
> "My father," she replied, "you have given your word to the Lord. Do to me just as you promised, now that the Lord has avenged you of your enemies, the Ammonites. But grant me this one request," she said. Give me two months to roam the hills and weep with my friends, because I will never marry."
>
> "You may go," he said. And he let her go for two months. She and the girls went into the hills and wept because she would never marry. After the two months, she returned to her father and he did to her as he had vowed. And she was a virgin.
>
> From this comes the Israelite custom that each year the young women of Israel go out for four days to commemorate the daughter of Jephthah the Gileadite.   (Judges 11:30–40)

The question of whether children should be sacrificed was again agonizingly considered in the story of Abraham going up to a high place to sacrifice Isaac. We are told God tested Abraham by commanding him to sacrifice his only son Isaac to Him. On the way to the mountain where the sacrifice was to be, Isaac asked,

"Father?"
"Yes, my son?" Abraham replied.

"The fire and the wood are here," Isaac said, "but where is the
lamb for the burnt offering?"

Abraham answered, "God himself will provide the lamb for the
burnt offering, my son." And the two of them went on together.

When they reached the place God had told him about, Abraham
built an altar there and arranged the wood on it. He bound his son
Isaac and laid him on the altar, on top of the wood. Then he reached out his hand and took the knife to slay his son. But the angel
of the Lord called out to him from heaven, "Abraham! Abraham!"

"Here I am," he replied.

"Do not lay a hand on the boy," he said. "Do not do anything
to him. Now I know that you fear God, because you have not
withheld from me your son, your only son."

Abraham looked up and there in a thicket he saw a ram caught
by its horns. He went over and took the ram and sacrificed it as
a burnt offering instead of his son.   (Gen 22:7–13)

After that all the Israelites' first-born boys were offered to God,
but were redeemed, and an animal was sacrificed in their place.
This resolved the issue in a very satisfactory way, and never
again would the Israelites need to consider sacrificing their
children to God. Nevertheless, the abomination of child sacrifice did occasionally occur in ancient Israel. The second book
of Chronicles mentions the wicked king Manasseh of Judah,
who:

"...sacrificed his sons in the fire in the Valley of Ben Hinnom."
(2 Chr 33:6)

Child sacrifice was, however, always seen as a perversion of
religion, and was never accepted by the prophets, who did
much to keep religious practice pure. The prophet Jeremiah
proclaimed:

"The people of Judah have done evil in my eyes, declares the
Lord. They have set up their detestable idols in the house that
bears my name and have defiled it. They have built the high
places of Topheth in the Valley of Ben Hinnom to burn their
sons and daughters in the fire — something I did not command
nor did it enter my mind."   (Jer 7:30–31)

It would seem very few children were actually burned by the Israelites, though, and that they largely avoided this form of sacrifice which was so prevalent amongst their Canaanite neighbors.

In a similar way again, although the Israelites accepted that the Canaanite god El was one and the same as their own God, Yahweh, by and large they were able to stay away from the other gods of the Canaanite pantheon, and remain monotheistic. This certainly distinguished them from the peoples living around them. Baal, the Canaanite storm god, was worshipped at times, as a passing perversion, but he never seriously took hold in Israel. The prophet Elijah helped make sure of that.[16] The Israelites were a loose group of tribes, initially without a king, and they would have needed to cooperate in something like a "federation" in order to survive and defend themselves against their enemies.[17] Their single God of national unity helped strengthen this federation. Yahweh was a "God of gods," a "King of kings," in whom everything known and unknown was united. He helped give the Israelite tribes the power to work together as a nation, even though they had no earthly king, providing they adhered to their side of the covenant by obeying His commands. The most important part of this law, the Ten Commandments, had been written by Yawheh on two stone tablets, which the Israelites kept in the "Ark of the Covenant," a decorated wooden box, which they took into battle with them.[18] The Prophets were traveling teachers of this law which united the Israelites, and they were an important force in fostering unity through the emphasis they placed on living by the spirit of the law.[19] This advanced concept of God, and the social organization which went with it, enabled a small group of poor people to survive as a separate nation against all the odds.[20] The humbleness of the Israelites' Canaanite origins and their helplessness without God are shown by this allegory from the prophet Ezekiel:

> "This is what the Sovereign Lord says to Jerusalem: Your ancestry and birth were in the land of the Canaanites; your father was an

Amorite and your mother a Hittite. On the day you were born your cord was not cut, nor were you washed with water to make you clean, nor were you rubbed with salt or wrapped in cloth. No-one looked on you with pity or had compassion enough to do any of these things for you. Rather you were thrown out into the open field, for on the day you were born you were despised.

"Then I passed by and saw you kicking about in your blood, and as you lay there in your blood I said to you, "Live!" I made you grow like a plant of the field. You grew up and developed and became the most beautiful of jewels. Your breasts were formed and your hair grew, you who were naked and bare."

(Ezk 16:3–7)

The Israelites' recognition that there was only one God, who was lord of all, and who was all their strength, was a very advanced concept for their time. While other civilizations were trying to understand the universe by splitting it up into many smaller parts and giving a god to each — a god of healing, a god of the weather, a god of war, a god of the harvest, and the list goes on — the Israelites saw the unity in creation, and realized there must be a single creator, a single upholder of the universe, who was the mystery at the center of all things. Only in the nineteenth and twentieth centuries has science begun to grasp this unity, in terms of Einstein's search for a "Unified Field Theory" in physics, the Big Bang Theory in cosmology, and Darwin's Theory of Evolution in biology. The great unifying theories of Organic Evolution and Plate Tectonics (which relates to continental drift) nowadays explain and tie together all of Biology and Geology. These modern theories illustrate how advanced the concept of a unifying principle at the center of all things really was in the world of 1000 B.C. The importance of this unification concept in the Judaeo-Christian tradition, from such early times, could be taken to support the stand of those in the modern church who believe in evolution, both of the physical universe and of life, and maintain it is compatible with Christian belief.

While the Israelites adhered to their covenant with Yahweh, all went well for them. The Bible books of Joshua, Judges, Ruth, Samuel, and parts of Kings and Chronicles, show ancient

Israel in her heyday. David took Jerusalem for the Israelites, and established an empire extending from the Red Sea to the Euphrates.[21] King Solomon accumulated great wealth through trade, built a substantial temple for Yahweh in Jerusalem, and was known for his "wisdom." His political wisdom was not great, though, as he created the seeds of a divided Israel by discriminating against the northern tribes and favoring Judah. After he died the north rebelled and became the separate kingdom of Israel, distinct from Judah.[22] A decline began, but the two kingdoms remained prosperous for another two hundred years. It was probably during this time that the first parts of the Bible were written: two of the sources of the Pentateuch, J and E.

There is little archaeological evidence of the Israelites' occupation of Jerusalem at this time, but in 1980, one of the few traces of it was found: a small rolled-up sheet of silver from the sixth or seventh century B.C., engraved with Hebrew writing, which turned out to be the priestly benediction from the book of Numbers:

> The Lord bless you and keep you;
> the Lord make his face shine upon you
>   and be gracious to you;
> the Lord turn his face towards you and give you peace.
>   (Num 6:24–26)

By this time the two kingdoms of Judah and Israel were sliding into decay. The Israelites often broke their covenant with Yahweh by hankering after the ways and gods of the nations around them, and terrible things began happening to them. They didn't seem to realize they had the best concept of God to start with. It was a case of "united we stand, divided we fall." When they lost the powerful integrity of guiding their lives and nations by the laws of Yahweh, the God of unity, their fall was catastrophic.

First the northern kingdom of Israel fell to the Assyrians (in 722 B.C.), and its population was dispersed, much of it finding refuge in Judah.[23] Then the fall of Judah began (in 701 B.C.)

when the city of Lachish, south of Jerusalem, was besieged and captured by the Assyrians. Prisoners were taken as refugees to the lands of Assyria and beyond. Jerusalem was also laid siege to, but it resisted capture. Much of the Bible was written during the next hundred years, as a result of the somewhat different religious traditions of Israel and Judah being thrown together. At the end of this hundred-year period the Babylonian king Nebuchadnessar, successor to the Assyrians, totally destroyed Lachish, and within two years went on to sack Jerusalem.[24] The Bible tells us King Zedekiah was captured while trying to flee from the besieged Jerusalem. His sons were killed before his eyes, then he himself had his eyes put out. He was bound in bronze shackles and carried off to Babylon. Jerusalem was then burned and its walls broken down. The chief priests and officials were executed, the temple treasures looted, and all but the poorest in the land were led off into exile in Babylon, or fled to Egypt (2 Kings 25:1–26). Hebrew was almost forgotten as a spoken language. Israel seemed utterly destroyed. Yet it had been promised in the Bible, through the prophet Nathan, that David's throne would last forever (2 Sam 7:13). And later on the prophet Ahijah had said God would "humble David's descendants...but not forever."(1 Kings 11:39) So despite David's dynasty of kings coming to an end at this time, the Jews never lost sight of the possibility that a descendent of David, a Messiah, might someday reclaim the throne and rule again. This had tremendous implications for both Judaism and Christianity.

In exile in Babylon, Israel's priests and scribes had time to sorrowfully and nostalgically reflect on their past glories, and on what had gone wrong with their covenant with Yahweh. Psalm 137 tells the sad story:

> By the rivers of Babylon we sat and wept
> when we remembered Zion.
> There on the poplars we hung our harps,
> for there our captors asked us for songs,
> our tormentors demanded songs of joy;
> they said, "Sing us one of the songs of Zion!"

How can we sing the songs of the Lord while in a foreign land?
If I forget you, O Jerusalem, may my right hand [wither][25]
May my tongue cling to the roof of my mouth
    if I do not remember you,
    if I do not consider Jerusalem my highest joy.

It is human nature to often not realize the value of something until it is lost. This was certainly true of the Jews in Babylon. Their response to their realization of what they had lost was to enter a new phase of the recording of the history of their relationship with their God, Yahweh. The exiles brought many sacred writings with them, but in Babylon a lot more of the Old Testament was written down. In the process of this reflection and recording, before, during and after the exile, the Israelites gained a sense of their nationhood, their culture, and the worth of their civilization based on their relationship with their one unifying and universal God of justice. They became what they had never been before: a civilized, determined, and self-disciplined people. Vital to this process, and unique to the Jews, was a new type of man which was able to exist for the first time in their type of society: the Prophet. In exile, the Jews carefully compiled and recorded the words of their Prophets. What sort of men were they? H.G. Wells paints this picture of them:

They were men of the most diverse origins...but all had this in common, that they gave allegiance to no one but to the God of Righteousness and that they spoke directly to the people. They came without licence or consecration...and exhorted the people against [their enemies] denounced the indolence of [the priests] and the sins of their kings...and turned their attention to what we should now call "social reform." ...[They warned that injustice] was hateful to Jehovah, the God of Abraham, who would certainly punish [the] land.

    These fulminations were written down and preserved and studied. They went wherever the Jews went, and wherever they went they spread a new religious spirit. They carried the common man past priest and temple, past court and king and brought him face to face with the rule of Righteousness. That is their supreme importance in the history of mankind. In the great utterances of Isaiah the prophetic voice rises to a pitch of splendid anticipation and foreshadows the whole earth united and at peace under one God. Therein the Jewish prophecies culminate.

All the Prophets did not speak in this fashion...Nevertheless it is the Hebrew Prophets of the period round and about the Babylonian captivity who mark the appearance of a new power in the world, the power of the individual moral appeal, of an appeal to the free conscience of mankind against the fetich sacrifices and slavish loyalties that had hitherto bridled and harnessed our race.[26]

It should be added that although this new moral power of the Prophets was unique in the world of the Mediterranean Middle East, in the Far East and elsewhere similar things were happening. During the century-and-a-half between 600 B.C. and 450 B.C., when the Prophets helped shape Judaism in Palestine, and much of the Bible was written, Gautama Buddha was teaching in India, Zoroaster taught in Persia, Socrates in Greece, Confucius and Lao Tse in China, and the Upanishads, the basis of modern Hinduism, were being composed in India. It was indeed an important time in the history of the human race.

After seventy years in exile in Babylon, during which the Israelites learned so much from their mistakes, they were, almost miraculously, given a second chance to make their nation of God work. And make it work they did. At a time when all the other Semitic civilizations were overrun by Aryan conquerors, only the Jews were able to hold together and maintain their independence. The Bible tells us that when the Babylonian empire fell, and King Cyrus of Persia came to power over the whole area, he felt moved to rebuild the temple in Jerusalem for "the Lord, the God of heaven," and to repatriate any Jews who wished to help in the reconstruction. He also returned the temple treasures which had previously been stolen (Ezra 1). It seemed Yahweh was giving the Israelites another chance to live by the covenant He had made with them. The Jews' absolute joy at building themselves a Temple again is recorded in the book of Ezra:

With praise and thanksgiving they sang to the Lord: "He is good;
his love to Israel endures forever." And all the people gave a great
shout of praise to the Lord, because the foundation of the house
of the Lord was laid. But many of the older priests and Levites
and family heads, who had seen the former temple, wept aloud
when they saw the foundation of this temple being laid, while
many others shouted for joy. No-one could distinguish the sound
of the shouts of joy from the sound of weeping, because the
people made so much noise. And the sound was heard far away.
(Ezr 3:10–13)

Ezra, who returned eighty years later, tried to ensure the cohesion of Judaea by banning the mixed marriages with people of
other countries which had come into fashion in the homeland
during the exile, and since the return. He even went so far as to
require the dissolution of mixed marriages which had already
taken place (Ezr 9–10). This inhumanity permanently poisoned
the relationship between the Judaean Jews and their neighbors,
including the Samaritans.[27] Nevertheless, for three hundred
years or so up until the beginning of the second century B.C.,
the Jews in Israel made great efforts to keep their covenant.
Although the Hebrew Bible had largely taken shape by then,
the compiling, editing and writing of the Old Testament
Scriptures continued. While the tolerant Persian empire lasted,
the Jews were able to live as they wished.

Not all the Jews had returned from the Babylonian exile.
Many continued to live in Persia, Egypt and elsewhere. This
scattering of the Jews around the world, came to be called the
"Diaspora." The Book of Esther relates the exploits of a beautiful young Jewish woman living in Persia under the reign of
King Xerxes, an emperor who ruled hundreds of provinces
stretching from India to the upper Nile. In this story Esther
becomes Xerxes' queen, uses her wiles, wisdom and courage to
defeat the treacherous plans of the enemies of the Jews, and
persuades Xerxes to give the loyal and hard-working Jewish
people in his lands the protection and privilege they deserve.
This story reflects how useful the Jews were found to be in

many foreign countries, and shows the confidence, born of success, which many of the Jews of the Diaspora felt.

However, the trials of the Jews in their homeland were by no means over. During the second century B.C. the influence of the Greek empire, "Hellenism," affected and threatened Israel. This was inevitable, since, as was mentioned earlier, Israel was the last Semitic civilization to hold out against Aryan conquest. What right had the Jews to resist progress and cling to their barbaric ancient ways, when the wonderful style and glamour of the Greek way of life was there to be had?

In the 4th century B.C. the new Greek ideas had been carried into the ancient East by Alexander the Great, who conquered everywhere, from Egypt to Persia, and founded many Greek trading cities. Their international Greek style became known as Hellenism, and it affected everything: buildings, language, and even religion. These cities held a lifestyle which the Israelites of Abraham's or Moses' times could not have dreamed of. This new way of life would change the Jews, affect the Bible, and alter their vision of God. The broad humanity of the book of Jonah, and the philosophical thought of Ecclesiastes, reflect the beneficial effects of Hellenism. Living in a Hellenistic city like Ephesus must have been exciting. Ephesus was cosmopolitan, like a modern city, and an enormous amount of trade took place: for instance, 10,000 slaves were traded out of Ephesus in a year. The Jews were important in these cities, from merchant princes to slaves. The Apostle Paul himself later lived in Ephesus for three years. For their prayer and worship in these cities the Jews had the synagogues (meeting houses) which had begun to appear since the exile. The Law was studied in them, and the Law was vitally important to the Jews. But the Jews, like everyone else, also wanted to be Greek — Hellenism had so much style. Jews living in these cities often spoke only Greek, and wrote their names in the Greek way. Jews wanted to join this new civilization, but at the same time not lose their Jewishness. When they went to the gymnasium to build up their bodies, and be noticed so they could get on in society, a problem arose: all training was done in the nude, and, being Jews, they stood out because they were circumcised. An extraordinary operation was devised, called an "epispasm," which disguised the effects of circumcision. The First Book of Maccabees (in Catholic Bibles, but relegated to apocrypha in the Protestant) shows us how this enthusiasm for Hellenism affected even Jerusalem:

> It was then that there emerged from Israel a set of renegades
> who led many people astray. "Come," they said, "let us reach an
> understanding with the pagans surrounding us, for since we
> separated ourselves from them many misfortunes have overtaken
> us." This proposal proved acceptable, and a number of the people
> eagerly approached the king [Antiochus Epiphanes from Hellenistic
> Syria] who authorized them to practice the pagan observances.
> So they built a gymnasium in Jerusalem, such as the pagans have,
> disguised their circumcision, and abandoned the holy covenant,
> submitting to the heathen rule as willing slaves of impiety.
>   (1 Mac 1:12–16, J.B.)

Then, after a campaign against Egypt, the Seleucid king Antiochus Epiphanes, one of Alexander's successors, invaded Judaea, looted the temple, set up a pagan altar there, established ritual prostitution in the temple precincts, and forbade the reading of the Torah, the practice of circumcision, and the keeping of the Sabbath. Thousands were put to death for not complying with these edicts. Antiochus may have thought he was bringing the advantages of Hellenism to these barbarous people—much as western colonizers and missionaries later thought they were benefitting African natives and American Indians by replacing their traditional ways of life with "commerce and Christianity." However, this was altogether too much for the Jews. They may have liked many things Greek, such as the gymnasium, but most Jews would rather have died than accept this annihilation of their religion. After much civil disobedience, they finally (in 168 B.C.) rallied around a dynasty of country priests called the Maccabees, and fought, with all their strength, a series of wars against Antiochus. They were joined by the community of Assidaeans, a Jewish party devoted to the Law who had already opposed pagan influences, and from whom both the Pharisees and the Essenes were soon to derive.[28] As the world has seen many times since then, an army defending its own country has an advantage over an invading one. The Jewish army led by Judas Maccabaeus pressed home this advantage, as well as the advantage which came from the Seleucids having been severely weakened by Roman attack.[29] They threw Antiochus out, and established a holy state of Israel with the Maccabees as priest kings. The origin of Hanukkah, the "feast of Lights," dates from this time. It is sometimes referred to as the "Jewish Christmas" because it is held for eight days starting on the 25th of Kisleu (approximately December), and gifts are often given. After desecrating the temple in Jerusalem by erecting a pagan altar in it (the Abomination of Desolation referred to by Daniel (Dn 9:27; 11:31)), Antiochus Epiphanes offered the first sacrifice to Zeus Olympius there on the 25th Kisleu, 167 B.C. This marked the winter solstice, a traditional pagan time of celebration. Judas Maccabee, after his initial victories, purified the temple, built a new altar, and dedicated it on the 25th Kisleu, 164 B.C., the third anniversary of its desecration. It was decided then that a feast should be held every year at this time to celebrate this re-dedication of the temple.[30]

The "Hasmonaean" priest kings, as the Maccabees were known, ruled in fierce succession for nearly a hundred years after this. They destroyed and annexed surrounding areas, forcing their populations to become Jews and be circumcised, or flee, and creating much ill-feeling between Jew and Gentile, which lasted for centuries. This offensive behavior continued until 63 B.C., when the Romans under Pompey conquered and annexed all of the Hellenistic East, and with it Judaea and Jerusalem. Many areas subject to Jewish domination received the Romans as liberators.

Although Israel had been conquered, the situation was still considered tolerable by most Jews. The Romans were happy to rule through local client kings, and, for all their ruthless self-interest, allowed subdued countries the freedom to practice their own religions. Because of this, Israel, though far from happy with its occupation, accepted it. An aggravating factor was that Herod the Great, the Roman puppet king in Judaea, was the most infamous and brutal of all the client kings, and identified more with Rome than with Judaea. In about 20 B.C. Herod decided to remodel the Temple of Jerusalem, and vastly extended and rebuilt it. The design was according to the Laws of Moses, but overtures to Rome were also made. To enter the new Temple, Jews had to pass underneath a huge carving of the imperial Roman eagle which Herod had placed over the main door. This upset the Jews, of course, along with many other things imposed on them, and bands of militant Jewish nationalists, later called Zealots, organized rebellions against Herod and Roman rule. Herod dealt with these by secretly executing rebels, or selling them into slavery. Rome's solution was to crucify rebels by the thousands. For over a hundred years, though, through until well after the crucifixion of Jesus, the Jews lived with the Roman occupation as best they could.

Herod the Great maintained political stability, even if harshly, but after his death in 4 B.C., under his successors, the situation rapidly deteriorated. In 6 A.D., at the request of the Jews, Rome started to govern Judaea directly. It didn't help the situation, though; it only caused the Romans to become hated, even more than Herod and his sons before them had been. During the second half of the first century, the rebels gained increasing support, until (in 66 A.D.) the Jews plunged themselves into a full-scale war against Rome. This led (in 70 A.D.) to the destruction of the temple, and much of Jerusalem. A final Jewish revolt (in 132 A.D.) was crushed by the Romans under the emperor Hadrian, and virtually the whole population of Judaea fled, or was deported or sold into slavery by the Romans. Jews were excluded, under pain of death, from ever returning to Jerusalem, which was rebuilt as a Roman city.

Chapter 3

The Pharisees, the Essenes and Jesus

Knowledge of the society Jesus was born into explains much about his teachings. It also reveals the origin of the Christian church, and gives some insights into the nature of the organization it became.

That the Prophets, by and large, got away with what they said, shows there was a measure of political freedom in ancient Israel, and that religious debate was allowed. This was certainly true in the half century or so leading up to, and including, Jesus' ministry, when Herod's secular rule encouraged dissent from traditional Judaism. The Jewish historian Josephus, who lived in the mid first century A.D., tells us that there were three main schools of Jewish philosophy at the time, represented by three parties: the Pharisees, the Sadducees, and the Essenes.[1] In addition there were the extremist Zealots who plotted a military defeat of the Romans, and a select few holy men, Hasidim, who called themselves sons of God and performed miracles.[2] Jewish society during the time Jesus was growing up was by no means conformist.

The Sadducees were the wealthy and conservative class of high priests and their retinues, with a vested interest in the status quo. They had power and influence in and around the temple in Jerusalem, and what is more, became wealthy from selling sacrificial animals and baptisms in the temple area, and by using threats and violence to ensure collection of tithes due to them. This corruption was attacked by Jesus, and there was widespread unhappiness with it.[3] Theologically, the Sadducees rejected the apocalyptic speculation which had become popular, especially the beliefs in resurrection and predestination. They believed that people are free agents, fully responsible for their actions.[4]

The Pharisees, on the other hand, were the progressives. They were liberal in allowing discussion about which of a number of interpretations of the law might be the most proper,[5] and were innovators in encouraging new religious festivals, and accepting gentile religious ideas into orthodox Judaism, such as the concept of the resurrection of men. This concept of resurrection, meaning immortality due to life being restored after death, had been around since the third century B.C., and probably arose from the Greek concept of the soul, and from the influence of the Alexandrian Egyptian trinity of Serapis, Isis and Horus. These were not regarded as separate gods, but more as three aspects of one god, where Serapis, the "savior of souls," dies, and Horus, Serapis' posthumous son, is born to Isis and grows up in the image of Serapis, avenges his death, and inherits his kingdom. Serapis himself is resurrected in the afterlife, where he becomes both the judge and the saviour of the dead. The resurrected Serapis (the old Osiris) lives in the night sky as the constellation of Orion, along with his consort Isis, who is the star Sirius, following him across the sky. Serapis not only governed the seed and the harvest, but, by a natural extension of thought, was also the means of human immortality. He was a divine hero who died and rose again. In the mystery cult of Isis and Serapis, each person was offered salvation and promised regeneration after death. Sins were confessed and forgiven through immersion in water. Isis' priests were the fishermen who rescued the soul from the sea, the evil world.[6]

As well as encouraging this innovation and borrowing from other religions, the Pharisees had also developed a high morality which Jesus reinforced and built on. Love of one's neighbor was seen as being the sum total of the Mosaic Law. Pharisees considered it was better to love God unconditionally than to fear Him, and the "golden rule," "...do to others what you would have them do to you," (Matt 7:12) had already been declared by the Pharisee Hillel in 20 B.C.[7]

In short, the Pharisees introduced many concepts which passed over into Christianity. It was a sincere and progressive movement, even though the Pharisees often became proud and legalistic, and considered themselves better than other men. It was for this neglect of the loving spirit of the law while passionately pursuing its letter, as well as for often not practicing what they preached, that Jesus branded the Pharisees hypocrites (e.g. Matt 23:3,13). Jesus was, however, closer to the Pharisees than to any other major party of his day, despite his criticism of them.[8]

The Pharisees had a certain amount in common with the Essenes, as they had both derived, a hundred years or so earlier, from the Assidaeans (Hasidim) who bravely and patriotically fought for the Jews in the Maccabean wars.[9] However, the Essenes were even further away from the main stream, and a lot more like the early church. They had taken the Assidaean apocalyptic speculation to a radical extreme, whereas the Pharisees had become more liberal, and didn't believe in predestination, or that the world was about to end. Instead they sought to achieve the kingdom of God in this world, through living morally.[10] This is, of course, also a crucial aspect of Jesus' teaching, although it is one the church doesn't usually acknowledge. Unlike the Sadducees, the Pharisees' piety did not require the existence of the temple. No sanctuary was required apart from man himself—another belief Jesus shared. This meant Pharisaic Judaism could survive the destruction of the temple in 70 A.D., and become the modern form of Judaism, whereas the Sadducees disappeared with the temple. It is said that a great Jewish teacher of the times told one of his students, who was distressed by the spectacle of the ruins of the Temple:

> My son, be not distressed! We have another atonement as effective as this—acts of loving-kindness, as it is said (Hosea 6:6): "For I desire mercy and not sacrifice."[11]

Both the Pharisees and the Essenes believed strongly in the coming of a "new covenant" to replace the old one made between Yahweh and Moses. Few Jews had been able to keep the old covenant, with its strict laws. To keep such laws while living with a worldly perspective was coming to be seen as impossible. It was being realized that an inner transformation must take place before a person can really keep God's laws.[12] As the prophet Jeremiah had said:

"The time is coming," declares the Lord, "when I will make a new covenant with the house of Israel and with the house of Judah. It will not be like the covenant I made with their forefathers...I will put my law in their minds and write it on their hearts."

(Jer 31:31–33)

The Essenes believed this new covenant applied only to them, and all the rest of humanity would be damned.[13] Jesus, however, didn't even begin to accept this exclusiveness, and his teachings were the basis of a new covenant which included all people.

Between the philosopher Philo, the historians Pliny and Josephus, and the Dead Sea Scrolls which are so far available, we are beginning to know quite a bit about the Essenes, and more is likely to become known during the next few decades. Much of the controversy over the Dead Sea Scrolls centers on the beliefs and activities of the Essenes. Philo said the Essenes: "live in a large number of towns in Judaea and also in villages in large groups."[14] One of the most studied of the Dead Sea Scrolls, the *Manual of Discipline*, is a rule book for an Essene monastic community, commonly supposed to have been situated at the "Qumran" ruins on the Dead Sea, near the caves where the scrolls were found. Some now question whether this really could have been the site of such a monastery. Pauline Donceel from the University of Paris, for instance, maintains it was a luxurious winter villa for wealthy Sadducees. But whether the Essenes lived at Qumran or not doesn't really matter. What is important, and what is agreed on, is that this scroll is the rule book for an Essene monastic community, and Pliny, as well as Philo, confirms many Essene communities existed, even if not at Qumran. One of the most fascinating things to emerge from the study of the Essenes, is the large number of ways in which their communities resembled the early Christian church, and even, in some cases, the much later church.

The Dead Sea Scrolls and other ancient sources show these parallels between Essene communities and early Christianity:

> Both had a sacred meal of bread and new wine, where the bread was consecrated before the wine, in contrast to the practice of consecrating the wine first.[15]

> Both held that baptism was necessary for atonement, unlike the Jews, and that it should be preceded by repentance (turning from wickedness).[16]

> Both communities held all their property in common. The way the Christians did this is described in the book of Acts.[17]

> Both expected a coming fiery judgment, heralding the end of the world and the coming of the messianic kingdom of God.[18]

> Both referred to themselves as the "Way" (Acts 9:2).[19]

> The Essenes called themselves "Sons of Light," a term also appearing in the New Testament.[20]

> Both believed in a "new covenant." The Essenes believed their community of the "Sons of Light" to be a spiritual sanctuary, fashioned by God by means of a New Testament (describing what would happen in the last days) which supplemented the Old Testament covenanted with Israel.[21]

Comparisons with some later manifestations of Christianity include:

> Having a celibate priesthood, a monastic order, and a belief that sex is sinful and should be avoided as far as possible except for propagating children, and (according to Josephus) that women are wanton temptresses who are inherently unfaithful.[22]

Believing in predestination—that mankind is divided into "Sons of Light" and "Sons of Darkness," the division being determined from the very beginning by God's free will. The Sons of Light are the elect of God's grace and have inherited the spirit which liberates them from the sins of the flesh.[23]

Believing in salvation by grace alone.[24]

Believing in everlasting damnation in a place of fire.[25]

Believing in the sinfulness of the flesh (God having "a dispute with all flesh").[26]

Being organized in a fixed and inflexible hierarchy,[27] whereas Judaism had a reassuring flexibility which took account of individuality. (An example of this is the *Mishnah* saying that the priest is superior to the Levite, the Levite to the Israelite, and the Israelite to the "bastard," but that the precedence is conditional. If the "bastard" is a man of learning, and the High Priest a "boor," "the bastard... precedes the High Priest."[28])

So many similarities in belief, organization and structure between the Essenes and the early church, right down to the common name of the "Way," combined with the fact that their communities co-existed, strongly suggests the organizations themselves overlapped. In short, it is difficult to escape the conclusion that the early Christian church was in fact a continuation of one or more Essene communities, and that the church has continuously existed from at least as early as 50 B.C., when Essene communities were known to have been well established. This early church was, of course, not yet Christian, and the moderation and compassion of Jesus' teaching were not present.[29] The Essene communities insisted on strict, even fanatical, observance of the laws of Moses,[30] unlike early Christians, and were priestly, in believing that lay people were inferior to priests and had to obey them. It would appear Jesus was closely associated with the Essenes, but that his beliefs were closer to those of the Pharisees, with whom he also associated. The Dead Sea Scrolls show the Essenes had a fine moral sense, and Philo confirms this. The Damascus Rule scroll, the non-monastic rule, says this about how their members should care for each other:

> They shall place the earnings of at least two days out of every
> month into the hands of the Guardian and the Judges, and
> from it they shall give to the fatherless, and from it they shall
> succour the poor and the needy, the aged sick and the homeless,
> the captive taken by a foreign people, the virgin with no near
> kin, and the ma[id for] whom no man cares...[31]

This was more like the modern welfare state than anything else of the time, nevertheless, the Essenes were, in many respects, a narrow and bigoted community. Though they have sometimes been portrayed as Tolstoy-like pacifists, or Jewish "Buddhists," the Dead Sea Scrolls give a more realistic picture. Their pacifism was conditional: they really hoped that they, the "Children of Light," would finally triumph over the "Children of Darkness" in a military victory, and their brotherly love was mainly directed toward members of their own community; they had little love left for the outer world.[32]

Christianity certainly was a dramatic reform of the Essene "church," and must have split it, with the new Christianity and the traditional Essene church continuing to exist side by side, and influencing each other for some time. And, of course, the more traditional Jewish sects also had an important influence on early Christianity. These Essene roots, in addition to its conventional Jewish roots, help explain much of the extra doctrine the church has, over and above that coming from Jesus' teachings. And, as will be shown later, they also put the letters of the Apostle Paul into a context which helps explain and interpret them.

Although much is known about the heterodox and non-conformist Jewish society Jesus was born into, very little is known about the birth and early life of Jesus himself. Everything we do know is based on the four Gospels, and they do not support each other all that well. Mark, the earliest Gospel, and John, regarded as the historically most reliable,[33] both say absolutely nothing about Jesus until he is baptized by John the Baptist in the last years of his life. Matthew says Jesus was born in Bethlehem during the reign of King Herod, was visited by wise men who gave him gifts of gold, frankincense and myrrh, and was taken by his parents to Egypt to escape Herod's plans to kill him. Herod had apparently relied on the wise men to tell him who the infant "king" they were seeking was, and where he was to be found, and when the wise men didn't come back to him, Herod was furious and had all male children two years old or younger in the area of Bethlehem killed, in order to be sure he did away with this rival "king." Matthew goes on to say that Mary and Joseph kept Jesus in Egypt until they heard Herod had died, then returned to Nazareth in Galilee, instead of Bethlehem, because they considered it safer. Since history tells us King Herod died in the year 4 B.C., it is assumed from this account in Matthew that Jesus must have been born some time before that year, probably in 6 or 7 B.C.

Luke tells quite a different story of the birth of Jesus. According to him Mary and Joseph were living in Nazareth at the time Jesus was conceived, and traveled all the way to Bethlehem (about 120 miles away) to register in Joseph's home town for a census organized by Quirinius, Caesar's legate in Syria. And while they were there, we are told, Jesus was born. There is no mention of the wise men or the flight to Egypt, but instead we are told that Jesus was circumcised and presented at the temple, where a lifetime of waiting by Simeon and Anna was blessed by his appearance. After this Jesus and his parents simply returned to Nazareth.

Which of these accounts is closer to the truth? There is a good reason for considering it to be Matthew's, and this is that Luke's account has at least two serious flaws. The first is that it is highly unlikely a woman of those times would have undertaken a week-long journey by foot, or on the back of a donkey, when she was just about to have a baby — especially when she herself was not required to go. Experts on Jewish customs of the times say it would never have happened: she would have stayed home with her family to have her baby, and Joseph would have gone if necessary and returned as quickly as possible.[34] Perhaps, however, we could just accept this extraordinary journey if it weren't for an even more serious problem with the story. History tells us that the census organized by Quirinius didn't take place till the year 6 A.D., about 12 years after Jesus was born! Judaea had only just become a Roman province, and Quirinius conducted the census to assess its taxable potential. This is well documented, as by 6 A.D. Judas the Galilean, a Zealot, was preaching open revolt against the Romans, and one of his main issues was that of the payment of the Roman poll tax heralded in by the census of that year. This was an important issue for the Jews, who did not consider Yahweh's Holy Land could ever be one of Caesar's possessions.[35] As we know, Jesus himself adroitly avoided being caught out by a trick question about whether taxes should be paid to Caesar (Matt 15:15–22).

Luke, like Matthew, places the nativity story in the reign of King Herod (Luke 1:5), and this has led some people to propose that there was an earlier census conducted by Quirinius. Indeed Luke says he is referring to "the first census that took place while Quirinius was the governor of Syria." (Luke 2:2) Unfortunately there is no historical reference to Quirinius being governor of Syria before 6 A.D. The Governorship of Syria is known right through this period, except for a few years after 4 B.C., so it is known Quirinius could not have been the governor of Syria in any of the few years up to and including 4 B.C., the last years of Herod's reign, during which both Luke and Matthew say Jesus was born.[36] One theory suggests Jesus was born in 12 B.C., and the star the wise men saw was an early visitation of Halley's comet in that year. However, that really causes problems for Luke, as Quirinius was the Roman Consul in that year, and could not have been governor of Syria at the same time. Another major problem with the theory that there was a Roman census of Judaea during King Herod's reign is that the Romans didn't directly rule Judaea until after 6 A.D.

Herod ruled Judaea as a client king, and it would have been up to him to hold a census if one were to be held, not Quirinius, who was a Roman official.[37] And there is no record of Herod holding such a census, on behalf of himself or the Romans, despite the fact that Josephus is very thorough in his coverage of Herod's last years. In point of fact, Josephus refers to the census of 6 A.D. as something new and unprecedented in Judaea.[38] In addition to this, Luke's statement about this being the "first" census discords with Acts 5:37 (Luke also wrote Acts) where he says, "Judas the Galilean appeared in the days of *the* census" (italics mine). This suggests Luke only knew about one census, and the reference to Judas the Galilean makes it clear it was the 6 A.D. census. It doesn't seem likely that the "first" census of about 6 B.C. ever took place, and since it was the very reason for Mary and Joseph traveling to Bethlehem, Luke's nativity story must come into question, especially as Matthew gives a different version of events. This is not to say Luke deliberately invented this story. He could have been reporting in good faith an existing legend which linked the birth of Jesus to "the census," and have not noticed the twelve year discrepancy. The word "first" could have been added before the word "census" by a scribe copying the manuscript at a later date, who saw the historical problem and presumed Luke must have been referring to an earlier census. Whatever the origins of the story, though, it would appear to be as historically inaccurate as it is improbable. Consequently, Matthew's version of events seems likely to be closer to the truth.

In fact, the Gospels contain a number of historical inconsistencies, and there are many scholars who do not regard them as being historically sound source documents.[39] An example quoted by the Church Father Origen is that the cleansing of the temple is placed early in Jesus' ministry by John, but late in his ministry, just before his crucifixion, by the writers of the other three Gospels. Origen concluded that the evangelists were describing a real temple, but were not even intending to write historically about God, since God cannot be confined to particular times or places.[40]

What the Gospels do agree on is the nature of Jesus' personality and teaching, and that he was crucified by the Romans, defeated death, and rose from it to appear to his disciples again in the flesh. Since the exile in Babylon, the Jews were used to carefully recording the words of their Prophets, and this written nature of their religion distinguished it from the religions around them. A generation or so after Jesus was crucified, while there were still eye witnesses left, the followers of Jesus continued this tradition, and recorded his words along with the prophetically and religiously important aspects of his life. The Gospel writers and their sources probably didn't know the exact details of Jesus' birth, but in writing these explanatory stories they were saying something symbolically important about Jesus. Gaalyah Cornfield, a Jewish expert on the life and times of Jesus, said that, among early Christians, the colorful story of Jesus' birth in Matthew and Luke was seen as evidence that he was the promised Messiah, descended from King David.[41] And Jesus being the Messiah is a central and very important part of the whole of Christianity, so it is not surprising the Gospel writers elaborated on the details of his birth to get this point across. The truth was seen in a different way in those times: compared to us, they had less regard for the literal letter of the truth, and more regard for its spirit and the message it held. It was an approach to truth more like that of an historical novelist than that of an historian.

It doesn't worry me that the Bible is not a reliable historical source. I would even go so far as to say that the Bible best serves its spiritual purpose by not being historically reliable, and that rather than being a flaw, it is actually a part of its genius.[42] This is because the many people down through the ages who wished to use Christianity to control society and learning typically appealed to the literal and historical truth of the Bible, its so called "inerrancy," to substantiate their claims — fundamentalists do to this day. The false claims to worldly power of these people are often shown up when Bible passages they insist are literally true are shown not to be, and are seen rather to have important symbolic significance to the way we should live our inner, spiritual lives. In this way the Bible helps steer the wise toward finding the inner spiritual life, and prevents the worldly from too long using it to justify their pursuit of outward power. This is, I believe, the true "inerrancy" of the Bible. Many examples of it will arise during the course of this book.

Chapter 4

The Mystery-Shrouded Life of Jesus

A young Jewish woman called Mary, betrothed to a man named Joseph, found, as a result of distressing and unexpected circumstances, that she was pregnant earlier than she would like to have been. However, both she and Joseph became convinced they should continue with the marriage, and that the child they would have was destined to do great things for God. They named the son born to them Jesus, and his destiny was apparent from the start. As an infant, wise men came to pay tribute to him, and leave him gifts, and there was reason to believe the king of the land was jealous of him and wanted to kill him. His parents were able to protect him, though, and he grew with the wisdom and grace of God. Each year Jesus went with his parents to the Passover Feast in Jerusalem, until one year, when he was twelve, he stayed behind when his parents left to go home. He wasn't missed for a day, as his parents presumed he was with the family party, then it took them two more days before they found him in the temple courts sitting among the teachers, listening to them and asking and answering questions. Everyone who heard Jesus was struck by his understanding. On seeing him, his parents were astonished, and his mother asked, "Son, why have you treated us like this? Your father and I have been anxiously searching for you." Jesus said, "Didn't you know I had to be in my Father's house?" Though she didn't fully understand his answer, and what had happened, Mary nevertheless treasured these things in her heart.

This is all we know about Jesus from the Gospels till he is about thirty years old, and none of the historians or philosophers of his day mention him at all, accept for a couple of brief references to his crucifixion. There is a period of eighteen years in Jesus' life, from the age of twelve to thirty, we know nothing about. Yet how crucial those years must have been to the man he became. One of the things we always want to know about great men and women is the story of their formative years: their home life, their schooling, how they interacted with their teachers, their early careers. With Jesus, we have always had to do without this insight (except for the one story, just told, of him in the temple when he was twelve). Many people have speculated about these "lost years," but without even a shred of evidence to go on, such speculation is worth little. In recent years, however, a theory about Jesus' lost years has come into this vacuum of knowledge, which is supported by a small amount of apparently real source material. These sources are not at all well authenticated, and could vanish into dust on closer investigation. Also, the theory is by nature controversial. Nevertheless, it is a plausible theory with at least the promise of documentary evidence, and even though it is far from established, it is very difficult to disprove, since there is no evidence to counter it. It is also a theory which opens up valuable new possibilities for Christianity, and that might be its greatest worth, even if evidence to fully authenticate it can never be found.

The theory is that Jesus spent most of his "lost" eighteen years in India, studying and teaching at universities, monasteries and various other places. It proposes the "wise men from the east" either came from India, the center of religious learning in the world at that time, or if they were indeed "Magi" (Persian priests) as Matthew's Gospel suggests, then they had close connections with India, as Persia and India shared a border in those days. In addition to paying homage to Jesus, the wise men were supposed to have extended an invitation to Jesus' parents to send him to India when he was older, to continue his education. Caravans had, for centuries, been plying their way along trade routes from the Mediterranean to India and back, so undertaking such a journey would not have presented insurmountable problems.

Luke's story of Jesus in the temple at the age of twelve actually ties in quite nicely with this theory. Jesus' thirteenth year, 6 A.D., was a time of much turmoil in Palestine. The introduction of the poll tax in that year caused open revolt against Roman rule by the Zealots. We know Jesus' parents were aware of how much he was beginning to be noticed by the teachers and others in the temple, who were "amazed" at his wisdom beyond his years. Since Jesus' later teachings were so revolutionary, no doubt some of his opinions as a twelve-year-old were also rather controversial, and that this was one of the reasons people were astonished by them. We know that although Mary didn't understand everything at the time, that she "treasured all these things in her heart" (Luke 2:51), and was an intelligent and caring person who responded to these sorts of mysteries by questioning them and pondering them (Luke 1:29,34). They had taken Jesus to Egypt as an infant to keep him from danger, and returned to live in Galilee instead of Judaea when Herod died, because his son had succeeded him as tetrarch of Judaea, and they were afraid of him. The situation became even more volatile when Judaea became a Roman province (in 6 A.D.), and since Jesus was calling the temple in Jerusalem his "Father's house" and starting to spend time there impressing people with what he said, it could well have occurred to Mary and Joseph that, at this unstable time, Jesus was in potential danger there. Jesus' parents could well have told him it would be unsafe for him to return to the temple in Jerusalem — perhaps for many years to come. Yet the Jerusalem temple was the only place in Palestine where Jesus could properly continue to learn and prepare himself for his ministry; it was, as he said, "his Father's house." In this circumstance, if Jesus had an invitation to go to the great centers of religious learning in Persia and India to study, both he and his parents could have seen this as an attractive alternative, and decided to pursue it. What is more, Jesus was approaching the age at which Jews often married,[1] so a decision about his future would have been called for.

Nor would Jesus have been worried about picking up foreign religious ideas from gentile nations. For a start, he already had a thorough grounding in Judaism, and a love and understanding of God which impressed even the teachers at the temple. But more importantly, these were not times of unthinking orthodoxy amongst the Jews. On the contrary, we have seen how the times since the exile in Babylon were times of great spiritual endeavor and creativity, when much of the Bible was written, the new free spirit of the Prophets was taken seriously, and the Pharisees introduced a number of compatible beliefs and practices into Judaism from the gentile religions around them. Jesus was even more of an innovator than the Pharisees, and it is reasonable to suppose he would have welcomed the opportunity to learn what he could from the priests of Persia and the Buddhists and Hindus of India, and ponder on the applicability of parts of their teachings to his native religion. In our day, some narrow Christians say, "Oh heathen religions; what an abomination!" In Jesus' day, history shows, most Jews just weren't like that.

The theory that Jesus went to India certainly doesn't conflict with what is known about his life and times. And it nicely explains why nothing more is heard about Jesus in the Gospels, after the incident in the temple, until he is about thirty years old. Just as he was starting to draw attention to himself, no more was heard from him. It is unlikely Jesus could have lived in Palestine and been totally unnoticed for eighteen years, after already creating such an impression at the age of twelve. It is more reasonable to suppose he totally left the area. So, especially considering Jesus could have been considered in danger in Palestine at that time, it does appear plausible that he left the country for some years. But is it plausible that he went as far as India?

Frequent caravan journeys meant it was quite feasible for Jesus to travel to and from Persia or India. But why go all the way to India when it would have been easier just to go to Persia to escape the danger in Palestine? It is here that the question of whether it would have been worthwhile for Jesus to travel on to India arises. Escaping danger would certainly not have been Jesus' only consideration. Opportunities to both learn and teach would have been at least as important. So, was India an important center for religious learning at this time? To cast some light on this, let's briefly look at how religion and scholarship were manifesting there.

In the sixth century B.C., Gautama Buddha lived and taught in India. Siddhattha Gautama, later given the title "Buddha," was the son of a wealthy aristocrat, and had every comfort and luxury life could bring, but amidst this a great discontent fell on him; his life seemed to him like a holiday which had gone on for too long. He decided to leave this aimless existence, face reality, and find out the truth about life. He left all his luxury and went to live in a cave as an ascetic, putting to test the popular belief that power and knowledge could be obtained by extreme fasting, sleeplessness and ascetic practices. He failed to find the truth this way, but ended up having a vision of a way of moderation through which enlightenment could be found, and this brought about a much needed reform to Hinduism, and came to be the inspiration for the new religion of Buddhism. Gautama taught that all suffering is due to greedy desires, and that until a man conquers personal cravings his life is all troubles and sorrow. But when desires are overcome, when the egoistic self has vanished, then suffering will cease, and the state of Nirvana will be realized. Gautama taught an "Eight-fold Path" to live by to reach desirelessness, which insisted on a right understanding of the nature of reality, right motivation, right speech, right conduct, honest livelihood, cultivation of right states of mind, mindful awareness of all actions, and the practice of concentration through formal meditation. Buddha taught that we do not have souls, but that our consciousness passes from life to life while we are still held by desires. He claimed no gods exist, and that the ideal state of Nirvana cannot be described, but only experienced. The closest we can come to knowing what Nirvana is, without actually experiencing it, is that the word itself means "blown out." But is this blown "out of sight, out of mind," or simply blown out like a candle? Or does it, as Alan Watts suggested, refer to the breath being blown out in a sigh of relief?[2]

It wasn't until Buddhism conquered the imagination of King Ashoka, one of the greatest emperors the world has seen, that it started to make real headway. After a crushing military victory (in 255 B.C.), Ashoka became so disgusted by the cruelty of war that he renounced it as a means of foreign policy. After a couple of years of careful consideration he became a Buddhist, and declared that in the future all his conquests would be conquests of religion. He founded hospitals, public parks and gardens for growing medicinal herbs, created a ministry for the care of aboriginal and subject races in India, and provided for the education of women. He gave huge endowments to Buddhist teaching orders, and encouraged them to a better criticism of their own literature, which had gained, on top of Buddha's simple teachings, much which was superstitious, corrupt or otherwise of little worth.[3] Ashoka expounded a new political philosophy called *Dhamma* (The Pali form of the Sanskrit word *Dharma*, meaning the Universal Law, Righteousness, or Religion), by which he promoted peaceful and just government, advised the subjects of his empire that happiness is rooted in morality, and sought toleration of people, and of their beliefs and ideas. At about this time the Buddhist church underwent major reorganization as a result of the meeting of the Third Buddhist Council. One of the decisions of this council was to send out missionaries, and make Buddhism an actively proselytizing religion. Ashoka himself sent diplomatic and religious missions to the kings of Syria, Egypt, Macedonia, Cyrene and Epirus, and he had close relations with the Seleucid empire (Persia), with which he shared a border. There was a continual interchange of envoys with the Seleucids though three generations of kings, and Ashoka's north-western provinces, having once been a part of Persia, had many Persian features.[4] Missions to the Middle East continued for centuries, and Buddhist missionaries were, at times, found in the great Hellenistic cities such as Ephesus and Alexandria in the first centuries B.C. and A.D. (Which makes it just possible that the wise men who visited Jesus were a group of Buddhist missionaries.)

After Ashoka's death, his political empire gradually crumbled, as various parts of it were taken over by conquerors such as the Greek kings who ruled the north-west in the second century B.C., and oversaw a mingling of Greek and Indian culture. One of these Indo-Greek kings, Menander, is remembered as a protagonist in a Buddhist classic, and was supposedly converted to Buddhism. Although Ashoka's empire was in decline, India's national identity and religion remained strong. One of the main factors which gave continuity to this whole period (200 B.C. — 200 A.D.) was trade, and the Indo-Greek kings encouraged contact with western Asia and the Mediterranean world. Roman demand for spices and other luxuries took Indian traders to south-east Asia, and brought Roman traders to southern and western India. The religions of the merchants, Buddhism and Jainism, saw their heyday during these centuries.[5]

The few centuries up to and including the life of Jesus were certainly ones of religious innovation and progress in India. And the Buddhist teachings had important areas of correspondence with those of Jesus, from the teaching that worldly desires lead to unhappiness and misery through to the common name of the "Way" used by the followers of both (as well as by the Essenes, who are thought by some to have had contact with Buddhists). That Hinduism, the most widespread religion in India, shares a monotheistic outlook with Christianity, Judaism and Islam is not often realized. The popular view is that Hinduism has many idolatrous gods. But these gods in fact represent the many aspects of one universal God, just as the many names of God do in Christianity. In *The Religions of Man*, Huston Smith says:

> It is clumsy to confuse Hinduism's images with idolatry and her many images with polytheism. They are but runways from which man's heavily sense-embodied spirit can take off for its "flight of the alone to the Alone." Even village priests will frequently open their temple worship with the following beloved invocation:
>
> > O Lord, forgive three sins that are due to my human
> >   limitations:
> > Thou art everywhere, but I worship you here;
> > Thou art without form, but I worship you in these forms;

Thou needest no praise, yet I offer you these prayers
and salutations.
Lord, forgive three sins that are due to my human
limitations.[6]

India was clearly a place of great religious interest in the
centuries around Jesus' lifetime, so it could be reasonable to
suppose he traveled there. However, the plausibility of such a
journey is no proof it actually took place. For that we must
look for actual documentary evidence.

One piece of circumstantial evidence of Jesus' possible
connection with India is his story of the "widow's mite." A
Buddhist narration, claimed to pre-date the New Testament,
contains almost exactly the same story: in a religious service
rich people gave large donations, but a poor widow who owned nothing but two coins donated them with pleasure. The
priest recognized her noble attitude and praised her without
recognizing the gifts of others.[7] The correspondence with the
Gospel story (Mark 12:41–44) seems too close to be coincid-
ental: if the Buddhist story really does date from a time before
Jesus was born, then Jesus could have heard it from Buddhists
in India, or from Buddhist missionaries in the Mediterranean
area, and told it himself to illustrate a point.

This is not enough evidence in itself to demonstrate that
Jesus went to India, though it is suggestive of it. Another
ancient Buddhist writing is, however, said to actually document
the visit. If it could be tracked down and authenticated it would
carry considerable weight. The Russian historian, Nicolas
Notovitch was one of the first to hear of this document. When
he arrived in Kashmir in northern India (in 1887), he heard
about the existence of scriptures concerning a prophet called
"Issa" who lived for a time in the area, and who sounded very
like Jesus. In an attempt to find the scriptures he traveled to the
distinguished monastery of Hemis in the adjacent province of
Ladakh. Here some scriptures referring to Issa were read to
Notovitch through a translator, and he copied them down. As
the document read to him was a collection of isolated verses,
he reordered them in a chronological sequence before publish-

ing them in *The Unknown Life of Jesus Christ*.[8] Here is a slightly condensed version of Notovitch's compilation of these Issa Scriptures:

> The earth has trembled and the heavens wept, because of the great crime recently committed in the land of Israel. For they have tortured and executed the great just Issa, in whom dwelt the universal spirit, which was incarnated in a simple mortal, that those degraded by sin might be brought back to a life of peace, love and happiness, through coming to know the one indivisible Creator, whose mercy is boundless. Merchants from Israel have recounted this.
>
> The prosperous people of Israel incurred the wrath of God through their sins, and were punished by being taken from their land and flocks, and being sent to slavery in Egypt. There they were treated more cruelly than animals, kept in a state of continual terror, and robbed of all semblance of humanity. In their dire distress, the children of Israel remembered their heavenly protector, and prayed to Him for mercy.
>
> The Pharaoh then reigning in Egypt had two sons: the younger one, Mossa (or Moses), learned much from the Israelites, and was loved throughout Egypt for his goodness, and compassion for all who suffered. He noticed that despite their intolerable sufferings, the Israelites refused to abandon their God, and he came to believe, himself, in this one universal God who gave them such strength. The teachers of the Israelites encouraged Mossa's ardor, and begged him to intercede with Pharaoh, his father, on behalf of their people. Mossa did this, but it only made Pharaoh become angry and impose more hardships on his slaves. Soon after this a great plague fell upon Egypt, and Pharaoh believed he had incurred the wrath of the gods, but prince Mossa declared to his father that it was the God of his slaves who was interceding in favor of his unhappy people and punishing the Egyptians. At this Pharaoh commanded Mossa to gather all the Jewish slaves, and take them far

away from his capital. Mossa announced to the Hebrews that he had delivered them in the name of their God, and led them out of Egypt back into the land they had lost. He gave them laws and told them to always pray to the invisible Creator whose goodness is infinite. After Mossa died the Israelites rigorously observed his laws, and God recompensed them for the wrongs they had suffered in Egypt. They became the most powerful kingdom in the world, and a long period of peace prevailed amongst the children of Israel.

Unhappily, just as man does not always obey even his own will, the fidelity of the Israelites to their God did not last long. They began to forget the favors He had showered upon them, and instead of invoking His name, they more often sought the protection of magicians and wizards. Their kings substituted their own laws for those of Mossa, and the temple of God and the practice of religion were abandoned. The nation gave itself up to pleasures, and lost its purity. Many centuries after they had left Egypt, God again resolved to punish them. Strangers invaded the land of Israel, destroying it and taking their people into captivity. Then pagans from Romeles (Rome) subjected the Hebrews to their rule. Nobles became warriors, women were ravished from their husbands, and the lower classes became slaves. All the children were put to the sword, till, throughout the land of Israel, nothing was heard but weeping and wailing. In this dire distress, the people remembered their powerful God, and implored his mercy and forgiveness. Our Father, in His inexhaustible goodness, heeded their prayers: the time had come when the supreme Judge, in His boundless clemency, chose to incarnate himself as a human being.

The Eternal Spirit, which dwelt in a state of complete inertness and supreme beatitude, awakened and detached itself from the Eternal Being for an indefinite period, in order to show, by assuming a human form, how people can identify with the divine and attain eternal joy. And he came to teach us, by his example, how we can become pure and separate the soul from its gross envelope, so we may attain the perfection necessary to enter the Kingdom of Heaven, where eternal happiness reigns. Soon after this a wonderful child was born in Israel; God himself, through the mouth of this child, spoke of the nothingness of the body and the grandeur of the soul. Poor but pious parents were rewarded for their perseverance on the path of truth by being given this divine child as their first born. He was named Issa (one of a number of Arabian names for Jesus, and one still used in India). He began speaking of the one universal God even in his most tender years, and exhorted people who had strayed from the path of righteousness to purify themselves of the sins they had committed. People from many areas came to listen and marvel at the words of wisdom which fell from his infant lips; all of Israel united in proclaiming that the Eternal Spirit dwelt in him. When Issa reached thirteen, the age at which an Israelite should take a wife, the modest house of his parents became a meeting place for the rich and noble who wished to gain for their son-in-law the young Issa, who was already celebrated for his inspiring discourses on the Almighty. It was then that Issa secretly left his father's house, departed from Jerusalem, and, in the company of merchants, traveled toward the Sindh (the Indus River), that he might become perfect in the divine word, and study the laws of the great Buddhas.

During his fourteenth year, Issa journeyed beyond the Sindh and settled among the Aryans in the beloved country of God. His fame spread along the northern Sindh, and when he passed through the country of the five rivers (the Punjab), the Jains begged him to stay with them. He went on, however, to Jagannath, where the priests of Brahma gave him a joyous welcome. They taught him to read and understand the Vedas, to heal by prayer, to teach and explain Holy Scripture, and to caste out evil spirits from the body. He spent six years in Jagannath (now Puri), Benares (now Varanasi) and other holy cities. The masses loved him, for he lived in peace with the lower castes, and taught them the Holy Scripture. The higher castes of priests and warriors tried to prevent this unauthorized revealing of Scripture to the lower castes of artisans and servants, but Issa would not heed them; instead he preached against the priests and warriors as men who robbed their fellow beings of their rights as men, saying: "God the Father establishes no difference between his children, who are all equally dear to him." He denounced their distortion of the Vedic teaching, into which polytheistic concepts had crept, saying, "The Eternal Judge, the Eternal Spirit, comprises the one, indivisible, soul of the universe, which alone creates, contains, and animates the whole." He added: "They that deprive their brothers of divine happiness shall themselves be deprived of it, and the priests and warriors shall become the servants [of these servants] with whom the Eternal shall dwell forever." The artisan and servant castes were struck with admiration, but the priests and warriors resolved to kill Issa.

Being warned of the danger, Issa fled by night from Jagannath and took refuge in the (Himalayan) mountains among people who adored the only and sublime Brahma (God). Here, for six years, he learned Pali and studied the sacred Buddhist Sutras, until he could perfectly explain them. Then he left Nepal, descended into the valley of Rajipoutan, and traveled westward, preaching as he went of the way to perfection — of the good we must do to others, which is the surest means of quickly merging ourselves with the Eternal Spirit. Issa said, "He who has recovered his primitive purity at death shall be forgiven his sins, and shall have the right to contemplate the majestic figure of God." "Just as a father deals with his children, so God shall judge men after death according to His merciful laws; never will He humiliate His child by causing his soul to emigrate into the body of an animal."

Issa's words spread quickly in the countries he traveled through, and many people abandoned their idols. Seeing this, the priests demanded he demonstrate, in the presence of the people, that their idols really were worthless. Issa replied: "If your idols and your animals are mighty, and really possess supernatural power, let them annihilate me on the spot!" To this the priests retorted, "Perform a miracle, and let your God confound our own, if they are loathsome to him." Issa's answer was, "The miracles of our God began when the universe was created; they occur each day, each instant; whoever does not see them is deprived of one of the most beautiful gifts of life. And it is not against pieces of inanimate stone, metal, or wood that the wrath of God shall find vent; rather it shall fall upon men, who in order to be saved, should destroy all the idols they have raised." Seeing the powerlessness of their priests, the pagans believed Issa and broke their idols. Issa went on to teach these people not to strive to see the Eternal Spirit with their own eyes, but to endeavor to feel it in their hearts, and to purify their souls to make themselves worthy of its favors.

The fame of Issa's sermons spread to neighboring countries, and when he reached Persia the priests were terrified, and forbade the people to listen to him. When they saw the villagers welcome him with joy, and eagerly listen to him, they arrested him and brought him before the high priest. He was asked: "Who is this new God of whom you speak? Do you not know, unhappy man that you are, that Saint Zoroaster is the only just one admitted to the honor of receiving communications from the Supreme Being who commanded the angels to draw up in writing the word of God, laws that were given to Zoroaster in Paradise? Who are you that dares blaspheme our God and sow doubt in the hearts of believers?" Issa replied, "It is not of a new god that I speak, but of our heavenly Father, who existed before the beginning and will still be after the eternal end. It was of Him I spoke to the people, who, even as innocent children, cannot yet understand God by the mere strength of their intelligence and penetrate his spiritual and divine sublimity. But as a newborn child recognizes the maternal breast even in obscurity, so your people, induced into error by your erroneous doctrines and religious ceremonies, have instinctively recognized their Father in the Father of whom I am the prophet." The priests then interjected, "But how could a nation live according to the laws of justice, if it possessed no preceptors?" Issa replied, "As long as the people had no priests, they were governed by the law of nature and retained their candor of soul. Their souls were in God, and to communicate with the Father, they had no recourse to the intermediaries of idol or animal, nor to fire, as you do here. You claim that we must worship the sun, the genius of Good, and the genius of Evil; well, your doctrine is an abomination. I say to you the sun does not act spontaneously, but by the will of the invisible Creator who has given it existence, and willed it to light the day and warm the labor and the crops of man. The Eternal Spirit is the soul of all that is animated; you commit a grievous sin in dividing it into the spirit of Evil and the spirit of Good, for there is no God save that of good, who like the father of a family, does good only to his children, forgiving all their faults if they repent of them. The spirit of Evil dwells on this earth in the hearts of men who turn the children of God from the right path."

After listening to Issa, the wise men decided not to harm him. In the night, while the city was wrapped in slumber, they took him outside the walls and left him on the highway, hoping he would fall prey to wild beasts. But, being protected by God, Saint Issa continued on his way unmolested, and was twenty-nine years of age when he arrived in Israel.

There Issa urged his countrymen not to despair under the yoke of pagan oppression. The Father said through him: "Children do not yield to despair, for I have heard your voices, and your cries have ascended to me. Weep not, O my beloved, for your sobs have touched the heart of your Father, and I have forgiven you as I forgave your ancestors. Do not abandon your families to plunge into debauchery, do not lose the nobility of your sentiments and worship idols that will remain deaf to your voices. Fill my temple with your hopes and your patience, and do not forsake the religion of your fathers, for I alone have guided them and heaped blessings upon them. Raise them that have fallen, feed them that are hungry, and help them that are sick, that you may all be pure and just on the day of the last judgment that I am preparing for you." Issa added, "Enter into the temple of your own heart, illuminate it with good thoughts, patience, and the unflinching confidence you should place in your Father. Your sacred vessels are your hands and your eyes; look and do what is agreeable to God, for in doing good to your neighbor you perform a rite that decorates the temple of the One who has given you life. For God created you in his image: innocent, pure of soul, with a heart filled with kindness, and destined not to conceive evil projects, but to be the sanctuary of love and justice. So I tell you, do not sully your hearts, for the Eternal being dwells there always."

Saint Issa went from place to place strengthening the courage of the Israelites, and thousands followed him to hear his preaching. The rulers of the cities feared him, though, and word was sent to Pilate, the governor of Jerusalem, that Issa was inciting people against the authorities. When Issa entered Jerusalem he was respectfully greeted, and the doors of the temple were thrown open for him. Issa said to those gathered there, "The human race is perishing because of its want of faith, for the gloom and the tempest have bewildered the human flock, and they have lost their shepherd. But tempests do not last forever, and the clouds will not hide the eternal light. The heavens shall soon be serene again, the celestial light shall spread throughout the world, and the strayed sheep shall gather around their shepherd."

The priests and old men listened to him, full of admiration, before asking him if it were true that he had attempted to rouse the people against the authorities of the country, as had been reported to the Governor, Pilate. He denied this, saying, "Worldly power is not of long duration, and it is subject to innumerable changes. It would be of no use to a man to rebel against it, for one power always succeeds another, and it shall be this way until the end of human existence." The learned old men then said, "It is claimed you deny the laws of Mossa and teach the people to desert the temple of God." Issa's reply was: "We cannot demolish what has been given by our Heavenly Father [nor restore] what has been destroyed by sinners; but I have recommended the purification of all stain from the heart, for it is the veritable temple of God. As to the laws of Mossa, I have striven to re-establish them in the heart of men; and I say to you that you are in ignorance of their true meaning, for it is not vengeance, but forgiveness, that they teach — the sense of these laws has been perverted."

Having heard Issa, the priests and learned men decided among themselves that they would not judge him, for he was doing no one harm. They presented themselves before Pilate and said, "We have seen the man you accuse of inciting our people to rebellion; we have heard his preaching and know he is of our people. The rulers of the towns have sent you false reports, for he is a just man who teaches the people the word of God. After interrogating him, we dismissed him that he might go in peace." Overcome with anger, the Governor sent disguised servants to spy on Issa and report back to him on all his actions and speeches. Nevertheless Issa continued to preach, and a multitude followed him wherever he went. Many stayed with him, and acted as his servants. Among the things he said to them was: "The secret of nature is in the hands of God; for the world, before appearing, existed in the depth of the divine mind; it became material and visible by the will of the Most High. When you wish to address him, become as children once more, for you know neither the past, nor the present, nor the future, and God is the master of time." One of the disguised servants of Pilate asked: "O just man, tell us should we do the will of Caesar or await our near deliverance?" Issa answered, "I have not said that you should be delivered from Caesar; it is the soul plunged in error which shall have its deliverance. There can be no family without a head, and there would be no order in a nation without a Caesar…"

Saint Issa taught the people of Israel for three years in every city and village, on the roadways and in the fields. During all this time Pilate's spies observed him closely, but without hearing anything which could be held against him. Nevertheless, Pilate became alarmed at the great popularity of Issa, and ordered his arrest on the charge of inciting the people, and wanting to be made king. He was tortured in a dungeon until he became extremely weak. Hearing of the sufferings and tortures inflicted on their saint, the principal priests and learned elders begged the Governor to release Issa on the occasion of an approaching great feast. Pilate refused, but they begged him, then, to bring Issa before the tribunal of the Ancients that he might be condemned or acquitted before the feast. This Pilate agreed to. The next day Pilate called together the chief rulers, priests, elders and law-givers, with the object of making them pass judgment on Issa. After being unable to trap Issa into condemning himself, the Governor summoned the witness, who, at his instigation, had betrayed Issa. This man asked: "Did you not claim to be the king of Israel in saying that the Lord of heaven had sent you to prepare his people?" Issa blessed him, then said, "You shall be forgiven, for what you say doesn't come from you." Turning to the Governor, he added: "Why lower your dignity and teach your inferiors to live in falsehood, when even without this you have the power to condemn an innocent man?" At this Pilate became violently enraged and ordered the death of Issa. After the Judges deliberated among themselves, they said to Pilate: "We will not take upon our heads the great sin of condemning an innocent man…" Having said this the priests and wise men went out and washed their hands in a sacred vessel, saying: "We are innocent of the death of a just man."

Issa was nailed to a cross, along with two thieves tried with him. At sunset the agony of Issa came to an end, and his soul departed from his body to become a part of the Divinity. Although persecuted, his followers continued to spread his teachings, and many people in many lands were won over, and abandoned their idols to sing the praises of the all-wise Creator of the universe, the King of kings, whose heart is filled with infinite mercy.[9]

The manuscripts read to Notovitch were from two volumes of Tibetan writings. He was told that the Pali manuscripts they were translated from were in Lhasa in Tibet.[10] Notovitch published these scriptures, amidst considerable controversy, in his book *The Unknown Life of Jesus Christ*, and there has been an enduring interest in his work.

Although most of the details of these Issa Scriptures square with what we know about Jesus from the Bible, one very significant difference stands out: all four Gospels blame the Jews for Jesus' death, whereas the Issa Scriptures clearly put the full blame at the feet of the Roman governor, Pilate, and actually credit the Jewish authorities with going out of their way to try to save Jesus. The significance of this lies in the fact that in recent years a number of Jewish and other scholars have been arguing the same contention. They have pointed out that the Gospels were gentile documents, written after the fall of Jerusalem in order to spread the teachings of Jesus amongst citizens of the Roman Empire, and that it is quite possible the blame for Jesus' death was shifted to the Jews so as not to offend the Roman citizens they were trying to convert.[11] This ties in, it must be said, with the lack of historical reliability of the Gospels (which was demonstrated in the previous chapter). Whether or not this is the case, though, what is certainly known is that the blaming of the Jews for the crucifixion of Jesus was a direct cause of the huge tide of anti-Semitism which inundated Europe for nearly two-thousand years. Considering this, it is not surprising modern Jewish scholars should question whether or not the Jews really were to blame for Jesus' death. In the light of this, it is interesting that this independent account of events, supposedly preserved in the storerooms of Buddhist monasteries in the Himalayas since the first or second century, should so unequivocally support the interpretation of these scholars that the Jews were not to blame for the crucifixion.

Notovitch's work was dismissed by many, and declared to be fraudulent by no less an authority than the great orientalist Max Muller. Nevertheless, over the years, the existence of the manuscripts about Issa, and the authenticity of Notovitch's work, have been confirmed by quite a few people.

Well before Notovitch went to Hemis, a Mrs. Harvey wrote of the existence of the scripts on Issa in *The Adventures of a Lady in Tartary, China and Kashmir*.[12] Then, after Notovitch, came a number of other confirmations.

Swami Abhedananda, a leading figure in the Ramakrishna Society, was known and respected throughout the world. He read Notovich's book while in America, and some years later (in 1922) finally had the opportunity to travel to Hemis to find out for himself whether Notovitch's story was true. He explained Notovitch's claims to the lamas, who confirmed they were true. Then he was shown a manuscript, which he was told was a translation into Tibetan of an original which was in a monastery at Marbour near Lhasa.[13] With the aid of one of the lamas, Abhedananda made his own translations, which closely agree with those of Notovitch. Abhedananda published his translations of the Issa Scriptures in *Kashmir O Tibbate* (In Kashmir and Tibet).[14]

The famous and widely respected expatriate Russian artist and intellectual, Nicholas Roerich, visited the Hemis monastery (in 1925), and published his account of the Issa manuscripts in his books *Heart of Asia* and *Altai-Himalaya*. Again they confirm Notovitch's story and add some extra details. Like Notovitch and Swami Abhedananda before him, Roerich made his own translation of parts of the Issa manuscripts. Where these three translations overlap, they agree quite well.[15]

In the summer of 1939 Madame Caspairi, a Swiss musician, went on a pilgrimage to India organized by a renowned religious leader Mrs Clarence Gasque. Mrs Gasque was known internationally as the head of the *World Fellowship of Faith*, and she and her party were most cordially received everywhere they went throughout the pilgrimage. In one case, an Indian maharajah literally rolled out a red carpet to greet them. At Hemis, although they arrived just after the annual performance of a mystery play was over, the lamas performed it a second time in their honour. What happened next was extraordinary:

> A few days after the performance, when seated alone on the roof of the monastery, Mrs Gasque and Madame Caspari were approached by the librarian of the convent and two other monks. They were carrying three manuscripts in ornate coverings, one of which the librarian ceremoniously unwrapped. He then presented Mrs. Gasque the parchment leaves and with great reverence said, "These books say your Jesus was here."
>
> ...While we have no reason not to take the monks at their word, unfortunately we do not know what the books said. They were written in Tibetan and neither of the two women asked for a translation. However, Madame Caspari did take a picture of the lama proudly displaying the book.[16]

In 1951, U.S. Supreme Court Justice William O. Douglas traveled to Hemis. In his *Beyond the High Himalayas*, he observed that there were many legends in the area concerning the monastery at Hemis, and that one of them related to Jesus. Some people believed Jesus visited Hemis, coming at the age of 14 and leaving at the age of 28, traveling under the name Issa. The legend described Issa's stay there in some detail.[17]

There are two other people who have stumbled upon this legend, even though they had never previously heard of Jesus being in India. Dr Robert S. Ravicz, professor of anthropology at California State University, visited Hemis (in 1975), and while there was told by a friend, an eminent Ladakhi physician, that it was said there were documents at the monastery which stated that Jesus had been to Hemis.[18] In the late 1970's Edward F. Noack was staying at Hemis when a lama at the monastery told him that a manuscript relating the story of Jesus' pilgrimage to Ladakh was locked in the storeroom."[19]

Finally, there is a confirmation of the accuracy of the Hemis Scriptures about Issa from another part of India altogether, and from a Hindu rather than a Buddhist source. It will be recalled that these scriptures said Issa spent six years in Jagannath (now Puri) and other holy cities of the Hindus, before going to live for a further six years in the Himalayas. Sri Daya Mata, president of Self-Realization Fellowship, went to India in 1959, and in an interview with one of India's great spiritual leaders, His Holiness Sri Bharati Krishna Tirtha, the Shankaracharya of Puri, she mentioned that she had been told that Jesus "spent some of his life in India, in association with her illumined sages. His Holiness replied, 'That is true. I have studied ancient records in the Puri Jagannath Temple archives confirming those facts. He was known as "Isha," and during part of his time in India he stayed in the Jagannath Temple. When he returned to his part of the world, he expounded the teachings that are known today as Christianity.'"[20]

There is certainly the promise of sound documentary evidence here, from two distinct sources, though neither is, as yet, well authenticated. If the original Pali sources of the documents at Hemis are still at Lhasa, in Tibet, and could be found and dated to the first or second century A.D. this would certainly add weight to the scriptures. Alternately, some of the other "thousands" of scrolls of Issa scriptures said to be in the archives at Lhasa could be found.[21] For about forty years there has been very little foreign access to Tibet, but at some stage this will change, and, although many scrolls are said to have been destroyed by the Communist Chinese, scholars may still have access to a great number of ancient manuscripts. This could prove to be an historical gold mine. Meanwhile, careful analysis and comparison of the three translations which have been made should provide a useful starting point. After all, we have no New Testament originals, and rely totally on a number of slightly differing copies for Bible translations.

A lot of careful research has to take place before this story of Jesus living for twelve years in India can really be authenticated. Until then it must remain merely a plausible and exciting possibility. The story does, however, have just enough weight of evidence behind it to make Christians take it seriously in this respect: it could well lead them to ask themselves what their attitude would be if future research does authenticate the story. Would this be a threat to Christianity? Or would Christians be able to constructively use the account of Jesus' stay in India to reach out and find common ground with Hindus and Buddhists?

Extraordinary as this story of Jesus visiting India is, some have taken it even further. Holger Kersten, in his book *Jesus Lived in India*, extends the story to even more incredible heights, backed up by even more sketchy evidence. We will just very briefly look at his theory, before moving on to better established knowledge about Jesus.

Kersten uses evidence from the Shroud of Turin (of much challenged authenticity) to maintain that Jesus was not dead, in the modern sense of the word, when taken from the cross, but just in a deep coma, and that, in the tomb, he rose from the teeth of death and made a remarkably quick recovery. If he could miraculously heal others, it seems reasonable to suppose he could do the same for himself. Indeed, Jesus inferred he would do this, when he said, referring to his body, "Destroy this temple, and I will raise it again in three days." (John 2:19). After this Jesus appeared to his disciples a few times, then left with his mother Mary to travel gradually, over a period of sixteen years, back to India. The by now elderly Mary died on the way, but Jesus continued on to Kashmir, and lived and taught there till he was about a hundred years old. There is even speculation that he attended the Fourth Buddhist Council, held in Kashmir toward the end of the first century A.D., and helped inspire the important reforms made to Buddhism at this council.

The second century Church Father Irenaeus wrote a celebrated book called *Against Heresies*, which was crucial in
establishing church orthodoxy. In this book he claimed Jesus
lived to be an old man, and remained in "Asia" with his disciple
John, and others, up to the times of the Emperor Trajan, before
finally dying. Trajan's reign began in 98 A.D., at which time
Jesus would have been just over one hundred years old.[22] This
is support, from a most unexpected quarter, for Kirsten's
theory.

Kirsten himself uses place names, age-old traditions, and
claims in certain documents, to give credence to this theory.
The story is that after Jesus appeared to his disciples, he went
to Damascus in Syria, where the Jews had been disliked since
the Maccabean wars, but where the Essenes had a spiritual
center, and where he would be safer than in Palestine. He was
still there about two years later when he dramatically appeared
to Saul on the road to Damascus, in order to win him over
from being the main persecutor of the Way to being the main
proponent of it (Acts 9:1–31). About five kilometers outside
Damascus there is to this day a place called *Mayuam-i-isa*,
which means "The place where Jesus lived," and the Persian
historian Mir Kawand has cited several sources claiming Jesus
lived and taught in Damascus after his crucifixion.[23] These
Persian sources claim that Jesus, while in Damascus, received a
letter from the King of Nisibis (now Nusaybin near Edessa in
Turkey), asking Jesus to cure him of a disease. He sent Thomas
to cure him, and later visited there himself, before leaving to
travel north west into the Kurdish territory in the north of
Anotolia. The apocryphal *Acts of Thomas* relates how Jesus
suddenly appeared there at the marriage festivities of a princess
at the court of the King of Andrapa. From there Jesus and
Mary apparently journeyed eastward over the old Silk Road,
where certain place names such as "House of Mary" (near
Ephesos on the west coast of modern Turkey), supposedly
suggest their stay. As Jesus gradually moved through Persia, he
increasingly became known as "Yuz Asaf," meaning "leader of
the healed." Tradition says he preached throughout Persia, and

converted vast numbers to his creed. Accounts such as Agha Mustafai's *Jami-uf-Tawarik* (Vol II) claim Yuz Asaf and Jesus were one and the same man, and the court poet of Emperor Akbar of India later backed this up when he called Jesus *Ai Ki Nam-i to: Yus o Kristo*, or "Thou whose name is Yuz or Christ."[24]

The Acts of Thomas describe the stay of Jesus and Thomas in Taxila (now in Pakistan) at the court of King Gundafor in the twenty-sixth year of his rule (47 A.D.). East of Taxila is a small town called Mari ("Murree" in English) near the modern border with Kashmir. In Mari there is a grave which has been maintained and honored as far back as anyone can remember, called *Mai Mari da Asthan*, "The Final Resting Place of Mother Mary." The grave is orientated east-west in Jewish fashion, rather than the Muslim north-south. Moreover, the area was under Hindu rule in Jesus' time, and the Hindus cremated their dead and scattered their ashes, so had no need for graves. When Islam took over this area in the seventh century A.D., all "infidel" monuments were destroyed, but they recognized this grave as being a relic of a "People of the Book," Christian or Israelite, and respected it. The grave continues to be honored as the final resting-place of Jesus' mother by Muslims, who consider Jesus one of the most important prophets of Islam.[25] The Qur'an states that Jesus (Issa or Isa) was saved from dying on the cross, which it considered an accursed death, unworthy of him (Deut 21:23), and has many other references to the "prophet Issa," supposedly to correct the distorted image in the writings of his followers. The most incredible of these is that Muhammad believed Jesus' prophecy of the coming of the "Spirit of truth" (John 16:12–14) referred to him.

After this Jesus supposedly traveled on to Kashmir, from where he made periodic journeys to other parts of India. There is a grave in the middle of Srinagar's old town which many people believe to be the grave of Jesus himself. The building later erected around the grave stone is called *Rozabal*, meaning "tomb of a prophet." Above the passage to the actual burial chamber is an inscription explaining that Yuz Asaf entered the valley of Kashmir many centuries before, and that his life was dedicated to the search for the truth. Within the inner burial chamber there are two long gravestones, the larger for Yuz Asaf, the smaller for an Islamic saint of the fifteenth century. Both gravestones point north-south in keeping with Muslim custom, but they are in fact only covers: the actual graves are in a crypt under the floor of the building. There is a tiny opening through which one can look into the true burial chamber below, and see that the sarcophagus containing the earthly remains of Yuz Asaf points east-west in keeping with Jewish custom. This clearly indicates Yuz Asaf was neither an Islamic saint nor a Hindu.[26]

The Indian Mogul emperor Akbar, in the sixteenth century, planned to unite India, then split into religious factions, with a single religion that would contain the quintessence of all the various faiths as its one "Truth." Akbar evidently selected at least one saying of Jesus to inscribe on the wall of his Victory Gate to the central mosque of the city he built for himself, for (in 1900) this saying, unknown in the west, and supposedly deriving from Jesus' stay in India, was found on a piece of wall amid the ruins of Fatehpur Sikri, the city he built 25 km from Agra:

> Said Jesus, on whom be peace! The world is a bridge, pass over it but build no house there. He who hopeth for an hour, may hope for eternity; the world is but an hour, spend it in devotion; the rest is worth nothing.[27]

Since Akbar had in common with Jesus a vision of one religion uniting the best from all religions, perhaps, if he had known about it, he would also have had Jesus' statement of this vision inscribed where the public could read it:

> I have other sheep that are not of this fold. I must bring them also. They too will hear my voice, and there shall be one flock and one shepherd.   (John 10:16 AT)

The Prophet Isaiah, we saw earlier, also had this vision of the whole earth united and at peace under one God (Isa 2:1–5). It is worth noting that this verse of Jesus', apart from being a vision of religious unity, is also suggestive of the fact that Jesus traveled and taught outside Palestine.

What are Christians to make of this supposed return of Jesus to India after the crucifixion? Despite the evidence for it being thin, perhaps we could, at least, ask this question: what if the inevitable further research into the theory does authenticate it? What if the remains of "Yuz Asaf" in Shrinagar are exhumed and are well enough preserved to show evidence of crucifixion? My own belief is that this should not adversely affect Christian faith. Whether Jesus actually physically died on the cross is a minor point. The important thing is that he suffered for the sins of all, and indeed, if he didn't physically die he would have suffered much more (have died a worse "death") due to the pain of recovering, than he would have if he had just quickly died and been miraculously raised to life. Later versions of the Nicene Creed say Jesus "descended into hell" for three days, which would be a good description of such an ordeal of recovery from terrible wounds while lying in a grave. In either case the Bible makes it clear that Jesus ended up very much alive in his original body, and that his body was not subject to decay during the ordeal (Acts 2:31). What is possible is that he was what we would now call "clinically dead" for a while, and that, like many patients in modern hospitals, he was restored to life. We do not, however, any longer think of "clinically dead" as really being dead — only when the brain has decayed so much as to lose its ability to function do we pronounce a person dead. And, as we have just seen, the Bible says Jesus' body was not subject to any decay. It is also worth noting that Jesus said there would be no miraculous sign to demonstrate his authority, except the sign of the prophet Jonah:

> For as Johah was three days and three nights in the belly of
> a huge fish, so the Son of Man will be three days and three
> nights in the heart of the earth. (Matt 12:40)

And Jonah did not die inside the fish before he emerged.

Jesus may have visited India, and he may even have returned there after his crucifixion. We just don't know for sure yet, one way or the other. The fact that there is room for speculation about this, and that it can't be ruled out, shows just how little we actually know about Jesus, and the importance of keeping an open mind about him and his teachings.

Chapter 5

Jesus' Teachings — Living in the Kingdom of Heaven

Jesus came to Galilee at about the age of thirty to be baptized by John. In reverence, John said it should be Jesus rather than he who did the baptizing, but Jesus wanted John to baptize him, in order to "fulfill all righteousness."[1] Although Jesus brought in a revolutionary new teaching, his aim was not to overthrow the existing religious Law, but to fulfill it, and many of his teachings refer to Old Testament passages, and are clearly developments of the old Law. Nevertheless, his teachings about how to live in the "kingdom of heaven" with God in the here-and-now were radically new, and have never been well understood, in his time or since.

The Jews were expecting a Messiah to establish a new "kingdom of God" in the form of a powerful Jewish nation which would rout the Romans and dominate the world. But although its name was the same, Jesus' kingdom was diametrically opposed to the kingdom of worldly power and wealth many Jews were looking for. For Jesus there was the way of the world, Satan's way, bound to lead to misery, or the way of God, leading to eternal happiness. We are free to choose either one, but we must choose between them. Jesus told us we can't serve both God and Mammon, just as a servant can't serve two masters (Matt 6:24). The Zealots almost certainly wanted to recruit Jesus to their cause. The devil, presumably in the form of one of these Zealots,[2] took Jesus "to a very high mountain and showed him all the kingdoms of the world and their splendor." He tried to entice Jesus to his cause, saying, "All this I will give you, if you will bow down and worship me." In modern words, we can imagine a Zealot saying, "Join and devote yourself to our cause — serve our interests — and I will make you king of all you can see from this high mountain and more!" Jesus, however, was beyond being tempted by worldly power, and replied, "Away from me, Satan! For it is written: 'Worship the Lord your God, and serve him only.'" (Matt 4:10)

Having set himself apart from worldliness, Jesus began to preach about the "kingdom of heaven," and drew together his disciples. In the Sermon on the Mount, Jesus gathered these disciples around him, and taught them how to live in the kingdom of heaven, showing them how joyful it is compared with living in a worldly way (Matt 5–7). In the Beatitudes he said,

> "Blessed are the poor in spirit,
> for theirs is the kingdom of heaven.
> Blessed are those who mourn,
> for they will be comforted."

The kingdom of heaven can only be lived in by those who are humble, and prepared to put aside their spirited, preconceived notions and surrender themselves, so they can learn as disciples. Those who place the greatest value on worldly riches, or even on knowledge of the world, cannot make much spiritual progress. But those who come to value spiritual things highly will consider themselves "poor in spirit," and mourn not having found God. Since they mourn their spiritual poverty more than any material lack, God will comfort them by revealing Himself to them. One might wonder how such humble people, not valuing material things, would survive in this world. The common view is that the meek will be trodden under foot. Jesus, however, had a different view. He said,

> "Blessed are the meek,
> for they will inherit the earth."

This is a strange statement, at first sight. When we consider the ways of the rich and power seeking, though, it begins to make sense. Those who possessively hunger for money and power often don't enjoy their lives much, as they are too busy making more money, and worrying about how to protect what they have. By contrast, the "meek" do not have these anxieties, and have the time, energy, and loving attitude necessary to really enjoy the world they live in. The world is their oyster. And being meek doesn't necessarily imply being unassertive and put-upon. Meekness, as the word is used here, rather embodies the virtues of not being possessive or power seeking, of preferring to give rather than take, serve rather than dominate, cooperate rather than compete, and of letting things unfold in a natural way rather than forcing issues. Jesus later elaborated on this meekness, advising people not to be anxious or worried about food, clothing or shelter, for:

> "...your heavenly Father knows that you need them. But seek first his kingdom, and his righteousness, and all these things will be given to you as well."   (Matt 6:32–33)

Jesus taught that there is a liberating freedom in living this way:

> "If you hold to my teaching, you are really my disciples. Then you will know the truth, and the truth will set you free."
> (John 8:31–32)

He also said,

> "Come to me, all you who are weary and burdened, and I will give you rest. Take my yoke upon you and learn from me, for I am gentle and humble in heart, and you will find rest for your souls. For my yoke is easy and my burden is light."
> (Matt 11:28–30)

The first of these three quotes introduces the concept of God's righteousness. It is also there in one of the Beatitudes:

> "Blessed are those who hunger and thirst for righteousness, for they will be filled."

What is this righteousness of God, which Jesus would have people hunger and thirst after? Quite simply, it is God himself, and his will for our lives. Our righteousness is our own view about what the right thing to do is; God's righteousness is His view. Jesus advised people to seek God's will rather than their own, and he lived to this himself, right to the bitter end, when he said, just before being crucified, "Father, if you are willing,

take this cup from me; yet not my will, but yours be done."
(Luke 22:42) Living by faith means actually being prepared to
do what God asks, even if it seems ridiculous or impossible at
first sight. People can become apprentices to God, the true
master of living, and go on a great adventure with Him, if they
are prepared to learn from Him. This can never happen,
though, while the ego is still in control, and insists a person
does things their own way. But by letting go of their own ideas
and anxieties, surrendering to God, and becoming receptive to
new possibilities, people can place themselves under the guidance of the Holy Spirit. Little children rarely spend much time
worrying about the past, or being anxious about the future, and
they have the humbleness and faith to accept the guidance of
older people. They live in the present much more than adults.
This is why Jesus said, "I tell you the truth, unless you change
and become like little children, you will never enter the
kingdom of heaven." (Matt 18:3) Fear comes from dwelling on
the past, and being anxious about the future. It also comes
from holding certain wrong attitudes with regard to other
people, which are bound to make us worry about what has
happened and might happen. Avoiding these negative, fearful
and selfish states of mind, Jesus called being "pure of heart."
One of the Beatitudes says: "Blessed are the pure in heart, for
they will see God."

Jesus goes on to explain that being pure of heart also means
having pure, unselfish, motives, yet he points out how being
this way is in a person's own enlightened self-interest in the
long run. He says people should not judge others, or it will
come back on themselves. Rather, they should readily forgive
and forget the wrongs others have done them, in order that
they can be forgiven for, and forget, their own past wrongs. It
is not sufficient to just avoid harming others; people should
also avoid even becoming angry, as this will separate them from
God and land them in misery.[3] They should be loyal and
faithful to their friends. They should not fight back when they
know they can win, and not get upset when people wrong
them. They should be kind and merciful, and do good deeds

out of love, without seeking recognition for them. Above all, they should love all others, even their enemies, as they love themselves. This is because all people are one in God, and God is love. In loving others they love themselves, and in hating others they hate themselves.

When people surrender themselves, and their intractable problems, to God, let go of their anxiety, and just live in the present, hungering and thirsting for the presence of God, they soon become pure of heart, and God reveals Himself to them. But how does God reveal Himself? Jesus is very clear about it. He explains that the kingdom of God is not found outwardly, as any external manifestation, for:

> "The kingdom of God does not come visibly, nor will people say
> 'Here it is,' or 'There it is,' because the kingdom of God is
> within you."   (Luke 17:21)

Through conscience and intuition God speaks to people, and through their inner thoughts they can talk to God. There are certain things people can do to foster this inner communion with God. The foremost is to spend time quietly alone, silently meditating and waiting on God, concentrating on the thought of Him, and letting worldly thoughts pass by. As Psalm 4 says, "Stand in awe, and sin not: commune with your own heart on your bed and be still." In this quietness, intuitive perception of God grows. Psalm 46 says, "Be still and know that I am God." Jesus spent much time like this, by himself, quietly absorbed in God. Luke says, "Jesus often withdrew to lonely places and prayed," (Luke 5:16) and "One of those days Jesus went out into the hills to pray, and spent the night praying to God." (Luke 6:12)

This is the basis of Jesus' teachings on the kingdom of heaven — an uncompromisingly spiritual teaching, yet a very practical one. He told many parables to illustrate it, often starting with the words: "The kingdom of heaven is like..." You can read the Gospels for yourself if you wish to explore these. For various reasons, which I will go into in later chapters, the established churches have always largely ignored Jesus' teachings about how individual people can attain the kingdom of heaven in their lives, and have concentrated instead on some of his words about himself, and a lot of St Paul's teachings about him. Many would agree with Wilhelm Nestle when he says, "Christianity is the religion founded by Paul; it replaced Christ's gospel with a gospel about Christ."[4] This was a problem Jesus had in his own lifetime. He said,

> You diligently study the Scriptures because you think that by them you possess eternal life. These are the Scriptures that testify about me, yet you refuse to come to me to have life.
> (John 5:39–40)

No doubt he foresaw it would be a problem in the future too. The teachings of the kingdom of heaven really are about how every person can individually come through the eternal Christ to an inner communion with God, to be guided by Him and have life in abundance. However, since the church is more concerned about who Jesus was, than with heeding his teachings, let's look briefly at what Jesus is recorded as having said about himself.

As a man, Jesus was very modest. He said, "By myself I can do nothing." (John 5:30) And when addressed as "Good teacher," he answered, "Why do you call me good? No-one is good—except God alone." (Luke 18:19) But Jesus also embodied the eternal Christ, which Paul defined as "the power of God and the wisdom of God." (1 Cor 1:24) In reference to this eternal Christ, Jesus made very exalted claims, but we must remember they were not personal claims, nor anything he took personal pride in or credit for, but statements about the universal Christ through which God created the world, which is the "Word" itself, the very reflection of God in creation. This Christ he talked about always existed, and always will, as that part of the fabric of the universe which is the one and only direct link between people and God, referred to in the Bible as the "only begotten of God." Consequently whenever and wherever people seek God and find Him, whatever race or religion

they come from, it is always this Christ which connects them
with God. It was in this context that Jesus said,

> "I am the way and the truth and the life. No-one comes to the
> Father except through me."   (John 14:6)

The church has often used this claim to say only followers of
Jesus can come to God, and all religions other than Christianity
must be invalid. This is denying the universality of Christ, a
universality that Paul was very aware of, stating that Christ was
the spiritual strength of the children of Israel during the Exodus, over a thousand years before Jesus was even born:

> Our forefathers were all under the cloud and...they all passed
> through the sea. They were all baptized into Moses in the
> cloud and in the sea. They all ate the same spiritual food, and
> drank the same spiritual drink; for they drank from the
> spiritual rock that accompanied them, and that rock was Christ.
>   (1 Cor 10:1–4)

Jesus affirmed this universality by saying "I tell you the truth,
before Abraham was born I am!" (John 8:58) And he stressed
that it was not his historical flesh-and-blood body which mat-
tered, but the spiritual essence of his teaching:

> "The Spirit gives life; the flesh counts for nothing. The words I
> have spoken to you are spirit and they are life."   (John 6:63)

Jesus referred to himself most often as "the son of man" to
emphasize his humanness and concern for humanity. Where his
humanness and divinity overlapped lay his power to redeem
humankind. He said,

> "I am the good shepherd. The good shepherd lays down his
> life for his sheep."   (John 10:11)

Christians very often, and quite rightly, quote this as a
reference to the importance of the crucifixion in saving people
from their sins, but rarely if ever mention the passage which
follows it:

> "I have other sheep that are not of this fold. I must bring
> them also. They too will hear my voice, and there shall be

one flock and one shepherd." (John 10:16)

Traditional Christianity, in its narrowness and exclusivity, does not like the scope this gives for other religions to share in the universality of Christ, so it ignores it.

Although the church gives more weight to who Jesus is than to his teaching, it is also fairly selective as to which of Jesus' statements about himself and his mission it quotes, as much of what he says doesn't fit comfortably with its doctrine. Another example of this is the church frequently referring to Jesus being the "son of God," but largely ignoring his teaching that we are all heirs to God's kingdom. When the Jews were about to stone Jesus for blasphemy for claiming to be God, Jesus answered: "Is it not written in your Law, 'I have said you are gods'?" (John 10:34) Jesus went on to argue: how can you say I am blaspheming for saying I am God's son, when you are divine too? He added, as one modern writer put it, that "the only difference between them was that he had been 'sanctified' by the Father, a fulfillment they had yet to achieve."[5] Jesus further emphasized that we can all attain to his heights when he said,

> "The disciple is not above his master: but everyone that is
> perfect shall be as his master." (Luke 6:40 AV)

The church has traditionally put a huge gulf between Jesus' perfection "up there" in heaven, and our baseness "down here" on Earth, with the gap being bridged after we die if we are good and do what the church says in the meanwhile. But this was by no means Jesus' attitude. Nor was it Paul's, which makes it doubly interesting that the church chose to override it. There are, in fact, understandable, though worldly, reasons why the church selectively ignored many of the teachings of Jesus, and these will become apparent in chapters to come.

Reform of existing religion was a vital part of Jesus' ministry. The early Christian church appears to have been continuous with the Essene "church," but encompassed many new teachings and reforms.[6] The three main areas of Essene belief and practice which Jesus reformed were: the existence of a privileged caste of priests who established themselves as intermediaries between man and God; a lack of moderation and compassion, including an insistence on the strict observance of the laws of Moses; and a belief in predestination, whereby it was claimed only a select few had been chosen from the very beginning to be saved, and the rest of the world was predestined to damnation. This last view was an excess peculiar to the Essenes, but the other areas of belief and practice needing reform existed right across Jewish religion.

The high-priestly Sadducees were corrupt, and Jesus was often in dispute with them, as when he threw the money changers out of the temple. (e.g. Mark 11:15–18) It is fundamental to the nature of Jesus' teachings that separate priests, acting as intermediaries between man and God, are not necessary — that all believers are their own priests. He taught that "the kingdom of heaven is within you," and that religion should be practiced in private:

> "When you pray, go into your room, close the door and pray to your Father, who is unseen. Then your Father, who sees what is done in secret, will reward you."   (Matt 6:6)

He also taught that "Where two or three come together in my name, there am I with them." (Matt 18:20) Jesus made it clear that all people can commune with God the Father directly, and this certainly makes a separate priestly class superfluous. Unfortunately, it didn't take long for this reform of Jesus' to be reversed and for priests to return to the Christian church as intermediaries between people and God. During the Reformation the principle of the "priesthood of all believers" was re-established in some denominations, but to this day the Roman Catholics, Orthodox, Anglicans and Episcopalians still have ordained priests as their leaders, and only these priests can preside over the Holy Communion or Mass.[7] How can so much of the church have so blatantly disregarded one of Jesus' most important reforms for so long? It is a question to keep in mind while looking at the history of the church.

Jesus certainly spoke and acted against blind obedience to the Laws of Moses, or for that matter to any teaching, and instead taught and acted out of thoughtfulness and compassion. Among the many examples of this are his healing on the Sabbath, and his justification of it to his critics by saying, "The Sabbath was made for man, not man for the Sabbath," (Mark 2:27) and "Stop judging by mere appearances, and make a right judgment." (John 7:24) In an appeal to the keeping of the spirit of the law, rather than its letter, Jesus elevated just two commandments above all the rest:

> "'Love the Lord your God with all your heart and with all your soul and with all your mind.' This is the first and greatest commandment. And the second is like it: 'Love your neighbor as yourself.' All the Law and the Prophets hang on these two commandments."   (Matt 22:37–40)

That Jesus thought the law should be looked at and taught in a fresh way, depending on the circumstances, is shown by his saying:

> "Therefore every teacher of the law who has been instructed about the kingdom of heaven is like the owner of a house who brings out of his storeroom new treasures as well as old."
>   (Matt 13:52)

Jesus' moderation and compassion fill the Gospels. The way he didn't judge the Samaritan woman at the well, even though he knew of her many sexual partners, but rather offered her "living water" by discussing great spiritual truths with her, is an inspiring example to all. And many Samaritans came to believe in Jesus as a result of the gentleness, love and respect he showed her (John 4:4–42). Then there is the story of how he saved the woman caught in the "very act" of adultery from being stoned to death under the Law of Moses, by saying, "He that is without sin among you, let him cast the first stone at her." (John 8:7 AV)

Yet how long did this compassion and moderation last in the Church? When you read about the Inquisition, it is hard to believe the medieval church had anything at all to do with Jesus. And what happened to the respect and equality Jesus showed to women? Even in our time, how does our compassion compare with that of Jesus? Yet his example did make early Christianity more moderate and compassionate than the Jews and Essenes were, and it has reached down through the ages and into the hearts of many, and made the world a better place than it might have been. And finally, in Western countries in the twentieth century, the laws of our lands have started to reflect Jesus' non-judgmental, caring attitude to moral offenders. Jesus was clearly saying that adultery, and other moral sins, should not be punishable offenses, yet it is only recently that laws against "moral" crimes have been repealed. Sadly, it has been humanists outside the church who have, for the most part, pushed for this new compassionate state of the law, and church people have often opposed it. It is a matter for concern in modern Christianity that large parts of the church are still pushing for a return to criminal status of homosexuality, prostitution and abortion. Jesus' example and teachings are finally being heeded in our society, but not as much by Christians as by non-Christians. What must well-informed, perceptive people think of this? Is it any wonder revival is not coming to the church in the West, and people are looking to New Age organizations and other religions for their spiritual well-being? If it is to regain Christ's mantle, the church and the people in it need to let go of their pride, and realize that "Not everyone who says to me, 'Lord, Lord,' will enter the kingdom of heaven, but only he who does the will of my Father who is in heaven." (Matt 7:21) It is not too late to change: it is time for people in the church who are still opposing Jesus' reforms to stop doing so. Jesus is no longer ahead of his time — his time has come, and the time has come for the church to fully accept his teachings.

Finally, in the matter of predestination, Jesus made it clear again and again that privilege plays no part in salvation, and that it will be those who produce the right fruit, and love and help their fellow human beings, who will be saved. In paving the way for Jesus, John the Baptist said,

> "Produce fruit in keeping with repentance. And do not think you can say to yourselves 'we have Abraham as our father...'"

(Matt 3:8–9)

Jesus told the story of the Good Samaritan (Luke 10:30–37), the parable of the Wedding Guests (Matt 22:2–14), and the story of the Sheep and the Goats (Matt 25:31–46) to bring home the point that anyone can qualify for salvation if they produce fruit in keeping with the kingdom of God. One of Jesus' other sayings talks of the additional need to come to him for salvation, but says that *whoever* does this will possess eternal life:

> "Whoever drinks the water I give him will never thirst. Indeed,
> the water I give him will become in him a spring of water
> welling up to eternal life."   (John 4:14)

Yet, despite this, St Augustine, St Thomas Aquinas, and the reformation theologians Martin Luther and John Calvin, all believed in predestination, and many in the church still believe in it. We should be aware that predestination is a belief which goes back to the Essene church, before it became Christian, and that it is not compatible with Jesus' teachings.[8]

It is sad to see how often Christians are prepared, "in the name of Jesus," to ignore many of Jesus' teachings and reverse his reforms. And in doing so they get a church which closely resembles the Essene church which existed before Jesus was even born. However, Jesus' life was by no means in vain. He knew his teachings would be written down and carefully preserved, even if they would not be properly understood for a long time, because the Jews had a tradition of recording the words of their Prophets. In this way, Jesus' teachings have survived to inspire people through the ages, and profoundly influence our laws and way of thinking, even if large parts of the church have never yet really come to grips with them. But this situation in the church can't go on forever; hopefully the church is on the verge of deciding to remodel itself on Jesus' teachings, and of deciding to focus its attention on what he considered important. The church, like society, consists of the sum total of its members, and these changes can only take place in the church if large numbers of individual Christians decide to embrace them. If and when this happens there will be a major revival of Christianity in western countries, and throughout the world. If it doesn't happen, Christianity will continue to dwindle, and could even be largely replaced as the bearer of Jesus' message of salvation by one or more other religions or spiritual movements.

Chapter 6

The Example of the Early Church

Although Jesus had many followers in Palestine during his ministry, the highly inspiring drama of his victory over the most horrible death of crucifixion and his re-appearance to his disciples certainly galvanized the early church into action. No longer was he just a revolutionary but loving teacher and friend who taught them how they could all, like him, be on intimate terms with their Father in the kingdom of heaven. No longer was he just a healer and miracle worker and reformer who went around doing good and standing up for the weak and oppressed. Now, through his victory over death, he became the focal point of a new religious movement which gave people lasting hope in a world of suffering. Soon this new way of living, with its new focus, came to be called Christianity, as a new and vital church grew up from its Jewish and Essene roots.

The early Christian communities seem to have been particularly close to Christ's teachings and spiritual power. The community of apostles and disciples, described in the book of Acts, experienced powerful spiritual manifestations, such as the descent on to them of the Holy Spirit on the day of Pentecost:

> Suddenly a sound like the blowing of a violent wind came from heaven and filled the whole house where they were sitting. They saw what seemed to be tongues of fire that separated and came to rest on each of them. All of them were filled with the Holy Spirit and began to speak in other tongues (languages) as the Spirit enabled them. (Acts 2:2–4)

Peter identified this as the fulfillment of a prophecy by Joel:

> In the last days, God says, I will pour out my Spirit on all people.
> Your sons and daughters will prophesy, your young men will see visions, your old men will dream dreams.
> Even on my servants both men and women, I will pour out my

Spirit in those days, and they will prophesy.
I will show wonders in the heaven above and signs on the earth
below, blood and fire and billows of smoke.
The sun will be turned to darkness and the moon to blood before
the coming of the great and glorious day of the Lord.
And everyone who calls on the name of the Lord will be saved.
(Acts 2:17–21, quoting Joel 2:28–32)

Because their involvement with worldliness was at an end, and they were living in their "last days" on this world, in accordance with Jesus' teachings, these early Christians of the book of Acts shared all their property, and lived in what we would today call a commune or a cooperative community:

All the believers were together and had everything in common.
Selling their possessions and goods, they gave to anyone as he
had need. Every day they continued to meet together in the
temple courts. They broke bread in their homes and ate together
with glad and sincere hearts, praising God and enjoying the
favor of all the people.   (Acts 2:44–47)

This is a model of Christian living which the modern world could well take seriously.

After a considerable period of persecution, the early church won over to its cause one of its chief persecutors, Saul of Tarsus. While Stephen was being stoned,

Saul was there, giving approval to his death. On that day great
persecution broke out against the church at Jerusalem, and
all except the apostles were scattered throughout Judaea and
Samaria. Godly men buried Stephen and mourned deeply for
him. But Saul began to destroy the church. Going from house to
house, he dragged off men and women and put them in prison.
(Acts 8:1–3)

Some time later Saul was dramatically converted to Christianity when Jesus himself confronted him:

Meanwhile, Saul was still breathing out murderous threats
against the Lord's disciples. He went to the high priest and
asked him for letters to the synagogues in Damascus, so that if
he found any there who belonged to the Way, whether men or

women, he might take them as prisoners to Jerusalem. As he neared Damascus on his journey, suddenly a light from heaven flashed around him. He fell to the ground and heard a voice say to him, "Saul, Saul, why do you persecute me?"

"Who are you, Lord?" Saul asked.

"I am Jesus, whom you are persecuting," he replied. "Now get up and go into the city, and you will be told what you must do."

Acts 9:1–6)

It took the church some time to accept as a convert someone who had been so vile to it for so long, but eventually it did. Saul changed his name to Paul, and went on to be the church's greatest proponent, and the most important molder of the theology and practice of the church. During Paul's time the church spread quickly through the Roman Empire. After consolidating in Antioch, churches were soon established in Smyrna (in Asia Minor), Alexandria (in Egypt), Corinth (in Greece), Rome, and many other places. Paul traveled to many of these centers to help found the churches, and wrote letters to encourage and correct them when he was unable to come in person. A number of these letters are preserved in the New Testament, and the churches have always given an extraordinary weight to them — often more than it has given to the Gospels.

Paul's letters are quite a contrast to the teachings of Jesus. Paul rarely refers to Jesus' words, and appears to some to be substituting his own teachings in their place, and to have a totally different way of thinking. So different can the two teachings appear, that it has prompted many modern critics of the church to say that everything good in Christianity comes from Jesus, and everything bad in it comes from Paul. One gets the impression that they think Christianity might have been better off if Paul had stayed its persecutor!

This is an interesting notion, but it doesn't stand up to close scrutiny. Examination of the nature of Paul's letters, in the context of the problems of the early church, shows that they do, in fact, support Jesus' teachings, even if they don't duplicate them, and that it is highly unlikely he was trying to compete with Jesus. Paul's letters are very specific documents, designed for the edification of particular first century churches, which had their own, often very individual, problems. While many of the problems Paul addressed in his letters are universal ones, some are highly specific to the particular church a letter was written to, and we need to be able to use our common sense to distinguish between the two. For instance, Paul said some controversial things about the role of women in the church. Unlike Jesus, whose teaching was timeless, and whose attitude of equality towards women still seems modern in the twentieth century, Paul was, probably like most men of his day, a male chauvinist. Nevertheless, some of his teachings about men and women are scrupulously balanced, for example:

> The wife's body does not belong to her alone, but also to her husband. In the same way, the husband's body does not belong to him alone, but also to his wife. Do not deprive each other except by mutual consent and for a time, so that you may devote yourselves to prayer.   (1 Cor 7:4–5)

This has the ring of general wisdom, which all could follow. However, Paul's injunction for women to be silent in church looks more like an answer to a particular discipline problem in a church containing some rowdy women. He advises:

> As in all the congregations of the saints, women should remain silent in the churches. They are not allowed to speak, but must be in submission, as the law says. If they want to inquire about something, they should ask their own husbands at home; for it is disgraceful for women to speak in the church.
> (1 Cor 14:33–35)

That this applies to general chatter during a church service, which neither men nor women should engage in, is shown by the fact that in the same letter Paul talks about women praying and prophesying in a way which makes it clear that women are free to do so with decorum. He says:

> Every woman who prays or prophesies with her head uncovered dishonors her head.   (1 Cor 11:5)

What relevance could this have had, if women were never allowed to speak in church? Incidentally, this is not, as has sometimes been considered, an injunction for women to wear shawls or hats in church, as later verses make it clear that Paul thinks a woman's own long hair is her "glory," and the best possible covering for her head, as it is given to her for this purpose. Also, Paul makes it clear that his observations on the question of dress decorum in church, including men wearing short hair, are only his opinions, and should not be the basis of contention in the church, as he concludes his thoughts on this question by saying, "But if any man seem to be contentious, we have no such custom." (1 Cor 11:16 AV)

One further area where Paul at first sight appears to be at odds with the teachings of Jesus is on the question of predestination. We saw in the last chapter how Jesus clearly taught that salvation was available for all who met certain conditions, yet in this celebrated passage from Romans Paul appears to be supporting predestination:

> For those God foreknew he also predestined to be conformed
> to the likeness of his Son, that he might be the firstborn
> among many brothers.   (Rom 8:29)

Taken out of context this seems to support predestination. However, the verse immediately before it helps place it in context and make its meaning clear. What God foreknew is that at any given point in time some people would love him and others would not, and what He predestined is that He would work for the good of those who loved him:

> And we know that in all things God works for the good of those
> who love him, who have been called according to his purpose.
>   (Rom 8:28)

You can hardly take a verse more out of context than to ignore the verse before it! Yet this is apparently what advocates of predestination like John Calvin have done, in addition to ignoring Jesus' teachings on the matter. Quite clearly, these verses of Paul's do not indicate that certain individuals are predestined from the beginning of the world to be saved while others are not, but that God decided from the beginning that all those who loved him would be treated in a special way. Paul confirms that everyone has the opportunity to be saved later in the same letter when he says:

> For there is no difference between Jew and Gentile — the same Lord is Lord of all and richly blesses all who call on him, for, "Everyone who calls on the name of the Lord will be saved."
>
> (Rom 10:12–13)

Why then, if Paul doesn't believe in predestination, did he even mention the topic? The answer is that it was an important issue in the early church because the Essenes did believe in a very narrow and restrictive form of predestination, and the early Christian church was a development from the Essene church (see Chapter 3). Despite Jesus' teachings to the contrary, a belief in predestination was obviously still common in the church, and Paul debunked the notion by explaining just what is predestined and what isn't. This is a good example of how a knowledge of the times Paul lived in helps us understand what he said in his letters. The problem of correctly interpreting Paul's teachings is one which will come up again in later chapters, but these two examples should demonstrate that even where Paul seems to be totally at odds with Jesus' teachings, he may, on closer examination, actually be in harmony with them.

As to the question of Paul not reproducing many of Jesus' teachings in his letters, this might not be because he didn't agree with them; it might be because he perceived them as holy, and didn't wish to appropriate them as his own. There was a particular tradition of word-of-mouth preaching of Jesus' teachings which Paul seems to have respected. Some of Paul's spoken words are recorded by Luke in the Book of Acts, and they include an otherwise unknown saying of Jesus:

> "...by this kind of hard work we must help the weak, remembering the words the Lord Jesus himself said: 'It is more blessed to give than to receive.'"
>
> (Acts 20:35)

Paul saw his letters as being a second-best substitute when he couldn't be at a church to preach himself, and he may well have deliberately confined himself in them to practical concerns and avoided the central teachings of Jesus, which were being spread, by himself and others, through this powerful word-of-mouth tradition. Paul would probably be surprised to see how seriously the church came to regard his stop-gap letters.

Spread by the spoken word, Christianity quickly became an international religion, with adherents all around the Mediterranean, and further afield. But soon after the end of Paul's ministry the Gospels were finally written down. It had reached the point where those who had personally known Jesus were old and beginning to die off. Afraid of losing the teachings, Christians decided to capture their oral tradition in writing. Different churches in different places wrote down their own versions of Jesus' life and words. Many Gospels were written, but only four were later accepted into the official Canon of Scripture. These Gospels are not direct biographies of Jesus, but they are the most authentic witnesses we have of a huge flood of faith which spread around the Mediterranean in the first century A.D.

Christianity was not the only Eastern religion to be popular in the first century Roman empire, and it was not the only one to be persecuted by the Romans. Mithraism and the Alexandrian religion were two others which Paul was well versed in, and which influenced his theology. Religions which practice side-by-side tend to influence each other. This was true of Judaism in Old Testament times, and it was equally true of first and second century Christianity. Mithraism had baptism and a sacred meal from a sacrificed bull, and bread and wine came to symbolize the bull's flesh and blood, and be eaten in their place. The sacred poetry of this religion includes the line, "And you saved us by having shed the eternal blood."[1] The comparisons with Christianity are obvious. Paul taught that Jesus, like the Alexandrian Serapis, was a god who died to rise again and give men immortality.[2] And the Egyptian *ankh* sign, representing the divine life force, and taking the form of a cross with a circle on top, became the cross of Christ, a sign of lives reborn.[3] These influences were, of course, only building on what there was already a basis for in Christianity. Other, more superficial things to come from these two religions include the shaven priest, the votive offering, altars with candles, and chanting.[4]

In addition to these two religions, there were many other small sects, and Christianity itself was divided into numerous sects. Foremost amongst these were the Gnostic sects, who believed that they, through initiation, became "children of the Father," the true and good God Christ represented, whereas the uninitiated members of the ordinary church were merely offspring of the *demiurge*, the creator of this world with all its evils, who reigns as king and lord, lays down laws, and judges those violating them. They identified this *demiurge* as the "God of Israel." Through their initiation Gnostics claimed they were released from the power of this false God who throws his weight around but cannot provide salvation, and received the charismatic gift of direct inspiration through the Holy Spirit, which they called *gnosis*. They also claimed to be no longer under the authority of the bishops of the established church.[5]

In the first centuries of Christianity there was no such thing as orthodoxy, but when orthodoxy was finally established, it was largely defined in argument against the Gnostic sects — "we are what the Gnostics aren't." This happened towards the end of the second century, mainly due to the tremendous battle waged by Irenaeus, Bishop of Lyons. His main method of promoting cohesion in the church was to attack the Gnostics, who were fragmenting it by denying clerical authority (and his own in particular).[6] He did this largely through his popular book *Against Heresies*.[7] Irenaeus succeeded in bringing some unity to the church, but at the price of a growing intolerance, and an increasingly hierarchical power structure in the church. Although he didn't use overtly political arguments, his book became a handbook for what was to be a very politically oriented church.[8] As a compendium of major heresies and their refutations, it also became the foundation for later inquisitions. Irenaeus gives an example in his book of the disruption of the church in his own district of the Rhone (around Lyons, in France) caused by one particular Gnostic:

> There is another of these heretics, called Marcus, who boasts of having improved upon his master. He is a skilled magician, and uses this to draw to him many men, and more than a few women. His inducement for them to join him is his claim that he has great knowledge and perfection, and has received the highest power from heaven above...
>
> ...He devotes himself especially to wealthy, well-bred and elegantly attired women. He draws them to him with seductive words like: "I am eager for you to partake of my Grace, since the Father of all continually beholds your angel before him. Now the place of your angel is between us, it is fitting for us to become one. Receive from me, and by me, the gift of Grace. Dress yourself as a bride expecting her bridegroom, that you might be what I am, and I what you are. Nurture the seed of light in your bridal chamber. Receive from me a spouse, and receive him while he receives you. Look! Grace has descended on you. Open your mouth and prophesy." When the woman replies, "I have never prophesied, nor do I even know how to," he continues his invocations. To confound his deluded victim he says, "Open your mouth, speak whatever comes to you, and you will prophesy." Then, puffed up and elated by these words, and greatly excited by the prospect that she herself is to prophesy, with her heart pounding, she reaches the required pitch of audacity, and idly and impudently utters some nonsense that happens to occur to her...After that she considers herself a prophetess, and is thankful to Marcus for giving to her of his own Grace. She rewards him, not only by giving him her possessions (through which he has emassed a large fortune), but also by giving herself to him, wishing in every way to be united and find oneness with him.
>
> ...A sad example of this was an Asian, one of our deacons, who invited Marcus into his home. His wife, a woman of remarkable beauty, fell victim in mind and body to this magician, and, for a long time, traveled about with him. When at last, with no little difficulty, the brethren converted her, she spent all her time in public confession, weeping and lamenting over the way this magician had defiled her.
>
> Some of his disciples, too, have become addicted to the same

practices, and have deceived and defiled many silly women.[9]

Even if the vast majority of Gnostics were respectable people, Irenaeus made sure this charlatan, and a few of his disciples, served to drag their name through the mud. Vilification tactics seem to have been much the same then as they are today.

Although other sects were persecuted by the Romans, as when Diocletian pronounced his edict against the Manichaens, Christianity was regarded with more suspicion than its rivals. This was because its followers would not worship the emperor as a god, which made it seditious, quite apart from being revolutionary due to the nature of Jesus' teachings. Also carefully noted was the fact that Christianity was a "book religion" which promoted education among its followers because the ability to read helped in understanding its doctrine. Older religions in the area, except for Judaism, made no such appeal to personal intelligence.[10] Christianity had the power to invade people's minds — a two edged sword if ever there was one — and later the Roman Empire and other political powers-that-be would put this to work in their quest for political control. For now, though, persecution took the form of confiscating Christian Scriptures and torturing and killing a few people who made a point of opposing the imperial divinity. The emperor Trajan initially tried to be tolerant of Christians, hoping they would be reasonable and respect his divinity, however this didn't last for long. In a testy interview, Bishop Ignatius of Antioch told the emperor that he was mistaken to believe in his own divinity, and for his pains he was sent to Rome in chains and thrown to wild beasts in a public stadium.

Other Christians were tortured to death by the Romans in the Lyons amphitheater. Many gave up their faith and avoided being butchered, but some would not submit. There is the moving story of a slave called Blandina who, after being brutally tortured until her whole body was distorted and covered in wounds, was still able to say she was a Christian, and not ashamed of it. After this treatment she was tied to a post in the arena, and exposed as food for the wild beasts let loose there.[11] When the beasts didn't attack her, she was returned to prison to be sacrificed on another day. Finally, the eye-witness account continues:

> On the last day of the games Blandina was brought in again with Ponticus, a boy of about fifteen. Every day they had been brought back to watch the others being punished, and attempts had been made to make them swear by the heathen idols. When they stood firm and treated these efforts with contempt, the crowd became so infuriated with them that the boy's tender age brought forth no pity and the woman commanded no respect. They put them through every horror and punishment in turn, trying again and again to make them swear, but to no avail. Ponticus bravely endured every punishment, encouraged by his sister in Christ, till he gave his spirit back to God. Finally, like a noble mother who had encouraged her children and sent them on in triumph to the King, blessed Blandina suffered all the ordeals of her children and sped to join them, rejoicing as if invited to a wedding supper, rather than being thrown to the beasts. After the whips, the beasts, and the griddle [a heated iron chair victims were forced to sit in which burned their flesh and suffocated them with the smell,[12]] she was put into a basket and thrown to a bull. The animal tossed her many times, but she had become indifferent to it, because of her surety in her faith of communing with Christ. When she was finally sacrificed, the heathen conceded that they had never yet known a woman suffer so much or so long.[13]

Blandina, though a weak, despised woman, had the power of faith, and not even the world's most powerful empire could make her do what she did not want to do.[14] In time, the spectacle of this woman and others, bravely facing torture and death rather than abandoning their beliefs, began to impress the spectators. The authorities stepped up the persecution, but many people came to the faith.

Although Christians would not admit the emperor's divinity, they were prepared to compromise with Rome in many other respects. As a result, not that many Christians were martyred, considering how widespread Christianity's following was. By the end of the third century almost ten percent of the population of the Roman Empire was Christian, yet the church father Origen testified that those who had died for the Christian faith had been few and could easily be counted.[15]

Origen was a writer and teacher about Christianity in the third century, and is regarded as the most important father of the early church, before Christianity became the imperial religion. Except for Augustine, he is still the most frequently studied Church Father.[16] He was one of the great creators of the mystical language and spiritual themes later used in the church. Origen wrote many Biblical commentaries, and a number of works of speculative theology, aimed at combating some of the more destructive heresies of his day. He was the teacher of most of the Christian writers of the fourth century, and gave an intellectual rigour to Christianity which played an important part in converting the Roman empire. Despite this, much of his work was later misunderstood, and in the late fourth and fifth centuries his speculative theology, under the tag of *Origenism*, was attacked as being heretical — rather ironically, as it had been written to combat heresies.[17]

Most of the "erroneous" doctrines Origen was later accused of can't, in fact, be safely attributed to him, when all his writings are taken into account. However, there was one doctrine, later declared heretical, which he clearly did believe in, and this was his favorite hypothesis of the pre-existence of souls, including that of Christ.[18] This hypothesis, developed from the Platonic doctrine of metempsychosis (reincarnation), was used by him to counter the Marcionite accusation that the Creator must be wicked since he was manifestly unfair in creating some creatures angels, others demons, and the rest an enormous diversity of people with very unequal prospects. Origen's answer was that in the beginning God created pure intelligences, all equal, which were given ethereal bodies. These spent their time contemplating God. All except Christ grew cold in their fervor and became souls...The depth of their fall differentiated them into angels, men and demons. God then created the material world and gross bodies to provide men a means for redemption.[19]

Under this theory all souls are created equal, and differences in condition are due to the choices made by each person. Evil thus comes from individual misuse of free will, and not from God. The pre-existence of souls before birth does not necessarily imply reincarnation, as souls could be created a relatively short time before being born, and each one could be allocated just one life in a physical body. Origen's version of this doctrine, however, does seem to imply reincarnation, and in his time, and afterwards, it was certainly taken to imply it. After all, how could the souls of the current generation of humans still be in physical bodies millions of years after first being given them at the creation of the world, as Origen maintained was the case, if they could only be allocated to a body once? The view that souls are pre-existent, and are reborn many times, is called *reincarnationism,* and is one of three schools within the development of Christian thought on the origin of the individual soul. The other two views are *creationism,* which maintains that God creates a new soul for each human being at conception, and *traducianism,* which claims the soul is transmitted along with the body by the parents. All three views have had their supporters at various times during the history of the church.[20]

That Origen believed in reincarnation is not to say that he held an heretical belief. Origen was a fighter against heresy, and would hardly have deliberately and openly persisted in heretical belief. Reincarnation had not yet been made an heresy, and Origen's belief in it suggests there was widespread acceptance of it among Christians of his day. There is certainly no record of any of his contemporaries criticizing him for the belief, though he was a controversial figure in other respects. This may seem surprising, but we should remember that for four hundred years the Hebrew and early Christian world had been very much under Greek influence. Middle Platonism was the philosophical foundation of Origen's theology, and Greek influences on the New Testament have long been noted. Add this to the fact that the doctrine of reincarnation (rebirth) was as elaborately developed in ancient Greece as it was in India, with the philosophers Pythagoras, Empedocles, Plato, and even Plotinus in the third century A.D., all teaching it, then it becomes clear why there was a widespread belief in reincarnation in the early Christian church.[21] Origen also took the position of believing there was no everlasting punishment in hell, as would be expected of a believer in reincarnation, and this, likewise, doesn't seem to have been an heretical position in the early church.[22]

The increasing intellectual sophistication of Christianity, following Origen, made it more appealing to Roman citizens. In this situation, the church became increasingly intent on wooing the Roman Empire, and gaining converts among people in high places. The compromises the church made with the political powers-that-be included accepting the legality of slavery, though trying to encourage masters to treat their slaves well. And the church certainly compromised the standards of meekness and separation from worldliness taught by Jesus. Martin E. Marty commented on the ethics of the time keeping up with its shifting standards: in the past, the meek were to have inherited the earth, but by the time of the conversion to Christianity of the emperor Constantine the church had cast its lot with the influential and worldly.[23] An hierarchical power structure had begun to emerge in the church as early as the beginning of the second century. At that time, Bishop Ignatius of Antioch, whose martyrdom we mentioned earlier, wrote:

> All of you follow the bishop as Jesus Christ followed the
> Father, and follow the presbytery as the Apostles; and respect
> the deacons as the commandment of God. Let no man perform
> anything pertaining to the church without the bishop...
> Wherever the bishop appears, there let the people be, just as,
> wheresoever Christ Jesus is, there is the Catholic Church.
> (Epistle to the Smyrneans, VIII)

This is in spite of the fact that only a century earlier, in the church of the Book of Acts, Bishops and presbyters only assumed the secular functions of overseeing finances and serving at tables.[24] Already the bishops and priests were in place again, acting as intermediaries between God and the people. It did not take the church long to compromise the principles Jesus laid down, in an attempt to find worldly security, and exercise power over people. Paul had foreseen that the church would become corrupt soon after he left it. These words of his were directed to the Ephesian elders in particular, but were certainly prophetic of the church in general:

> "I know that after I leave, savage wolves will come in among you and will not spare the flock. Even from your own number men will arise and distort the truth in order to draw away disciples after them."   (Acts 20:29–30)

Having already moved this far from its founding principles, the church did not have to move all that much further to accommodate the compromises sought by Constantine. The church had already begun to "sell its soul" to the empire, and couldn't wait to sign it away altogether, in return for Christianity being made the official state religion. At the Council of Nicaea (in 325 A.D.) the church was eating out of Constantine's hand.

Chapter 7

The Church Becomes Mistress of the State

"Alas!" Emperor Vespasian, destroyer of Judaea, jested on his death bed, "I think I am turning into a god."[1] It had long been supposed that Roman emperors became gods when they died, but later Roman emperors, starting with Aurelian, took the inevitable further step of declaring themselves gods while they were still alive. The emperor Diocletian, for instance, went to considerable lengths to use his "divinity" to impose order on his unruly empire. He split his empire into two halves, each under an emperor, and further subdivided it into administrative *dioecese*, named after himself, governed by officials called *vicarii*. Diocletian outlawed Christianity, and ordered its clergy to submit to the imperial cult, its churches to be shut, and its sacred books to be destroyed. He was the god, a personification and emanation of the chief god of the Roman pantheon, Jupiter.[2] His palace included a vast hall designed for his subjects to worship him in. Subsequently, churches and cathedrals were modelled on this hall of worship, with its rows of Roman arches high on Corinthian columns leading to a facade based on a triumphal arch. Diocletian sat on a throne underneath the semi-circular triumphal arch, where the Bible on its altar was later placed; the silks and gold, pearls and precious stones which decked out the emperor, were later used to cover and decorate imperial altar Bibles. Incense was censed around the throne.[3]

Despite the grandeur, Diocletian wasn't a very convincing god. He abdicated as emperor well before he died, after suffering a kind of nervous breakdown, and went back to his palace in the country to grow vegetables.[4] In a letter to his friend and former co-emperor Maximian, who had tried to draw him into leadership again to help establish his son in the succession to the imperial throne, Diocletian said that if he could only see the splendid cabbages he had planted in the palace gardens with his own hands, he would no longer urge him to give up his enjoyment of happiness for the pursuit of power.[5] At the same time he continued to hold court as a god. But a god growing cabbages as a hobby can't have been very convincing.

Other attempts at state religion before Diocletian also had their heyday, before being absorbed into Roman life. Septimus Severus insisted on only marrying a woman who had been born under the same sign of the zodiac as himself. He found the wife he was looking for in the daughter of the High Priest of the Syrian national cult of Sol Invictus. The couple portrayed themselves as personifications of the gods Sol and Luna on coins of the time.[6]

Once the Syrian High-Priestly family had married into the Roman Imperial dynasty, the stage was set for some remarkable happenings. After Septimus Severus died, his sister-in-law engineered a coup through which her fourteen-year-old grandson, the hereditary High Priest of the sun god Sol Invictus, became the Roman emperor. Because he was beautiful, and the high priest of their chosen religion, the Roman Army rallied behind him. He became the emperor Marcus Aurelius Antonius, though he preferred to be called Elagabalus. He went to Rome with the particular purpose of placing his beloved Sol Invictus Elagabal above Jupiter, as the premier god of the Roman pantheon. He left the government of the empire to his grandmother, and concentrated on just two things: trying to win everyone over to his cult, and living a carefree, voluptuous life. He quickly became disliked by many in Rome, because he didn't even try to adapt to a Roman lifestyle. (It would seem he failed to obey the dictum: "When in Rome, do as the Romans do.") He treated Roman customs with contempt and insolence: he would wear only his Asian costume of purple silk embroidered with gold, and adorned with necklaces and bracelets. He enthusiastically celebrated the orgies of his god, and, surrounded by his harem of women and eunuchs, lived a life of decadence and debauchery.[7]

He was still held in high esteem by most of the public, though, and his soldiers loved him. This gave him the scope to perpetrate many more enormities in Rome, including the establishment of a senate of women, and dressing and behaving like a woman himself. He set out to combine all religions, and make them subservient to Sol Invictus Elagabal. Rome could have accepted this syncretism, as it was heading that way anyway, and some of the changes Elagabalus brought in did survive, but the young emperor was too brash, domineering and inconsiderate of the ways of Rome to be able to achieve what he wanted. Repugnance of his sect grew when its deviant behavior intruded on Roman life — when, for instance, sex organs amputated in honor of Sol Invictus were, in a religious rite, thrown into the temples, and when the most beautiful young children were sacrificed to the Sun God. The thing which finally brought the rage of Rome down on Elagabalus's head, though, was divorcing his first wife and marrying Aquila Severa, a Vestal Virgin. By doing this he hoped to unite his cult with the honored cult of Vesta, and so further the acceptance of Sol Invictus. But by violating all that Rome had held most holy for centuries, in marrying a renunciant from a sacred order of nuns, he provoked widespread anger and retaliation. Revolt was only averted when he was persuaded to dissolve the marriage, and even then his reprieve was temporary. Within a few months the hate his loathsome behavior had engendered caused him to be murdered, and led to every reminder of him being banished from Rome. His much more reasonable and respectful cousin, Alexander Severus, became emperor, and brought normalcy back to Rome.[8]

Although even the memory of Elagabalus was expunged from Roman life, the worship of Sol Invictus continued, and fifty years later, under the emperor Aurelian, was ripe for a revival. Aurelian again made the worship of Sol Invictus the official religion of the empire, and used it to promote political unity. Unlike Elagabalus, he succeeded, and he did so by pursuing his goal with moderation and intelligence, and by combining it with a successful re-unification of the empire.

Rather than imposing something foreign on the Romans, he adapted the cult to Roman tastes, so it became a Roman nationalistic religion. Elements drawn from all the cults of the sun were used to give it a Roman character. All the old gods were held to be equal, then Sol Invictus became the sum of these deities, a Roman super god, "Deus Sol Invictus." This was a perfect syncretism, and, what was more, it created a specifically Roman cult, for the Roman people. A great circular temple was constructed for Sol, and on December 25th, his official day of celebration, circus games were held in his honor.[9]

Aurelian was convinced the cult of Sol Invictus was the mortar he needed to cement his political system into a solid, long-lasting structure. Part of the reason was that it brought an aura of divinity to the office of emperor.[10] Aurelian was the first emperor to take the title *Deus* during his lifetime. His subjects regarded him as being at one with the Sun God, and an emanation of him. To ensure the religion's continuation he established a college of priests, who were chosen from Senators and the most aristocratic families. The cult had been turned into a powerful political weapon, but an even more powerful force was knocking at the door: Christianity. Aurelian mounted a campaign of persecution against the Christians (in 275 A.D.), but within a year he was murdered. The cult of Deus Sol Invictus was obviously not a final answer to Rome's problems, but it did survive in strength for another hundred years. All the following emperors up to and including Constantine supported it. Diocletian, although he elevated Jupiter to the position of principal god, by no means abandoned Sol. Constantine, the first Christian Emperor, initially styled himself the "Sun Emperor," the personification of Sol Invictus on earth.[11] But as we shall see, Constantine also went a step further in enlisting the support of an even greater god, the creator of the sun and everything else. This ultimate god, who was becoming more and more popular amongst Romans, was the God of Christianity.

Constantine, the son of Constantius, emperor of the West, grew up in Diocletian's court. After Diocletian abdicated, the young Constantine became a hostage of Galarius, the new emperor of the East. A year later Constantine was called to York by his dying father, and his flight to his father, traveling by forced marches, and killing the post horses behind him to defeat pursuit, is the stuff of legends.[12] At the age of twenty-one, in 306 A.D., immediately following his father's death, Constantine was proclaimed emperor of the West by his father's legions. Galarius was forced to acknowledge this *fait accompli*, and accepted him as Caesar of the West under Severus, the old Caesar, whom he advanced to Augustus (emperor). He would have hoped to render Constantine harmless in this way till he could be dealt with later, but this was not to be. After seven years of brilliant campaigning, during which he adopted Sol Invictus as his patron deity, Constantine entered Rome in triumph, having defeated a much larger army, and killed a rival emperor, Maxentius, in the final battle. He'd had a dream that he would win if he fought the battle under the sign of a monogram used by Christians, which consisted of the Greek letters Chi-Rho, the first two letters of "Christ." He had all his troops paint this monogram on their shields, and won the decisive battle of Milvian Bridge. However, the coins minted in celebration of this great victory were dedicated to his legions' favourite god, Sol Invictus, and the victory arch erected in his honour, which stands to this day beside the Colosseum, was adorned with traditional pagan symbols.[13]

Constantine was now undisputed emperor in the West, and the only other emperor was Licinius in the East, who, as Galerius's comrade, was Constantine's implacable enemy. Nevertheless these two *Augustii* met in Milan, and agreed to ban the persecution of Christians. Constantine had already been involved in church politics for some time, adjudicating in disputes and receiving petitions. This was an ideal situation for the church: no longer persecuted, but still independent. It was not to last, though. Twelve years after the Milan conference, Constantine accused Licinius of reviving persecution of Christians in the east, and attacked and defeated him. Licinius' life was initially spared at the request of his wife Constantia,

Constantine's sister. Two years later, however, only a few months after the Council of Nicaea, where he helped lay down the guidelines for a united imperial Christianity, Constantine went on a killing spree. He put Licinius to death on a charge of treasonable intrigue, then went on to kill his own son Crispus, who had ably and loyally served him as a general, and the younger Licinius, his sister's son, who was, at the most, twelve years old. Next he put to death his wife Fausta, reputedly by boiling her alive in her own bath, and went on to kill a number of his friends.[14] By determination, ruthlessness, and military genius, Constantine had made himself the most powerful man in the world, but he was obviously anxious about his grip on power, and prepared to do anything to ensure it. His giant ego is testified to by the colossal statue he had made of himself in Rome. Judging by the huge marble head, the entire statue must have been at least fifty feet tall. An even greater monument to himself was the city of Constantinople, which was extravagantly adorned at the expense of a looted empire. Constantine was certainly no humble follower of Jesus — there were other reasons for his courting of Christianity.

Almost immediately after uniting the empire under himself, Constantine had convened the first general council of the Christian church at Nicaea. Having seen human "gods" like Diocletian fail as a binding force for the empire, and noting the wide appeal of Christianity, and the futility of Diocletian's attempts to persecute it, Constantine was determined to use Christianity as the "glue" to hold his empire together. At this council of Nicaea (in 325 A.D.) the precise nature of Christian faith was negotiated, and its relationship to Constantine and his successors established. The way Constantine orchestrated the council was brilliant. He seized the initiative from the eastern bishops who had called a smaller council to excommunicate some heretics who didn't believe in the full divinity of Jesus. In a letter announcing his imperial convocation, Constantine wrote:

It had been agreed that the Synod of Bishops should meet at

Ancyra of Galatia, but, it seems to us on a number of counts, that it would be better for a Synod to assemble at Nicaea, a city of Bithynia, both because the Bishops of Italy and the rest of Europe are coming, and because of the excellent temperature of the air, and so that I may be present as a spectator and participator in the things that will be done...[15]

He didn't mention the excommunications; his desire was for unity, not confrontation. And moving the council to Nicaea brought it under his control. The bishops were summoned by the emperor to a place only a few miles from the palace where the recently defeated (and soon to be executed) Licinius lived. Constantine filled the church council with his imperial presence and purpose, and carefully created the grandeur of this first image of Christendom. Church leaders from the four corners of the world attended it. One eyewitness declared: "It might have seemed the likeness of the Kingdom of Christ." Later generations even believed this council had been directly guided by the Holy Spirit. And to this day, as Dean Stanley has pointed out, every church feels it has some standing in the Council of Nicaea.[16]

The most important results of the Council of Nicaea were twenty statements containing rules of behavior for clergy, and the famous creed of faith known ever since as the *Nicene Creed*. Here is an early form of it from Rome at about 340 A.D.:

I believe in God almighty.
And in Christ Jesus, his only son, our Lord
Who was born of the Holy Spirit and the Virgin Mary,
Who was crucified under Pontius Pilate and was buried,
And the third day rose from the dead
Who ascended into heaven
And sitteth on the right hand of the Father
Whence he cometh to judge the living and the dead.
And in the Holy Ghost
The holy church
The remission of sins
The resurrection of the flesh
The life everlasting.[17]

Later versions have seen fit to add that Jesus "died" and "descended into hell." Perhaps this was because the original creed didn't mention hell, reflecting its lack of importance in the early church, and the medieval church, whose allegiance was largely built around the fear of hell, thought a reference to it should be added to help keep the thought of it uppermost in people's hearts and minds. The reference to Jesus dying could have been added to counteract the popular contention that Jesus didn't die on the cross, but merely went into a swoon resembling death.

This creed, still used by most churches as a basic statement of faith, was a result of careful compromise at the Council. Other creeds were rejected before this Jerusalem baptismal creed, which had its origins in the earliest days of the church, was selected. It is an inspiring creed, and everybody was able to agree with what it said, so it fostered unity in the church emerging from Nicaea. Most Christians, even today, see it as being profoundly true and beautiful. It is, however, a limited statement, as notable for what it *doesn't* say, as for what it does. It is far from being a balanced statement of Christian belief, let alone a comprehensive one.

Missing from the Nicene Creed is any reference at all to Jesus' teachings, especially his all-important teachings on the kingdom of heaven. Missing is any suggestion that we can all, individually, come into God's presence in prayer, and know Him during this life. Missing is Jesus' teaching that you can't serve both God and worldly ambition. The very practical basis of the spiritual life, which Jesus taught, is totally missing from this creed. This was, of course, necessary for the creed to be acceptable to Constantine, who was a worldly and ambitious man, and who didn't want Christianity to be a practical teaching which could guide people's lives, but rather a romantic, other-worldly faith. Constantine wanted to be the absolute ruler on earth, and have God far away in heaven, fully accessible only after death, and in the meanwhile only in a limited way through an hierarchy of priests and bishops. And most bishops wanted the same thing as Constantine, because they were a part of the power structure which was emerging. Any suggestion that people could attain salvation directly from God, without the help of the church as an intermediary, would undermine their importance, privilege and power. So the bishops forgot Jesus' teachings, and were willing collaborators with Constantine in molding Christianity into an instrument to serve the ambitions of the power hungry. Admittedly there were some who later regretted signing the Nicene formula. After returning home, Eusebius of Nicomedia wrote: "We have committed an impious act, O Prince, by subscribing to a blasphemy from fear of you."[18] But it was too late then to change what had happened. The course of history for over a thousand years to come had been established.

The Nicene Creed portrayed God as a remote and unknowable unity of Father, Son and Holy Ghost. The only direct contact with God was seen as having been in the remote past, when Jesus walked the earth. God was, in these later times, only approachable through the hierarchy of the church, and Constantine stood at the top of this pyramid of power, which reached down through the bishops and priests and deacons to the people. The church took over the forms of worship created by Diocletian for himself, and Sunday, the day of the god *Sol Invictus*, became confirmed as the official day of worship at the expense of Saturday, the Jewish Sabbath. The date and form of the celebration of Christmas were also adopted from the cult of *Sol Invictus*. Up until the middle of the fourth century Christ's birthday was observed, though not much celebrated, on Epiphany, the 6th of January. On the 25th of December pagan celebrations were held in honor of *Sol Invictus*. A day or two after the winter solstice, when the sun's warmth had waned to a minimum, and had just begun to grow again, the rebirth of the sun's power was celebrated, accompanied by a profusion of lights and torches, the decoration of branches and small trees, and the giving of gifts. So popular was this festival, that even after being converted to Christianity, Romans continued to celebrate it. The Church Fathers of the fourth century saw this as a danger, so they shifted the celebration of the birth of

Christ to that day, and informed the people that from then on it would be held in honor of the true Sun God, who had created the world and everything in it.[19]

In this new packaging of Christianity for the Roman Empire, Jesus was reduced to a figurehead, a mere sacrificial lamb of the past, and his reforms were reversed and his teachings ignored. The bishops were so enthusiastic about Christianity becoming the official religion of the empire that they don't appear to have even noticed that they were selling their souls, giving in to the very temptation to hold worldly power that Jesus resisted during his forty days in the wilderness. They were rendering the church to Caesar, and celebrating the process. Diocletian may have fed a few individual Christians to the lions, but Constantine, with the cooperation of the bishops, threw Christianity itself to the lions of the decaying Roman Empire, and put the dismembered pieces back together into an instrument of conquest and control which bore little resemblance to the gentle, visionary, peace-loving Jesus. This was a syncretism which surpassed even Aurelian's creation of Deus Sol Invictus. The metamorphosis of the church into a monster passed the point of no return at Nicaea. The medieval Christian church was born.

Chapter 8

Doctrinal Bickering—Preparing the Way for Islam

The early medieval church is particularly remembered for its "ecumenical" councils, where differences in belief were aired and the church attempted to establish a common canon of doctrine in which it could be unified. Once a canonical belief had been established, dissenters could be declared heretics, and be expelled from the church and persecuted. Although these councils were called "ecumenical," and superficially had the same aim as the modern ecumenical movement, to formulate doctrine acceptable to the whole church, in fact they were very different. Their aim was to force a common doctrine on to all whether they liked it or not, whereas modern ecumenicalism aims to try and find genuine common ground, and foster understanding and tolerance of dissenting views, which are allowed to co-exist.

During the time of the ecumenical councils, the popes (bishops of Rome) were generally more tolerant of dissenting views than were the emperors of Constantinople. These emperors, following in the footsteps of Constantine, were the real rulers of the early medieval church, and they attempted to rule the church the way they ruled their empires: as dictators, establishing an absolute and fixed order. Only the bishops of Rome were strong enough and independent enough to attempt to stand up to the emperor, and although they often came out of clashes with the emperor the worse for wear, most continued to insist on exerting a measure of independence.

Although Constantine fused the church with empire, and made it very much a political organization, at least he was diplomatic and moderate in his pronouncements. Not all the emperors who followed were so reasonable. In 380 A.D. the Emperor Theodosius made this decree from Thessalonica:

> We desire that all peoples who fall beneath the sway of our
> imperial clemency should profess the faith which we believe to
> have been communicated by the Apostle Peter to the Romans and
> maintained in its traditional form to the present day...And we
> require that those who follow this rule of faith should embrace
> the name of Catholic Christians, adjudging all others madmen
> and ordering them to be designated as heretics...[1]

This policy was sanctioned by the sword, and it prevailed. One
modern Protestant reaction to this decree is: "This was the
WORST CALAMITY that has ever befallen the Church."[2] The
rationalistic historian Gibbon concurred; he was convinced the
genius of Rome died with Theodosius.

The nature of Jesus' divinity and humanity was the issue
which the bishops had originally planned to discuss at the
council which Constantine broadened into the Council of
Nicaea. Arius had denied the eternity and full divinity of Jesus.
His position was discussed and rejected at Nicaea, the council
asserting that Jesus, as Son of God, is "begotten, not made,"
and "of the same substance as the Father." The council excommunicated Arius and his followers. This same issue of the
nature of Jesus, often called "Christology," went on to dominate all the early councils. While the medieval church largely
ignored Jesus' teachings, it was obsessed with establishing an
exact definition of who he was within the Trinity, and, to the
modern mind, the hair-splitting that took place is quite aston-
ishing. The adverse consequences to Christianity of the stupid-
ity which accompanied it were, as we shall see, staggering.

Theodosius I convoked the second ecumenical council (The
first council of Constantinople, of 381 A.D.). Its purpose was
to confirm Nicaea's insistence on the full divinity of Jesus as
Son, and to condemn those who denied that the Holy Spirit is a
distinct individual within the Trinity.

The Council of Ephesus was called (in 431 A.D.) to resolve
a bitter dispute between Nestorius, bishop of Constantinople,
and Cyril, bishop of Alexandria, over the proper way of
conceiving the relationship between the divine and the human
in Jesus. It was also to decide the propriety of calling Mary

"Mother of God," as Cyril insisted on doing, but Nestorius refused to allow, arguing that Mary could only be the mother of Jesus' humanity.[3] The two sides refused to meet, and the council ended abortively with both sides excommunicating the other. Two years later, Cyril reached an agreement with the more moderate of Nestorius's supporters to accept the title *theotokos* (Mother of God) as valid, and to excommunicate Nestorius, but nevertheless recognize that Jesus has two distinct natures, human and divine, united without confusion in a single individual. On the basis of this agreement which accepted a moderate form of Nestorianism as valid, the Meeting of Cyril's party at Ephesus came to be regarded as the third ecumenical council.

Despite this agreement, argument continued over "whether the humanity of Jesus constituted a distinct and operative reality or 'nature' after the incarnation of the Word."[4] This led the emperor Marcian to convoke a meeting of 350 bishops, the Council of Chalcedon (of 451 A.D.), and forced them to formulate a doctrine on Christ which would accommodate a variety of theological traditions. A Nestorian "two-nature" Christology, favored by the popes in Rome, was again adopted, but it did not resolve the dispute. In fact it fueled the fire of controversy, and caused the "Monophysite" Christians, who opposed the dual nature of Christ, and considered he was just the incarnate divine word, to break from the official church. After a century of recriminations, the emperor Justinian again attempted to resolve the issue. We will look at his attempt in some detail, as it is a good illustration of the dynamics of the early medieval church.

Justinian at first ruled the empire for his uncle Justin, then after nine years (in 527 A.D.) became emperor himself. During the early part of his rule he did his best to heal the rift which had developed with Rome. As a result, the pope congratulated Justinian on his zeal for promoting peace in the church, and Justinian vigorously persecuted the break-away Monophysites throughout the empire, including the Syrian Arabs. Monophysites found shelter in Egypt, though, and continued to spread their teaching. Both religious zeal and political expediency moved Justinian to a position of agreement with the pope. While he was Consul (in 521 A.D.), however, something happened to Justinian which would cause him to totally change his attitude to the church: he met Theodora.

Theodora was the second of three daughters of a bear-keeper at the hippodrome. She was sent into child prostitution and on to the stage by her widowed mother to help keep the family, and, as she grew up, her beauty, intelligence and wit soon charmed and scandalized Constantinople. She became famous for the follies of her entertainment, the boldness of her manner, and the large number of her lovers. Later she served as a concubine to the governor of Africa. After this, however, she returned to Constantinople, determined to better herself. She earned a quiet living spinning wool, and set herself the incredible goal of becoming empress. Amazingly, she captured the attention of Justinian, then heir to the throne and effective ruler of the empire, became his mistress, and soon had him charmed and in love. To please Justinian, the emperor conferred on Theodora the high title of Patrician, and then, to allow a marriage to take place, abrogated the law by which alliances between senators or high officials and actresses were forbidden. Justinian married Theodora shortly before he ascended the throne, and Theodora was crowned with him on Easter day (in 527 A.D.). When Justinian became emperor later in the year, on the death of his uncle, he made Theodora an independent and equal co-ruler, to the point of inserting her name with his own in the oath of allegiance taken by provincial governors.

Justinian's harsh and corrupt administration led within five years to a dangerous uprising against his rule called the Nika Riot. Fires raged in Constantinople while Justinian shut himself up in his palace in despair, panicked, and thought to save himself by fleeing from the capital. At this point, when Justinian had ordered the imperial treasure to be loaded into ships, Theodora took charge. She rose in the council and said, "When safety only remains in flight still I will not flee. Those who have worn the crown should not survive its fall. I will never live to see the day when I shall no longer be saluted as Empress. Flee if you wish, Caesar; you have money, the ships await you, the sea is unguarded. As for me, I stay. I hold with the old proverb which says that the purple is a good winding sheet."[5] This display of courage and leadership roused the generals to stand and fight for the capital. A frightful battle ensued, in which a crowd of at least 30,000 rioters in the hippodrome were killed. Order was restored, and Justinian returned to an even more absolute rule than before, but it was Theodora who had achieved it.

Even before the Nika Riot, Theodora began promoting the cause of the Monophysites, who had been kind to her in Africa. She sheltered their bishops in her own quarters, and helped them establish churches and monasteries in Constantinople. Although Justinian initially championed the position of the Council of Chalcedon, favored by the popes, he gradually came around to Theodora's position and into conflict with the papacy. It was Pope Vigilius who bore the brunt of the attack. He tried to insist on upholding the decrees of Chalcedon, and on Rome being the final arbiter of high faith. Vigilius accepted Justinian's dogmatic edict condemning Origen, but three years later when Justinian condemned the "Three Chapters," the writings of three Nestorians, he fought back. The next year Vigilius was captured by the emperor and forced to sign a secret agreement with Justinian and Theodora that he would move against the Three Chapters.

After Theodora died (in 548), Justinian's position hardened even further; he became very intent on establishing the theological position favored by his late wife. The fight between the pope and Justinian heated up, and when the pope sent an encyclical letter to all Christians portraying his side of the argument, Justinian responded by ordering his arrest. The pope took refuge in a church, and clung to the columns of the altar to prevent the arresting officers from carrying him away. In the scuffle the altar was actually pulled over! At this the officials withdrew in disarray and the people rescued the pope.

The standoff continued until Justinian convoked the Second Council of Constantinople (of 553), to resolve the issue. When equal representation of Western and Eastern bishops was not allowed, the pope boycotted the council, suspecting, along with most Western bishops, that it would be used to weaken the stated faith of Chalcedon in the interests of political unity. He decided to submit his judgment in writing instead. He took a compromise position of condemning the doctrines attributed to two of the Nestorians, but exonerating the third, and of not condemning the men themselves, as they had died in peace with the Church. This document was condemned by Justinian, and the seventh session of the council, acting under his orders, condemned Vigilius and insisted he should repent. Justinian continued to harass Vigilius for some months, until he caved in to his demands. The pope, finally a broken man, wrote an admission of his error, saying he had been deceived by Satan into staying away from the council.

The council condemned the Nestorian writings (the Three Chapters), and, in pronouncing a series of anathemas, attempted to purge the church of Nestorianism. The council also pronounced anathemas against Origenism. Justinian had previously condemned Origen, in a letter, accusing him of believing in metempsychosis (reincarnation), and saying "Whoever teaches the fantastic pre-existence of the soul, and its monstrous restoration shall be damned." But at the council he actually raised the question of the conduct of certain Palestinian Origenists, rather than of Origen himself, and the anathemas against Origenism do not appear in the council's official acts, nor are they among the council proceedings subsequently endorsed by the pope.[6] Although Origen was seen as suspect by the Byzantine church, he continued to be widely studied in the Latin West until the thirteenth century. As a result, although this council is generally seen as being the place where the church declared reincarnation an anathema, it is doubtful whether this anathema, or any of those against Origen, can be considered to have been properly ratified by the council at all.

Just why Justinian should have objected to Origen, and in particular to his belief in reincarnation, is not clear. It could well be, as with his stand against Nestorianism, a case of him fighting for Theodora's theological beliefs. In support of this is a claim that Theodora didn't like the concept of reincarnation, as she felt that under it she would have to return in another life to pay the price for the immorality of her youth, and the cruelty to the many people she had ordered killed, and that she consequently set about having it abolished.[7] Although this has a certain logic to it, it should be noted, before putting too much store by it, that the contemporary historian Procopius' *Secret History* shows that many people hated Theodora, and probably as much out of jealously of her success as for dislike of her brutality. As a result, scurrilous rumors about her were bound to be floating around.[8] This story, then, may be no more than a rumor, but it is one theory, at least, and an intriguing one, suggesting motives typical of the times, about why Justinian set about trying to discredit the belief in reincarnation.

The Second Council of Constantinople didn't solve much. The pope's eventual acceptance of much of the proceedings resulted in decades of controversy in Italy and Africa, which spilled over into later councils. The church eventually came to see the earlier Chalcedon position as normative,[9] effectively rejecting Justinian's efforts at Constantinople as a distortion of Christianity. One of the effects of Justinian's council was to contribute substantially to the growing rift between the Eastern Church in Constantinople and the Western Church in Rome, which built up to the final schism between Roman Catholic Church and the Eastern Orthodox Church in 1054. Rome initially sought more political power to protect its independence from the emperors of Constantinople, but once this was established, used it for many centuries to control the life and politics of Western Europe.

Another quite astounding, but little heard of, consequence of this doctrinal bickering in the sixth century, was that it paved the way for the rise of Islam, which has ever since been the Christian world's greatest enemy, and fiercest competitor. The western Arabs in Syria had long been Monophysite Christians, and as such had been greatly persecuted by those favoring a dual-nature Christology, including Justinian himself, before he met Theodora. Mundhir, a late sixth century leader of the Syrian Arabs, like his father before him, proudly protected the Arab Christians from the Persian Arabs, who were pagans. He twice defeated the Persians, who were also the enemies of Constantinople and the Christian Empire, breaking their power. Conscious of the service he had rendered Constantinople, Mundhir wrote to one of Justinian's successors asking for money to pay his tribes for their military service. Not only did he receive back an insulting refusal from the emperor, but by mistake he also received a letter intended for the imperial commander, who had also been fighting the Persians, ordering him to invite Mundhir to a conference and kill him! Not surprisingly, this treachery caused Mundhir to withdraw his support, and this in turn allowed the Persians to regain their strength, regroup, and defeat the weak Greek forces. Mundhir was not, however, about to allow the Persians to plunder Christian Syria, so he once again fought on the side of the Greeks, and achieved a great victory over the Persians. This time he brought home huge amounts of booty, and was finally able to handsomely reward the tribes the emperor had refused to supply money to pay. After this Mundhir did his best to heal the rift in Christianity which kept his countrymen fighting each other, and had long been a cause of their persecution by the Greeks. He traveled to Constantinople (in 580 A.D.) to plead with the emperor to put a stop to the theological disputes which were ruining Arab Christianity, and to beg for tolerance of the Monophysite position. The emperor received him with honor, pledged his support, and called the disputing bishops together, getting them to agree to live in peace with each other. Unfortunately the disputing factions did not keep their promises, and were soon persecuting each other again.

Consideration of the political and military machinations of church leaders in those days shows why "bishops" are among the title pieces in the game of chess, along with knights, castles, kings and queens. Mundhir's appeal to the emperor obviously created resentment amongst some of the bishops, for the upshot of it was that a plot was laid against him. A false friend asked him to visit him to discuss a religious matter, and while Mundhir was away from his guards, accused him of treachery, seized him, and sent him in chains to Constantinople. He ended up in permanent forced exile in Sicily. This outrage, on top of all the persecution they had received from the empire, greatly angered the Arab Christians, and this anger soon hardened into an implacable hatred of the Greeks. From this time on the Syrian Arabs joined forces with the Persians, their former enemies, and the supremacy of the Christian Arabs ended. Although Christianity persisted amongst them, it became less popular, as it was seen to be associated with their loathsome enemies, the Greeks. This end of the predominance of Christianity amongst the Arabs, and their seeking instead unity amongst themselves, was a direct consequence of the treachery and intolerance of the Imperial Christian Church. The church would pay dearly for this treachery, and for its long history of shameful treatment of Arab Christians: Muhammad, the founder of Islam, was just at this time approaching manhood.[10]

Within two centuries Muhammad's powerful and united Islamic empire would advance as far as France, and threaten the very existence of Christian Europe. Constantinople itself, the capital of the early Christian empire, later fell to the Muslims, and remains Islamic to this day, as the city of Istanbul. Justinian's exquisitely beautiful church of Haghia Sophia, in this city, has been a Muslim Mosque since the fifteenth century. If the sixth century Christian establishment had been able to be even reasonably tolerant of Monophysite Christianity, and had been able to avoid even just the grossest of their treachery, then Muhammad would not have had fertile ground in which to plant his new religion, which was, in the beginning, only very reluctantly accepted by the Arabs, and it is highly likely the Arab world would be Christian today. Instead, the policy of the

Imperial Christians was, in the words of one modern scholar, "as foolish as it was wicked. Henceforth they stood for tyranny and injustice in the eyes of the Arabs, and through them Christianity was associated with perfidy."[11]

As a result of the rise of Islam, Eastern Christianity, while surviving, became much less influential, and the center of the Christian world shifted westward to Rome. It could be claimed that the rise of Islam was a necessary corrective for a corrupt Christianity. Certainly, the Enlightenment in the West in the last few centuries was made possible, at least partly, by the Islamic impetus to scholarship which was picked up by Europe from Muslim Sicily and Spain. As we shall see in later chapters, this Islamic influence helped drive the Renaissance and the push for the secular state in Europe and America. Of course, even more important forces were at work, too, such as the innate desire for freedom causing progressive people to join together to promote reform. The Freemasons were one of the earliest and most important reform groups, who worked behind the scenes to pave the way for the Enlightenment at a time when open advocacy of progressive ideas was met with swift and brutal retaliation by the church, both Protestant and Catholic. It is to the course of Western civilization that we will now turn our attention.

Chapter 9

Power Games of the Western Church

As the remains of the Western Empire sank into the dark ages following the sacking of Rome by the Goths (in 410 A.D.), two men, more than any others, were responsible for providing the Roman Church with an intellectual and philosophical framework which would allow it to survive four hundred years of the dark night of Europe, and see it emerge into the middle ages in a powerful position. These two men were Saint Jerome and Saint Augustine. Jerome provided the church, for the first time, with an accurate Latin translation of the Bible. This was essential for the Western Church's authority and independence from the Eastern Church. Augustine's theological brilliance gave the Roman Church the philosophy which became its justification in the course it pursued. Many would question whether Augustine's theology was soundly based on the Bible, but there can be no doubt that it was just what the medieval church was looking for, both in terms of answers to personal religious anxieties in a spiritually weak age, and in terms of justifying the political pretensions of the church. So appealing to the church was Augustine's theology, that much of it survives in church doctrine to the present day.

The church's struggle for survival had for some time been based on it being built on three pillars: a canon of Scripture (with books not included often being destroyed); a canon of doctrine (with opposing doctrine having anathemas declared against it); and the historic episcopate (a power structure of bishops, priests and deacons, with the bishops supposedly in a direct line of succession from the apostles, with what they supposed had been their function as intermediaries between man and God.)[1]

Jerome greatly bolstered the authority of the canon of Scripture by spending much of his life accurately and meticulously translating the Bible into a Latin version known as the *Vulgate*. It was polished enough to appeal to the sophisticated and intelligent Roman taste, and it lent great weight to the Roman church's claim of primacy. For a struggling church, it was valuable beyond price. With a few revisions and correct-ions, this was the Bible used by the church right through till modern times, and it was the inspiration down through the ages of the saints who were the spiritual strength of Christian-ity. What the Bible says may have been much ignored and misunderstood by the church throughout its history, but the church has always highly revered the book itself, and time and time again has gone to great pains to preserve it accurately.

The other two pillars of the church, the canon of doctrine and the historical episcopate, were stoutly bolstered by August-ine's theology. As a young man Augustine excelled in his literary education, but was anything but pious or virtuous. He had a vulgar manner and a violent temper. His passions were fervent, and he often gave way to sensual temptation. He was involved in an illicit relationship, from which a son was born. His loving Christian mother, though, never forsook him, and was, in the end, able to rescue him from this path of "sin."[2] For a long time after this he was a very unconventional, indeed an heretical, Christian. Reading a work by Cicero converted him to the love of divine wisdom, but he remained repelled by the apparent barbarity of the Bible. He started following Manichaeism, a Gnostic sect with a dualistic theology which encouraged asceticism and intense devotion to Christ. This appealed to him because of the out of control battle between the dualistic forces of good and evil taking place in his own soul. He remained in this sect for nine years, before becoming disillusioned with it and going to Rome, where for some time he despaired of finding any certainty of belief. After being appointed Imperial Rhetorician at Milan, he came under the influence of Bishop Ambrose and the ideas of Neoplatonism. From these influences he learned that Christianity could be eloquent and intelligent, and that the Old Testament stories he found barbaric could be treated as allegories. At the age of thirty-three Augustine's conversion to Christianity came suddenly and dramatically. He just couldn't bear his old life anymore. He described what happened in his autobiographical *Confessions*:

> I probed the hidden depths of my soul and wrung its pitiful secrets from it, and when I gathered them all before the eyes of my heart, a great storm broke within me, bringing with it a great deluge of tears...For I felt that I was still the slave of my sins, and in my misery I kept crying, "How long shall I go on saying 'Tomorrow, tomorrow'? Why not now? Why not make an end of my ugly sins at this moment?"
>
> I was asking myself these questions, weeping all the while with the most bitter sorrow in my heart, when all at once I heard the sing-song voice of a child in a nearby house. Whether it was the voice of a boy or a girl I cannot say, but again and again it repeated the chorus, "Take it and read, take it and read." At this I looked up, thinking hard whether there was any kind of game in which children used to chant words like these, but I could not remember ever hearing them before. I checked my flood of tears and stood up, telling myself that this could only be God's command to open my book of Scripture and read the first passage on which my eyes fell. For I had head the story of Antony, and I remembered how he had happened to go into a church while the Gospel was being read and had taken it as an instruction addressed to himself when he heard the words, "Go home and sell all that belongs to you. Give it to the poor, and so the treasure you have shall be in heaven; then come back and follow me." By this divine message he had at once been converted to you.
>
> So I hurried back to the place where Alypius was sitting, for when I stood up to move away I had put down the book containing Paul's Letters. I seized it and opened it, and in silence I read the first passage on which my eyes fell: "Not in orgies and drunkenness, not in immorality and debauchery, not in dissension and jealousy. Rather, clothe yourselves with the Lord Jesus Christ, and spend no more thought on how to gratify the desires of the sinful nature." I had no wish to read more and no need to do so. For in an instant, as I came to the end of the sentence, it was as though the light of faith flooded into my heart and all the darkness of doubt was dispelled.[3]

The nature of Augustine's past life, and this sudden conversion, helps explain much of his subsequent theology. He very much thought he had no free will because it had always failed him in the fight against sin, and that it was only through God's grace that he was able to achieve anything at all. Luther and Calvin both strongly identified with this view. Luther, an Augustinian monk, said he was more indebted to Augustine than to any other writer. Calvin constantly quoted him, and eulogized him as the best of the Fathers. Many people in all ages have identified with him. Yet Augustine's position was an extreme one, which can't be adequately justified from a balanced reading of the Bible. An example of this is his firm belief in the predestination and perseverance of the "fixed number of the elect." Many of Augustine's beliefs are among the items of church doctrine which are questioned by a growing number of people in modern society. And indeed they came into question in Augustine's own lifetime — this was what the famous Pelagian controversy was all about.

Pelagius was a British monk who came to Rome in the last decade of the fourth century. A well-educated, clear-headed man, sober and strict in his morals, he was appalled at the laxness of conduct he observed in Rome, even among the clergy. He attributed this moral weakness to the doctrine of man's helplessness, which he could see no basis for believing in. Pelagius had not, like Augustine, wrestled in agony with temptation and been defeated. He had been able to discipline himself, and no doubt believed Augustine and his followers were indulgent and weak-willed, and had given up the fight against temptation far too easily. Perhaps the most unfortunate consequence of Augustine's position was that it logically led to a belief in the predestination of a fixed elect. If people have no real free will to choose right from wrong, to choose to love God rather than the world, but are indeed helpless, and totally dependent on God drawing them to him and saving them by the power of His grace alone, then who gets saved must totally depend on God, and it is a nonsense to say that the good will be rewarded for their virtue, and the bad punished for the lack of it, for there is, in this case, no such thing as merit or virtue. Some are lucky, a part of an elite they have done nothing to earn their way into, and others are not. This is a sort of holy "apartheid." Augustine clearly believed this, despite the fact that if it were true it would necessarily mean God is partial and unjust in His dealings with people. This belief in predestin- ation, which is quite out of step with the teachings of both Jesus and St Paul, and harks back to Essene teaching, was rejected by Pelagius, who regarded it as destructive of human responsibility.

The arguments in this controversy were quite involved. Augustine considered divine energy was perpetually needed in the lives of men, and forever exerted, whereas Pelagius believed the world and men were given, at the start, sufficient powers to enable self-improvement and self-guidance. Pelagius maintained freedom lies in the power of choice, and that the power to choose differently is always available. Augustine claimed true freedom is the union of the will with the divine law, resulting in voluntary yet spontaneous obedience, where freedom and necessity coalesce. Both agreed that the first sin was Adam's free act, and that he could have chosen either way, but August- ine claimed that Adam's choice to sin brought on him, and the whole human race, physical death, guilt, and bondage of the will, an inherited dominion of sin in the soul. In Adam, human- ity acted and was corrupted. We are responsible at birth for that act, and share all its consequences. Pelagius, on the other hand, held that we sin only by imitation of our first parent, and that there is no such helpless slavery of the will as Augustine claimed. He claimed physical death is a natural necessity, and has nothing to do with the primal transgression of Adam. Augustine considered conversion to be due wholly to the efficiency of divine grace, which is irresistible, and bestowed on those whom God has decided to recover to himself. Pelagius, of course, denied this. He saw grace as largely the effect of the teaching of the Gospel, and believed the sinner has the option of whether or not to respond to the call of the Gospel, and whether to persevere with it once he has chosen it.

As the controversy wore on, a very reasonable compromise position called "Semi-Pelagianism" was proposed by a man called Cassianus. In this, the innate tendency to sin and the need for the grace of the Spirit were strongly asserted, but inborn guilt was denied, and conversion was seen to come from the joint influence of God's grace and our freedom of will. Some distinguished people held this position in the fifth century and afterwards, but such was the influence of Augustine, that both Semi-Pelagianism and Pelagianism were condemned (in 529 A.D.) by two church councils, the Synod of Orange and the Synod of Valence. The church hierarchy was inclined to support Augustine, as he was very much an organization man, a strong supporter of the authority of the church. And, of course, the view that people are helpless of themselves lent authority to the church. Augustine placed so much trust in the church that he even said that he should not believe in the Gospel if he were not moved to do so by the authority of the church! And he was happy to leave the interpretation of the canon of Scripture entirely to the church.[4]

Augustine's major apologetic work, in which he justified the church's political power, was his influential book *City of God*. Written just after the fall of Rome (in 410 A.D.), it didn't specifically refer to Rome, but was obviously alluding to the pope ruling the world from Rome in the tradition and power of the former secular emperors. This book laid the foundations for a "theocratic" society in which the leaders of the Church would have an important role in government.[5] Augustine argued for theocracy (government of the world by God through the church) in this way:

> The true God from Whom is all being, beauty, form and number, weight and measure; He from Whom all nature mean and excellent, all seeds of forms, all forms of seeds, all motions both of forms and seeds, derive and have being;...it is in no way credible that He would leave the kingdoms of men and their bondages and freedoms loose and uncomprised in the laws of His eternal providence.[6]

In other words, God controls everything in nature so precisely and carefully, that it is inconceivable He would give people the freedom to do whatever they want.

In Augustine's time, the Donatist heretics believed that the note of the true church is the holiness of its members. Augustine countered this by contending that being catholic is the real criterion. He meant by this that the church is the visible organization, spread over the earth, containing the apostolic sees. He claimed this church should be considered holy, even if it contains unworthy members, for, although they are in it, they are not of it.[7] This illustrates the elevated way in which Augustine viewed the institutional church. What he wanted done about the Donatists illustrates what he considered were the rights of the church in the secular area. He wanted secular power used against the Donatists, not because he believed the state had any right to interfere in ecclesiastical affairs, but rather because he felt the church had a right to use earthly power to its ends.[8] Over the next thousand years the Roman Catholic Church certainly did claim this right, and used and abused earthly power repeatedly until people throughout Europe became heartily sick of its abuse of power, and reacted to it with the Reformation and the Enlightenment.

Critics of Augustine could say that he opposed the reality of free will in human beings, and was such an organization man and apologist for the institutional church, precisely because his own free will was paralyzed by his weakness of character. They could go on to say that a stronger man might have continued to struggle to acquire the will power needed to constructively exercise his free will, but that being a weak, though brilliant, man, he was content to indulge his weakness, and instead built up an elaborate philosophical justification for his personal lack of free will, which boiled down to his saying that no-one else has any free will either.

After Augustine, the church weathered the dark ages in Europe, while the Goths, Vandals, Vikings and other marauders laid waste to the former Roman Empire and caused it to revert to feudalism. The beginning of a dawn after this long night of wars, feudalism and illiteracy, was the rise to power of Charlemagne, whom the pope crowned the first Holy Roman Emperor — emperor of the West — on Christmas Day 800 A.D. As the marauders settled down in their new lands, and the advance of the Islamic empire was finally halted by the military genius of Charles Martel, Charlemagne's grandfather, at the battle of Tours, eventually the stage was set where Charlemagne was able to inherit a large kingdom, extend it, and rule it in a stable and enlightened way.[9] The papacy of the time, a refuge of culture, found a strong supporter in Charlemagne. Most of Charlemagne's nobles were illiterate, as was the pattern in that brutal age, but Charlemagne himself valued learning highly, and wanted to educate his realm. He founded public schools in which, for the first time in centuries, learning and literacy were cherished. Anyone, even a peasant, who wanted to learn could attend these schools. He also established scriptoria, where Bibles and other books were copied and decorated. At the start of Charlemagne's reign there were not enough books in the whole of Western Europe to fill a modern local library, but this began to change. The beginnings of modern free education can be traced back to Charlemagne's schools, and a new sense of the worth of people arose, irrespective of their station in life, and in this can be seen the seeds of modern democracy.[10]

Although the Papacy had been a shelter for culture, the only place where a strong literary tradition had been preserved was in certain Irish monasteries. Only in them was Greek still taught. Charlemagne's minister, Alcuin, who was given the major literary task of overseeing the revision and copying of the Latin Vulgate Bible, was an Englishman educated in Ireland. By this time Irish monks had been to Egypt and measured the pyramids, which they called "the granaries of St Joseph," and in their written account of the journey they cited more than thirty classical authors. Irish scholars in that age were known to travel a lot, and one of the reasons was the presence of Danish longboats sailing the north seas, plundering the area, and often making even those in monasteries feel unsettled:

Bitter and wild is the wind tonight
Tossing the tresses of the sea to white.
On such a night as this I feel at ease
Fierce Northmen only course the quiet seas.[11]

At around this time, it is said two Irish monks landed at a French seaport and went into the streets offering knowledge for sale. They were quickly taken to Charlemagne, who for a time kept them at his court and set them to work as teachers. After a while Charlemagne sent one to Italy to collect books and manuscripts, while retaining the other to help establish his first public school.[12]

Gothic civilization in medieval Europe started to emerge with Charlemagne, slowly at first, but then with growing enthusiasm. Some maintain the dark age continued into the tenth century, as Charlemagne didn't attempt to preserve his empire, but rather divided it up among his children, and political chaos reigned again. Nevertheless, the cultural and economic climate continued to improve. The seeds which bore fruit in the twelfth and thirteenth centuries had been planted. Under monks' directions new land was opened up to agriculture; forests were cleared, drainage channels cut. New harnesses made draught animals more efficient, and water mills became much more effective and widespread. This has been called the first industrial revolution. In the four hundred years after Charlemagne, Europe's population almost trebled to over one hundred million, and about three thousand new cities were founded. By the twelfth century Gothic cathedrals were expressing the aspirations of an optimistic new society. For the first time in many centuries, the world rose from abject filth and squalor,[13] and was seen as a beautiful place. The cathedrals were seen as symbols of society as a whole, based on the order and beauty of the Bible, but containing the image of society, in all its parts, as well. Cathedrals were usually financed by subscription, with a large variety of people from kings to craftsmen donating to them. People often donated stained-glass windows illustrating Biblical themes relating to their own profession. A guild of coopers donated a window showing Noah, who was a carpenter and also the first man to plant a vine. French kings donated windows showing their patron saint St Denis.[14] All parts of society felt united in these adventurous new buildings which flung themselves up toward heaven in grandeur and beauty.

And in this society the Bible was the guiding principle, the common truth, the rule book which justified and explained the world, right down to and including all its physical manifestations. Science was yet to provide its elegantly simple and powerful explanations of the physical world, so the Bible was asked to say it all. In the thirteenth century, Thomas Aquinas built a complex system of thought around the Bible, which sought to explain everything there is to explain, and which was a machine that created proofs of faith. Aquinas' writings, especially his *Summa Contra Gentiles* and *Summa Theologica*, have remained an important basis of Catholic theology to this day. As science later began to unravel the secrets of the universe, it came into conflict, again and again, with Aquinas' edifice, which the church was loath to let go of, or see modified in any way.

Like most of the Scholasticism of the time, Aquinas' world view was firmly based on the philosophy of Aristotle, who was, of course, the man who thought the earth stood at the center of the universe, and had the sun and all the planets revolving around it. Christian scholars of that time often considered Aristotle an infallible oracle, who had exhausted the resources of the human mind. The other great influence on Aquinas was Augustine, to whose theology, including that of predestination, he largely subscribed. Not all the Scholastics followed Augustine, though; Duns Scotus, for instance, was more inclined to Semi-Pelagianism. Aquinas, like Augustine, was an organization man, and staunch supporter of the absolute authority of the institutional church, so it is not surprising that the church so enthusiastically adopted his theology and view of the physical world. The concept of implicit faith was coming to be taken to mean unlimited submission of the mind to the authority of the church. With this the power of the pope increased, and the idea of papal infallibility, though not yet an official doctrine, began to take root, and was sanctioned by Aquinas.[15]

The high officers of the church really were in a frame of mind where they thought they could do no wrong, and where they thought they had a right, even a duty, to impose their views and ways on all levels of European society — and, what is more, by the twelfth century the church found it was often in a politically and militarily powerful enough position to exert this supposed right. But although the leaders of the church were often corrupted and made arrogant by power, up until this time most of the common priests, monks and nuns lived exemplary and faithful lives. Ironically, it was upon the confidence created by the example of these lives that the much-abused power of the church depended. And when, in the fourteenth century, the power of the popes waned, it was partly because people had come to see that many priests were no longer good men, that they were now often hunting around for money and legacies, and ways to throw their weight around.

The twelfth century was the height of papal power. Popes claimed the power to excommunicate a prince, absolve his subjects from their allegiance to him, and recognize a successor. They could put a nation under an interdict, where nearly all priestly functions would cease, and priests could not hold church services, marry people, or bury the dead. The most recalcitrant princes were overawed by these powerful weapons. Scotland, France and England were all placed under interdict during this century. But the popes were silly enough to use these powers so frequently that they staled their effect, and they preached crusades against offending princes until the crusading spirit died. This, combined with a neglect of the common touch — its ties with everyday people — led the church to its downfall. Up till the eleventh century Roman priests could marry, and had close ties with the people they lived among. Gregory VII made priests celibate, cutting them off from too great an intimacy with laymen in order to bind them more closely to Rome. The church also intruded its heavy hand into civil life by having its own law courts. Cases involving priests, monks, students, crusaders, widows, orphans, wills, marriages, oaths, and all cases of sorcery, heresy and blasphemy, were reserved for these clerical courts. The responsibility for producing wealth, and fighting wars to defend it, fell largely to the layman, yet he could very easily fall foul of the church and be tried for his life in a clerical court. In this atmosphere a jealously and hatred of priests grew up.[16]

The Roman Catholic church never seemed to realize that its greatest power was in the consciences of ordinary men and women. Religious enthusiasm should have been its ally, but it fought against it, and brutally forced doctrinal orthodoxy on honest doubt and liberal opinion. The Waldenses, in the south of France, were a sect teaching a return to the simplicity of Jesus in their faith and life. The church would have done well to encourage them, but Pope Innocent III instead preached a crusade against them, and allowed them to be suppressed by being burned, hacked to death, raped, and subjected to the most abominable cruelties. Even the Franciscans, followers of St Francis of Assisi, were persecuted, imprisoned and dispersed. Four Franciscan monks were burned alive at Marseilles (in 1318). On the other hand, the fiercely orthodox Dominicans, the order Thomas Aquinas was soon to join, were strongly supported by Innocent III. Early in the thirteenth century Innocent III and the two next popes, with the help of the Dominicans, revived and strengthened an organization first established 200 years earlier. Its new form was designed to even more thoroughly and systematically hunt out and destroy heresy and stifle free thought: it was the Holy Inquisition.[17] It is revealing to note that the Inquisition was strengthened and formalized, into its final insidious form, not during the church's rise to great political power, or even during its time of greatest power, but rather afterward, as its power was declining, in a desperate effort to hang on to the influence it had grown accustomed to wielding.[18]

The Holy Inquisition was a special court with power to judge intentions as well as actions. It consisted of one very powerful official called an inquisitor, who was prosecutor,

judge and jury all in one, and a number of other officials including delegates, who handled preliminary investigations and
formalities, familiars, who were guards, prison visitors and
secret agents, and notaries, who carefully collected evidence,
and filed it for future use. Mere suspicion was enough to be
summoned to appear before the Inquisition, so those being
tried were classified as lightly suspect, vehemently suspect, or
violently suspect. The web was carefully woven to trap suspects, and it was often simpler for people to confess than to try
to defend themselves. Typically, an inquisitor would suddenly
arrive in a town and deliver a sermon to the people calling for
reports of anyone who might be suspected of heresy, and for all
who felt heresy within themselves to come forward and confess
within a period of grace. When this "general inquisition" was
over, the "special inquisition" began with summonses to suspected heretics, who were then imprisoned until trial.

The proceedings of the trial were not public, usually only
the general nature of the charges was revealed, and evidence
from two witnesses, even if they were of the most questionable
character, was enough to bring a conviction. Suspects could not
obtain defense lawyers, as lawyers quickly discovered that defending a suspected heretic could result in them being summoned for heresy themselves. Trials often continued for years,
while the suspects languished in prison. Torture was often used
to secure repentance, and though it could not be repeated, it
could be continued. Torture of children and old people had to
be relatively light, but only pregnant women were exempt, and
then only until after the delivery. There were three levels, or
degrees, of torture. In the first degree a lot of people got
through without confessing. In the second degree nearly everyone confessed, as the torture was monstrous. In the third
degree of torture, if they didn't die in the process, everyone
ended up confessing. This is where the expression of giving
someone the "third degree" comes from. The penance required
following confession was light for some heretics, but for others,
the "unreconciled," who were classified as insubordinate,
impenitent or relapsed, the fate was far worse. The first two

categories could still save themselves from the flames by confessing, and secure a lesser punishment, but for the "relapsed,"
along with those found to be witches, there was only one
possible punishment: being burned at the stake. The Inquisition
handed offenders over to the secular authorities for burning, as
canon law prevented the church from shedding blood.[19]

Three main categories of people were targeted by the
Inquisition during its centuries-long reign of terror. The original targets were religious heretics. These included groups such as
the Cathars and Waldensians. The Cathars, also known as
Albigensians in France, believed, like the earlier Manicheans, in
two gods, a good god who created the invisible spiritual world,
and an evil god who created the material world. The evil god,
who they identified as the God of the Old Testament, was
supposed to have imprisoned the soul in its earthly body, and
death merely caused the soul to migrate to another body,
human or animal. Salvation could only be obtained by breaking
free from this cycle, and Christ, the Son of the good God, had
been sent to humanity to show the way of this salvation. Christ
was a life-giving Spirit, whose earthly body was only an
illusion. They accepted the New Testament, but rejected all the
church's sacraments, replacing them with the one sacrament of
spiritual baptism by the laying on of hands. They held Christ
instituted this baptism to give recipients the Holy Spirit. They
claimed this baptism had been handed down from the apostles
by a succession of "good men" but that the church had perverted Christ's teachings and had become enslaved by the evil
god of matter. Cathars were divided into two classes, the
Perfect, who had received their spiritual baptism, and the
Believers, who had not. The Perfect lived in strict poverty as
ascetics. They lived in chastity, often fasted, ate only vegetarian
food, and renounced marriage and oaths. The Believers followed the Perfect with great veneration and unquestioning
obedience, as only the Perfect could pray directly to God. Most
Believers delayed receiving spiritual baptism until they were in
danger of death, as they felt the discipline required of a Perfect
would be too much for them. The holiness and austerity of the

Perfect contrasted starkly with the riches of the Catholic Church and the corruption of many of its clergy. Many found the Cathars answered their spiritual needs in a way Catholicism did not. At the beginning of the thirteenth century it seemed as if southern France might become entirely Cathar, and this provoked Innocent III's crusade against them, which (between 1208 and 1250) destroyed their political power and ruined the civilization and economy of the area where most of them lived. The Inquisition was very much involved in this process.[20]

The Waldensians were followers of Peter Waldo, who had been a wealthy merchant in Lyons until he was converted to Christianity (in 1175). He gave away his worldly goods in order to live a simple life of poverty and preaching, in imitation of Jesus. He had a French translation of the New Testament made from the Latin to help with his evangelism. Many devoted men and women supported him. Initially Pope Alexander III gave his approval to this ideal of illiterate lay people living in simple poverty, on the condition that they must obtain the permission and supervision of local church authorities before doing any preaching. But in spreading the message of the Bible (otherwise not much read by lay people in those days), and exalting the virtues of poverty, they were a living condemnation of the wealth and laxity of the established church. Within two years the Archbishop of Lyons prohibited them from preaching from the Scriptures at all. They responded by preaching all the more zealously. Three years later they were excommunicated by Pope Lucius III, who also ordered that they be eliminated by episcopal inquisition and secular punishment. Within ten years this enthusiastic popular movement had been branded a heresy. Rather than submit to the church, the Waldensians fled from Lyons and organized their own church, with their own bishops, priests and deacons. They claimed to be the true church, and became well established in some areas. Pope Innocent III denounced them as heretics and set to work to persecute them through the organization he was establishing to wipe out heresy — the Inquisition. The pope's outbursts had the effect of convincing the Waldensians that the

Catholic Church really was the "Whore of Babylon" and needn't even be acknowledged. Although they were continually hounded by the Inquisition, the Waldensians infiltrated most of Europe, and strongly influenced Protestant thought. The Catholic Church's two main objections to the Waldensians were their unauthorized preaching from the Bible, and their rejection of the role of priests as intermediaries between people and God. It was largely for these two reasons that they were declared heretics.[21]

Even the gentle Franciscans were persecuted by the Inquisition. Shortly after St Francis of Assisi died, his order ran into trouble with the church. The Franciscans split over the question of whether they should be allowed to own property, or whether they should keep to St Francis' original ideal of poverty. Pope Innocent IV supported the right to own property, the "Conventual" position. The "Spirituals," who supported the ideal of poverty, finally decided to cut all ties with the order, since it owned property. Pope John XXII ordered them to rejoin the other Franciscans. Spirituals who refused to obey were judged by the Inquisition, and four were executed. The Spiritual Franciscans were a thorn in the side of the Papacy because they drove home the point that poverty was the ideal practiced by Jesus and his disciples. From this came the idea that the church hierarchy should be aloof from entanglements in the world. It put the massive wealth and worldly power of the Papacy under scrutiny. The pope condemned the Franciscan doctrine of poverty, and some Franciscan leaders were excommunicated. Nevertheless, those favoring poverty eventually predominated in the order.

The second category of people persecuted by the Inquisition were scientists. The burning of Bruno at the stake, and the famous trial of Galileo, are amongst the most remembered acts of the Inquisition. The scientific community has, quite rightly, never allowed the church to forget its persecution of scientists and its obstruction of scientific progress. The church stuck obstinately to the world view of Aristotle which it had adopted through Thomas Aquinas. In its pride it thought it should be able to dictate the nature of the truth about God's universe. It never had the modesty and discernment to see that Aristotle's cosmology, useful though it was, should have been seen merely as a starting point, which scientists could modify and add to in the process of discovering the way God's universe actually works. The church alienated large numbers of educated people through its obstruction of science, and is still, to some extent, doing so today.

So successful has been the scientific community's highlighting of the atrocities it suffered at the hands of the Inquisition, that it is easy to form the impression that this was the main evil of this barbaric institution. This is far from being the truth, though. The third, and by far the largest, group of people to suffer under the Inquisition were women. Only now, in the late twentieth century, are historians coming to realize the extent of the holocaust perpetrated by the church through the Inquisition and Protestant courts. Some have estimated that as many as nine million people were tortured and executed for witchcraft, over three centuries, and that eighty-five percent of them were women.[22] Others claim the figure should be much lower, on the basis that only about 200,000 people in western Europe between 1450 and 1700 were killed as a result of formal investigations that we know about.[23] Considering, however, that only a minority of the people persecuted as witches were formally tried,[24] accurate records were often not kept,[25] and that over the centuries many, if not most, of the records of trials and executions are likely to have been lost, it is reasonable to suppose that the 200,000 documented cases are just the tip of the iceberg, and that the real figure must run into the millions. Both the Inquisition and the Protestant churches were guilty of this slaughter — in fact the Protestant church in Germany was the most vehement burner of witches, and persisted for the longest in doing so.[26] Both Luther and Calvin fully supported the burning of witches,[27] and just about everywhere their Protestant theology spread, this hideous practice went with it.[28] Any woman who claimed a degree of independence or influence, or who was at all unusual or mysterious, was in danger of being declared a witch, and the punishment for being a witch was to be burned to death at the stake.

Toward the end of the "dark ages," the Emperor Charlemagne had forbidden the burning of supposed witches, and decreed the death penalty for anyone in the newly converted Saxony who did so. Shortly afterward, in the ninth century, the church repudiated the belief that witches had supernatural powers, and declared anyone who believed in them to be an infidel and a pagan. This statement was accepted into the canon law, and became known as the *canon Episcopi.*[29] Up until the fourteenth century the church retained this sensible policy that witches don't exist, but then the reversal of thinking began. The Dominicans, who had been entrusted with the task of fighting heresy through the Inquisition, began to see witchcraft behind the other heresies they were fighting, and once these heresies had been brutally suppressed, brought pressure on the popes to allow the Inquisition to go on to eliminate the witchcraft.

Finally, in the fifteenth century, two Dominican inquisitors, Heinrich Kramer and Jakob Sprenger, convinced the pope to act. Pope Innocent VIII issued the bull *Summis Desiderantes Affectibus* (of 1484), which deplored the spread of witchcraft in Germany and authorized his "beloved sons," Kramer and Sprenger, to "extirpate" it. Two years later these two Dominicans published the *Malleus Maleficarum*, "The Hammer of Witches," a handbook on how to detect and eradicate witches. With this book, one of the first to be widely distributed through Europe after the advent of the printing press, witchcraft came to be considered a terrible heresy, and the main purpose of the Inquisition was seen to be to eliminate it. The two hundred years of torture and slaughter that resulted came to be known as the "witch craze."[30] Even then, the persecution of witches looked like dying out soon after it began, in the early sixteenth century, until it was fired up again into two centuries of intolerance, hatred and mass carnage by the Reformation and the Counter Reformation. Witchcraft came to be identified with paganism, and the competition between Protestants and Catholics in evangelizing and converting the many pagan areas left in Europe led to a huge harvest of supposed witches, who were burned at the stake to cleanse newly converted areas and eradicate old pockets of paganism, such as those in the Alps and Pyrenees.[31] This Reformation evangelism had a lot in common with modern fundamentalism, including a fervent return to the belief that the end of the world was about to occur, and that the Millennium would soon be established.[32] Without any effective separation of church and state, havoc reigned.

There are a number of reasons why medieval society was able to take this sinister turn. The reduced political power of the church after Innocent III, leading to its fragmentation during the Reformation, was one contributing factor. As the church lost its political power to princes, it increasingly concentrated on exerting its power over the life style of ordinary people. The church was intent on imposing an hierarchical, male-dominated power structure, such as it had within itself, onto all parts of society. It faced stiff opposition in doing so, though. For thousands of years the village life style over most of Europe had been quite a fair and equal one. Women and men worked side-by-side, and both often held positions of prestige, and were looked up to as leaders and healers. In particular, most of the healers were women, as they did so in the tradition of their society's pagan past, where earth goddesses were worshiped. Healing has, in all societies and at all times, been considered a divine function,[33] so the practice of healing fell largely to women, who were more intuitively in tune with the feminine "earth" nature of their most important gods. As healers, these women were often looked up to as wise counselors, and were much respected. In these times the word "witch" was not associated with darkness and evil as it later was; rather it signified someone wise. The word came from the Anglo-Saxon root *wic* — to bend or shape, and a witch was someone who could bend or shape consciousness or events in life. Their powers were descended from the old shamanic tradition, which induced altered states of consciousness without using drugs, through simple techniques like meditation, chanting and singing.[34]

｜Priests were enraged when village wise women received the honor and gratitude the church claimed for God alone. The church believed in a male God, and that, consequently, men were superior, and should occupy all the prestigious positions, particularly those involved with healing. It claimed this reflected the divine order. The church also believed it had a right to impose its views on society by force, if necessary, and it set about destroying the ancient social order of Europe, and establishing a new structure in its place. This new structure was hierarchical, dictatorial, conservative and male-dominated, and expected slavish, unquestioning loyalty from each level of the hierarchy to the level above it. It was a hardened form of the dictatorships of the Roman Empire, and closely resembled modern Fascism. One of its aims was to domesticate women and make good housewives of them. By the time the witch craze ended in the eighteenth century, it had largely succeeded in doing this.

Even after men had come to dominate most areas of medicine, women continued to be midwives, and to be in demand for their general healing ability.[35] This led the Inquisition to announce that no-one did more harm to the Catholic faith than midwives. They eased the pain of labor, God's punishment for Eve's sin, and they interfered with God's will through the use of birth control and abortion. New laws proclaimed that any woman who dared heal people without having studied was a witch, and must die. Since most women were barred from universities, the rise of the male medical profession was guaranteed. Women healers who continued to practice lived in constant fear of their lives. An example is Alison Peirsoun of Byrehill, who had a reputation as a gifted healer. The archbishop of St Andrews sent for her to try and heal him, as he suffered from various disorders which other practitioners had been unable to bring him relief from. Alison cured him, however, in response, he not only refused to pay her bill, but also had her arrested. She was charged with witchcraft and executed.[36]

This was a battle between the traditional leaders and informers of society, and the church, which was intent on assuming the role. Although the church faced strong resistance from the traditional wise women and men of European society in establishing its antithetical hierarchy and values, it had an ally which ruling establishments have long used to get their way: the intolerance and fear of non-conformity of the masses of ignorant people. The church exploited this mercilessly.

In these superstitious times, Jews were hated and persecuted, and were the main target of the Spanish Inquisition.[37] And women were feared by men, often just because they were different — because the sexes always find it difficult to understand each other. Women were also feared for their sexuality and procreative power, which, again, men didn't understand. This enabled the officially sanctioned witch burnings to grow into an almost out-of-control holocaust. It was an application of the technique of "divide and conquer." In largely Protestant Germany alone, one hundred thousand witch burnings have been carefully documented. At the turn of the seventeenth century, a contemporary observer noted that: "Germany is almost entirely occupied with building fires for the witches. Switzerland has been compelled to wipe out many of her villages on their account. Travelers in Lorraine may see thousands and thousands of the stakes to which witches are bound."[38] In Germany inquisitors had ovens built to handle the mass burning of witches, of much the same design as those later built by Hitler for the Jews. The prince-bishop of Würzburg, one of the places where these ovens were built, stated that man's greatest misfortune was to have been born from the stinking private parts of women. In Würzburg, and many other parts of Germany, even the most virtuous, beautiful and modest girls were burned, and three hundred children were burned, many having been accused of having had intercourse with the devil.[39]

\Just about every sort of unexplained misfortune was blamed on witches. If a cow failed to give milk, a witch was blamed. The witch could be anyone the accuser disliked or distrusted, or anyone who was unusual or had been seen near the cow. Identification and execution of the witch were believed to reverse the troublesome condition. It was believed impotence could be cured if the witch causing the problem could be found and punished or killed. The justification for this was that Thomas Aquinas had earlier written into church records that a witch was likely to be to blame if a man's penis wilted.[40] King James I of England believed that plots and supernatural forces threatened his life, and it was he who commissioned the first translation of the Bible containing the word "witch." Exodus 22:18: "Thou shalt not suffer a witch to live," was used to help justify the murdering of hundreds of thousands of women. This is despite the fact that as early as 1584, Reginal Scot pointed out that the Hebrew word in question, *Kashaph,* is not accurately translated as "witch," and would be better rendered as "poisoner." He was ignored, and the witch burning went on.[41]

This witch hysteria was exacerbated by the conditions in Europe during the fourteenth, fifteenth and sixteenth centuries. The plague pandemic called the Black Death raged during this time and halved the population of Europe. It returned again and again to ravage society. In one year alone (1478), the Black Death killed off one third of the population. At the same time many other diseases, such as syphilis and small pox, took their toll. Women seemed to be more resistant to the Black Death than men, and this, along with the toll on men taken by wars, meant that there were many more women in society than men. The large number of women who were unable to marry lived independent lives, not under the control of husbands, and this threatened the male hierarchy.[42] Also, life had been made cheap by the devastation of disease, and the economy had suffered in the process. Much property ended up in the hands of elderly widows and spinsters. Such women became objects of suspicion and envy, and consequently were vulnerable to charges of witchcraft. They became scapegoats for communities plagued by war, disease, and rapid social change. Pressure was taken off the establishment by convincing people that their difficulties arose from the fact that witches were present, blighting the harvest, causing barrenness in the marriage bed, and striking people down with disease. People were easily enough convinced that it was not the state, nor the pope, nor the bishop who was the source of their problems; but that it was, rather, the accursed presence of witches.

There was great social upheaval during these times. Peasants were forced off their land into cities, so land owners could establish larger farms, and calls for reform, and peasant rebellions, led to charges of witchcraft being laid against them. Repression increased. The helpless, mysterious and nonconformist were victimized. Punishments became public spectacles. Many suffered, but women most of all. Husbands were advised from the pulpit to beat their wives, not in rage, but out of charity for their souls.

The Inquisition was also a good way of redistributing the wealth which accumulated in the hands of elderly women. The bureaucratic state and capitalism were emerging. A new profit ethic was beginning to take hold. Witch hunts were a profitable business. There was meticulous bookkeeping. Each step of the trial was costed and charged for. There were charges for seizing the witch, escorting her, and locking her up. Her torture and execution were charged for. If the witch owned any property, it would be confiscated to pay for these costs. It generated widespread employment opportunities for lawyers and judges, torturers, and those sitting on tribunals and helping in many capacities.[43]

Anyone could be accused of witchcraft. One accusation by a neighbor could set the wheels in motion. After having been in jail for some time, and probably already having been tortured, a woman accused of being a witch would be brought before the Inquisition. Nearly all witch trials were in small country towns, and took place in the town square, which was usually in front of the church. Nearly everyone came out to look at the spectacle. The suspected witch was brought out, then stripped of all her clothes, as it was thought she may have a spell in her clothes, or an item sown into the hem which was made of something sinister like the skin of an unbaptized child. Both the hair on her head and her pubic hair were shaved, as hair had always been thought to have a lot of power, and when women braided their hair they were thought to braid men's fate. She then had to approach the Inquisitor walking backwards so she couldn't give him the evil eye. After this the trial would proceed through the first, second and third degrees of torture, in order to obtain the desired confessions. Finally the convicted witch would be handed over to the secular authorities for burning.

This is a contemporary description of the torture of a witch:

> The torturer made her sit on the rack, undressed her, and applied the thumb screws. When the thumb screws were applied to her toes she cried out louder than before. The Inquisitor inserted the mouth pear and demanded that she confess. When it was removed, she told her story. Ten years ago it happened that the devil came to her in the guise of a man. First they danced, then they dined, then she and others knelt before the goat and kissed him. Here she named eight neighbors.[44]

Only one letter from a suspected witch survives. It was written in 1590 by Rebecca Lamp:

> Oh husband, they take me from thee by force. How can God suffer it? My heart is nearly broken. Alas, alas, my poor dear children orphaned. Husband, send me something that I might die, or I must expire under torture. If thou canst not today, do it tomorrow. Write to me directly. R.L.[45]

When the records of witch trials were studied, it was found that witches right across Europe made much the same confessions under torture. When women made a contract with the devil, it appeared almost always to be finalized by some sexual act, and the women always seemed to say that sexual union with the devil is a very painful thing, and never enjoyable.

Apparently the devil's penis is as cold as ice. This discovery caused much consternation, for if there wasn't such a thing as witchcraft, what could the explanation be for all these women responding in such a similar way? It turned out the reason was that Inquisitors were all supplied with handbooks specifying the type of questions to pose, and the particular confessions to seek from the tortured women. The most popular handbook was the *Malleus Maleficarum* (Hammer against Witches). This is a highly sexual book, involving a lot of repression and projection of men's fears about many things, including women and sexuality.[46] The nature of the confessions sought, and the way women were stripped and shaved of all their hair before being tried or tortured, both confirm that there were strong sadistic overtones to the witch trials. St Thomas Aquinas belonged to the Dominican order during the decades when the Dominicans were first entrusted to run the Inquisition, and there can be little doubt he was a sadist; this is obvious from his infamous statement about the pleasures of heaven. Aquinas wrote that next to contemplating God, the greatest pleasure for the blessed ones in heaven would be watching the tortures of the eternally damned.

Near the city of Trier in Germany, in the space of one year (in 1585), the Inquisition left two entire villages with only one female inhabitant alive in each, and in the following eight years twenty-two more villages were decimated.[47] Yet all this was just a part of a continuing carnage. People in Trier have now forgotten that for hundreds of years women there lived in terror, and that six generations of children watched as their mothers burned at the stake. The reason they have forgotten this is that history is written by the winners, and for hundreds of years little has been said about this holocaust.[48] Instead, history has concentrated on the Renaissance, the Reformation and the scientific revolution, which were happening, in a very male-dominated way, at the same time that women were being tortured and burned into submission.[49] However, the effect of these burning times still smolders in the church and in society, in their relationships with women, and in the suppression of the "feminine," feeling, side of men, and will continue to do so until the problem is addressed. One way it can be addressed, and indeed is already beginning to be, is to bring the issue right out into the open, and fully acknowledge the terrible wrongs that were done. The witch craze haunts our society in much the same way as suppressed and un-dealt-with childhood traumas haunt the lives of many adults.

When the execution of witches finally stopped in the eighteenth century, it was not so much because of a realization of the horror of burning women as witches — there were two quite different reasons. One was that the witch craze had largely achieved its goal; the "housewification" of women was virtually complete. The other was that the church's power had greatly waned, as the ideal of human freedom promoted by science and the Enlightenment irresistibly attracted people, and led them to demand that secular governments stem the church's wanton violence and intrusion into people's lives.[50]

It took the church two hundred years of terror and death to transform the image of paganism into devil worship, and folk culture into heresy. This holocaust all but destroyed a way of life which had endured for thousands of years. In modern times, groups of people within certain New Age organizations, and some of those endeavoring to reform the church from within, such as the former Dominican Matthew Fox, are gradually restoring some of the best of this heritage of pagan folk culture to our society. Churches which wish to be freed from their guilt in this area need to let go of their collective pride, acknowledge their past wrongdoing, and cooperate in the process of restoring the culture they once so wantonly worked at destroying.

The witch craze was the church's darkest hour. The church had become vicious and out of control — megalomaniacal. It had forgotten all about the teachings of Jesus. But social forces at work in Europe gradually brought it under control — straitjacketed it, sedated it, and largely reduced it to ranting and raving every now and then. And that's basically where much of the church is still — alive and vicious, but caged. Of course, now as then, there are large numbers of fine Christians around the world, living and giving and loving in the spirit of Jesus. But the institutional church? There are far too many indications that the organization men and women in it — the modern Augustines, Aquinas's and Calvins: the fundamentalists — still hanker after the heady medieval days when the church, Catholic and Protestant, lorded it over the life of Europe.

Chapter 10

The Church is Brought Under Control

Gradually, modern society brought the church under control. The first efforts to do so date right back to the zenith of the church's power under Pope Innocent III. In 1198 Emperor Frederick II inherited his kingdom at the age of four, and Innocent III was made his guardian, by his mother's will. This would seem to have been an ideal opportunity for the pope to mold the future emperor into a supporter of the church, but somehow it didn't quite work out that way. Innocent was not as good a parent as he was a politician. Sicily had only recently been conquered and consolidated by the Normans, after being occupied by the Muslim Saracens, and the Imperial Court was still half Oriental, and full of highly educated Arabs who helped teach the young king. Frederick's education consequently included a Muslim view of Christianity, as well as a Christian view of Islam, and the net result was his gaining the view, exceptional for his time, that all religions were impostures. He talked about it freely, and his heresies and blasphemies are on record. The famous blasphemy that the world had been deceived by three imposters, Moses, Muhammad and Christ, was attributed to Frederick by Pope Gregory IX.[1]

As Frederick grew up, he often found himself in conflict with the pope. His guardian demanded far too much from him. Before he could succeed as emperor, Innocent III made him agree to a long list of conditions. Frederick was to relinquish his crown in Sicily and south Italy, and promise to put down heresy in Germany with a strong hand. He was to undertake to free the German clergy from all taxation, and pursue a crusade against the Waldenses in Germany, similar to the one being waged in France. As well as all this, Innocent III even made him promise to mount a crusade against the Muslims to recover Jerusalem. Frederick agreed to all these things, but with no intention of keeping his word. He was much more heretical than the heretics he was being asked to eliminate, and objected to crusades, and it would seem, even to being told what to do by a religious leader.

Having secured his imperial crown, Frederick II stayed on in Sicily, and ignored his promises to the pope. Innocent III, otherwise one of the most powerful popes in history, went to his death baffled and frustrated by Frederick's behavior. The next pope succeeded no better, but the following pope, Gregory IX, came to power determined to bring the by now thirty-year-old Frederick into line. For failing, after much procrastination, to keep his vow to go on a crusade, Frederick was excommunicated by Gregory, and denied all the "comforts" of religion. In Frederick's half-Arab court in Sicily this in fact produced very little discomfort. Gregory followed this up by addressing a public letter to the emperor reciting his vices, heresies and general misconduct. To this Frederick replied with a document of consummate eloquence, directed to the crusaders and princes of Europe. It was a turning point in history: the first clear statement of the issues which stood between the pope and princes. It included a shattering attack on the manifest ambition of the pope to become the absolute ruler of all Europe, and suggested the princes unite to prevent it. It also specifically drew the princes' attention to the vast wealth of the church.[2]

| Frederick followed up his attack on the church by finally deciding to keep one of his promises to the pope. He went on a crusade (the Sixth Crusade, of 1229). As a crusade it was farcical, yet, ironically, it was the most successful of all the crusades. Frederick II went to Egypt, and had discussions with the Sultan. Both men were religious sceptics, and got on remarkably well. They made a commercial treaty to their mutual advantage, and as a part of the deal agreed to transfer Jerusalem to Frederick. This crusade by private treaty succeeded in recovering Jerusalem, where all previous military attempts had failed. And it was led by an excommunicated man. Frederick had to be content with a purely secular coronation as king of

Jerusalem. He took the crown from the altar with his own hands. The only fighting Frederick did was on his return to Italy, to chase the papal armies which had invaded his territories back into their own. As a part of the peace which followed, Frederick forced the pope to grant him absolution from his excommunication.

Gregory IX was not content to let sleeping dogs lie, though. Ten years later he excommunicated Frederick for a second time. Again it was the papacy which suffered in the public abuse-slinging match which followed. Gregory removed himself from the firing-line by dying, so it was Innocent IV who had to weather the devastatingly prophetic letter which Frederick wrote. In it Frederick denounced the irreligion of the clergy, and maintained all the corruptions of the time were due to their pride and wealth. He proposed to his fellow princes that there should be a general confiscation of church property, for the good of the church. In this letter, the political seeds of the Reformation were sown. Though Frederick did not live to see it, his suggestion was later put into effect in many countries.

As well as hastening the Reformation by thumbing his nose at the church, Frederick also did much to promote the spirit of learning and free inquiry which became the Renaissance. He gathered Jewish, Muslim and Christian philosophers at his court. Through him Arabic numerals and algebra were introduced to Europe. He founded the University of Naples, and expanded the important medical school at Salerno University. He has been called the first of the moderns.[3]

The concept of Christendom continued to decay during the thirteenth century, until its power over the minds of men had largely gone. Early in the fourteenth century a French king was able to send an agent to arrest Pope Boniface VIII, after obtaining the consent of the council of the Three Estates of France (lords, church and commons), and there was little disapproval of the action from anywhere in Europe. Later in the same century the authority of the papacy was even further eroded by the "Great Schism." Dissenting cardinals declared the election of Pope Urban VI of Italy invalid, and elected another pope, the "anti-pope," Clement VII, who ruled from Avignon. Rival popes ruled in competition with each other for forty years.

Toward the end of the fourteenth century John Wyclif, an Oxford scholar, began criticizing the church and the corruption of the clergy. One of his beliefs was that the church consisted of God's chosen people, who did not need priests to mediate between them and God. He believed priests should preach, and do so from a Bible in the congregation's own language. He initiated an English translation of the Bible, and his followers, the Lollards, spread his beliefs widely in England and Europe. The genuineness of the Lollards urge to reform is indicated by this statement from their writings:

> We ask God then of his supreme goodness to reform our church,
> as being entirely out of joint, to the perfectness of its first
> beginning.   (The Lollard Conclusions, 1394)

Although Rome raged at Wyclif, and ordered his imprisonment, Wyclif died a free man. Such was the bitterness against him, though, that a decree of the Council of Constance, thirty years after his death, ordered that his remains were to be dug up and burned. Over ten years later again, Pope Martin IV saw to it that this order was actually carried out. The papacy lowered itself to officially desecrating graves. In this atmosphere, Wyclif's followers were persecuted, but they continued to thrive in some parts of England, and helped prepare the way for the Reformation there.[4]

At the end of the fourteenth century Jan Hus gave a series of lectures on Wyclif's teachings at the University of Prague. These teachings quickly spread past the educated classes to the population in general, and aroused great public enthusiasm. Seventeen years later (in 1415), Hus was invited to the Council of Constance under the emperor's promise of safe conduct. Once there he was seized, put on trial for heresy, and burned alive. Far from stemming the calls for reform in Bohemia, this treachery caused the Hussites to openly rebel. Pope Martin V preached a crusade against them. In the end five crusades were launched, but all of them failed. The successful resistance of the

Hussites was the beginning of the end of Latin Christendom. Small nations now knew they could stand up to the church. By the end of the fifteenth century printed Bibles and other books became widely distributed, encouraging more and more people to think for themselves. Ever since Frederick II, European princes had dreamed of extricating themselves from the sway of Rome, and recovering the great wealth the church had accumulated in their lands. Now they began to feel confident about doing so. The church was corrupt enough, confused enough, and had alienated enough of its support, to open it up to a successful attack.

In Germany the attack gathered around an ex-monk called Martin Luther. Luther provided the theological justification for breaking with Rome; the princes took advantage of this by supporting him, and making sure Hus's fate didn't befall him; the printing presses did the rest. In many European countries, and in England, the church split from Rome and was brought under the control of secular government. In each case there was some genuine reform of the way religion was practiced, as this was required as a justification for the split. Apart from this, though, the reform of the church during the Reformation was quite limited; only the most blatant corruptions were addressed. The basic worldliness of the church, as revealed in its doctrines from Augustine to Aquinas, remained unchanged in the new Protestant churches. One of the major problems was that both Luther and Calvin still believed in the predestination of a fixed elect, and all this entails. Bound up with predestination is the doctrine of man's lack of free will, and inherent helplessness. As pointed out by Pelagius in Augustine's time, this doctrine leads to moral weakness and is destructive of human responsibility. Consequently, the major Protestant churches introduced very few changes in belief on how people should behave toward each other; if anything their attitude was even more self-centered and selfish than that promoted by the Catholic church, as salvation was seen as being by "faith alone," and the value of good works was discounted. Nor was there any real spiritual renewal. Protestants saw the spirit as being directed through the Bible, rather than through the pope and bishops. There was even less scope in Protestantism than in Catholicism for direct personal experience of God.

The similarity of the position and methods of the Protestants and Catholics is shown by their joint reaction to the Anabaptist movement. The Anabaptists believed the Christian's relationship with Christ must go beyond inner experience and acceptance of doctrines, and must involve a daily walk with God, where Jesus' teachings and example shape a transformed life. They believed the principle of love should guide their lives in a practical way. As a result, they were pacifists in dealing with their persecutors, rather like Gandhi and Martin Luther King in modern times, and would not take part in coercion by the state. As in the church of the book of Acts, they helped each other, and redistributed wealth within their own communities. Decisions were made by the entire membership on a consensus basis. Separation of church and state was called for. They considered Christians to be "free, unforced, uncompelled people," that faith is the free gift of God, and that authorities exceed their competence when they "champion the Word of God with a fist." The Anabaptists believed the church to be distinct from society, even a so-called Christian society. These beliefs alarmed the established leaders of Protestant and Catholic Europe alike. Protestants were additionally concerned that the Anabaptist's emphasis on life as well as belief was a challenge to the basic Reformation principle of salvation by "faith alone." The Anabaptists protested that their ethical teachings were not a means of gaining salvation, but rather a necessary expression of the new life in Christ which resulted from it. Their protests were in vain, though, which is not surprising, as they served to point out the bankruptcy of the standard Protestant position, and this merely made the Protestants hostile. The Reformers determined to use all necessary means to root out Anabaptism. The Catholic authorities took the same line. Both Catholics and Protestants considered the Anabaptists dangerous heretics who threatened the religious and social stability of Christian Europe. Over the next twenty-five years thousands of Anabaptists were put to death, by burning in Catholic areas, and by drowning or the sword under Protestant regimes. Many more Anabaptists were forced to recant. Remnants of the Anabaptists survive today as certain groups of European "brethren," the Hutterites and the Mennonites. In order to survive, these groups shed many of their Anabaptist characteristics, and became legalistic and isolationist. With the safety of recent times, though, the Mennonites are experiencing revival, and their numbers have more than trebled to nearly a million over the last forty years. It will be interesting to see if they can play a significant role in the transformation of the church in our time.[5]

The basic lack of change in Protestantism is reflected in the fact that the same bad old fruits kept being produced by the new churches. The way the Anabaptists were treated is just one example of this. Another is that the burning of witches went on just as relentlessly in Protestant areas as it did under the Catholic Inquisition. Indeed, as we have seen, the competition between Protestants and Catholics resulting from the Reformation led to a renewal of intensity of witch burning on both sides, when it had looked like it might otherwise have died out.[6] The real reform, a return to Jesus' teachings of toleration, love and living in "the Kingdom of Heaven," quite simply just didn't take place in the main-stream Protestant Reformation, or in the Catholic Counter Reformation. And, arguably, genuine reform couldn't yet take place, as the conditions in Europe were still so superstitious and brutal. But at least the break-up of the church started to bring it under the control of governments. Eventually, as governments became more democratic and enlightened, this would cause the church's more barbaric excesses to be curbed. Within two hundred years the witch burnings ceased, and the time finally arrived when scientists were able to get on with their work without living in fear of their lives.

Although the Reformation was politically significant, in starting the process of bringing the church under secular control, it was very much a non-event in spiritual terms. Perhaps

the biggest single misapprehension holding the Protestant
church back in our time, is the notion that it has already gone
through all the major reform it needs, in the Reformation, and
that all it needs to do now is get around and "witness" to as
many people as possible, and tell them how wonderful it is.
Most of the reform the church needs, both Catholic and
Protestant, is yet to come, and their witness will be unimpres-
sive until after this real reform takes place.

Although the Protestant churches were sponsored by secular rulers, they continued to exert a lot of control over the
government of society. In the Reformation days it was still
considered appropriate for churches to do this. To John Calvin,
the church was supreme, and should not be restricted in any
way by the state.[7] It meant the Protestant churches were very
little different from the Catholic church in the way they
controlled society—they just did it on a smaller scale, and were
more answerable to secular rulers. Church and state were still
closely linked; the Reformation did little to change that. It was
not until the Enlightenment and the spread of democracy in the
last two hundred years that this started to change.

The American President and founding father, Thomas Jef-
ferson, was a champion of religious freedom. He was, however,
also a champion of the then revolutionary concept of the separation of church and state. In 1802, he wrote to the Danbury
Association of Baptists that he would see built and retained "a
wall of separation between church and state." The First Am-
endment to the American Constitution (of 1791) had laid down
that there should be neutrality in religion, that there should be
free speech and right of assembly, and that "Congress shall
make no law respecting an establishment of religion." The
Constitution also rejected all religious tests for office-holders.
The United States became the first modern secular state. Some
parts of the church have never accepted the necessity of the
separation of church and state, yet under it a wide variety of
churches have flourished in America.[8] Under the *Separation
Law* of 1801, a similar separation of church and state was
achieved in France.

This was a critical point of departure for the church. Different parts of the church have made different responses to the separation of church and state. Some have accepted it as reasonable and moved forward into the modern age. Others, the fundamentalists, baulked at it, and have been fighting it and stagnating ever since. These religious conservatives often say they do accept the separation of church and state, but, as we shall see, their beliefs and actions belie them.

The papacy responded to its progressive loss of political power by increasingly emphasizing what it called its "spiritual" power — its power to control people's lives. It policed its edicts on how people should conduct their personal lives both directly, through religious courts such as the Inquisition, and indirectly, by playing on people's anxieties about their sexuality, and their fears about what would happen when they died. The church's edicts on morality to this day so often focus on sexuality and reproduction because this is the domain of every person's control over themselves, where people make choices which don't directly affect others. The church has gained its control over people's sexual and reproductive lives by the divide-and-conquer tactic of making people feel guilt-stricken and fearful about such a normal and reasonable thing as enjoying sex, whether it be through masturbation, or through the use of contraception to enable people's sex lives to extend beyond reproduction into the area of recreational sex.

This extension of control and manipulation over the lives of individual people is what the Counter Reformation was really about. As with the Protestants, there was a certain amount of genuine reform. The sale of indulgences, which precipitated the Reformation, was stopped. The Oratory of Divine Love, a society of progressive and influential Catholics, and a number of saints, such as Teresa of Avila and John of the Cross, contributed to some important spiritual renewal which was lacking in main-stream Protestantism. In addition to this, though, the Catholic church used the Inquisition in a big way to enforce its authority over people, and the Jesuits to spread Catholic ideas through education and missionary effort. The familiar Jesuit saying, "Give me a child until he is seven, and he will remain a Catholic the rest of his life," reflects their philosophy. The Catholic church also tried more than ever to control people's thinking, and insist on the absolute authority of the papacy. The Council of Trent issued the *Tridentine Index* of prohibited books, which was kept and updated until it was finally abolished in 1966. In the sixteenth century it censored nearly three-quarters of all the books in print.[9] Pope Pius IX's bull of *Ineffabilis Deus* (of 1853) established the doctrine of the immaculate conception of the Virgin Mary, claiming that from the moment of her conception she was entirely free from original sin. This provided a solid basis for the veneration of Mary, and at the same time strengthened Pius's own authority. Ten years later Pius's *Syllabus of Errors* condemned political liberalism, rationalism in all its forms, liberal theology, Freemasonry, religious toleration, and even the Bible Societies. At the first Vatican Council (of 1870) Pius IX capped off his elevation of the "authority" of the papacy with his dogma of "papal infallibility," which taught that the pope is infallible when speaking *ex cathedra* on matters of faith and practice.

This was the pope's response to the growing influence of rationalistic thought, such as that promoted by Darwin's Theory of Evolution. Many subsequent popes have used this power to lay down the law to Catholics. Often this has been done in a very arbitrary way, as when Pope John XXIII's successor, Paul VI, ignored the advice of his wide-ranging and respected committee, and issued the encyclical *Humanae Vitae* prohibiting the use of artificial birth control by Catholics. The overwhelming consensus in the church was to allow artificial birth control, but the pope totally ignored what his church was telling him, and decided against birth control purely on the basis of his own "infallibility," and in the tradition of wielding "spiritual" power to gain control over people, which the church practiced down through the centuries. This return to hard-line conservatism and arbitrary authority, after the enthusiasm generated by the reform of the second Vatican Council (1962–65), in fact greatly undermined the real authority of the papacy. An increasing number of people had become liberated, through education, from the hold of this sort of manipulation, and were coming to see the manipulation itself as being wrong. Many Catholics felt angry and betrayed by the pope indulging in such arrogant behavior. It is common knowledge that most educated Catholics in western countries have blatantly disregarded this encyclical on birth control; only in third-world countries has it been widely obeyed, and there it has greatly contributed to the population explosion, and the consequent misery this has produced. In 1993, right against the tide of change in his church, Pope John Paul II reaffirmed the Catholic Church's insistence that artificial birth control is intrinsically evil, in his encyclical *Veritatis Splendor*. Its release was accompanied by many claims of its irrelevance to most Westerners, but fears as to its adverse effect in third-world countries like the Philippines, where Catholicism is taken very seriously, and where there is massive overpopulation and widespread poverty. At this time, throughout the world, there were 23,000 new unwanted pregnancies occurring every day, about eight million each year. For many Catholics, the actual evil of the human misery caused by the ban on artificial birth control far outweighed any theoretical "intrinsic evil." This encyclical was an acknowledged attempt to stem the tide of liberalism in the church, but the pope may as well have been King Canute, sitting on his throne on the beach, ordering the tide not to come in. Its greatest effect, in the West, has been to cause large parts of the church to dismiss the papacy as being irrelevant to *their* church. There is nothing in the world so powerful as an idea whose time has come, and this is what liberalism is in Western Catholicism.

The liberal papacy of John XXIII, and the reform of Vatican II, stand out as bright lights in the darkness of Roman Catholic History. The second Vatican Council was called to improve the pastoral work of the church, and ushered in a new era of Catholic thought. It showed an openness to many theological questions, including dialogue with Protestant churches and other religions. The Jesuit Karl Rahner, who typified the post Vatican spirit, believed that the people of God extend beyond the Catholic church, and even the other churches, to include all of humanity.[10] The early sixties was a stirring time to be a Catholic, and the early return to arbitrary conservatism, after John XXIII died, was bitterly disappointing to progressive Catholics around the world. Many sincere and devoted Catholics left the Roman church at this time, but many also stayed, and kept their progressive ideas, continuing to work quietly for reform, in spite of the papacy. In the interests of unity, the papacy has, for a long time, largely tolerated these rebels, who, to a large extent, act independently of the Vatican. Only pope John Paul II has seriously attempted to suppress them, and in vain.

In South America, Liberation Theologians adapt Catholicism to cater to the urgent needs of oppressed people, and go as far as using Marxist analysis to help determine the way the church should care for society. They have achieved impressive results in improving the lot of the poor. In North America the former Dominican Matthew Fox is one of the main advocates of a widespread Catholic Feminist theology. To make up for past wrongs, he advocates changing the Bible to make its language gender inclusive, and proposes the adoption by the church of the essentially pantheist perspective of "Creation Theology," incorporating a renewed worship of ancient earth goddesses. He believes we are all heirs to God's "original blessing" rather than to original sin.[11] He has also been a major force in bringing to light the evils of the witch craze, which, in the Catholic Church, via the Inquisition, was perpetrated by his own Dominican order. The Catholic priest Bede Griffiths ran an Hindu-style ashram in India, and preached around the world on the similarities between Hinduism and Christianity, and of the urgent need for them to cooperate to revitalize each other.[12] This progressive side of Catholicism is in stark contrast to the official church, which continues to be conservative and authoritarian. Issues such as birth control, celibacy of priests, the sexual abuse of children in the church's care, and ordination of women, are racking the Catholic church. While the Vatican continues to fail to properly address these issues, and others raised by liberals, Roman Catholicism will keep on stagnating. Yet at least there are the seeds of renewal within Catholicism, in its saints and in its liberals. If it can let go of the dead wood of its past, acknowledge its corruption, and see that much of its tradition just isn't worth keeping, then the Catholic liberals and the main-stream may well be able to work together. The Roman Catholic church might then be able to go permanently into "Vatican II mode," and create a church which really would be able to meet the spiritual needs of the sophisticated, concerned, and discriminating people of the twenty-first century. If such an accommodation is not achieved, though, the Catholic Church will effectively split. The papacy will become like a diseased branch, cut off from the nourishment of the vine, gradually withering away, while liberalism will blossom, as its roots become more and more firmly established in the community.

The dead hand of the past, and the seeds of renewal, are also present in the Protestant church. Within Protestantism they manifest differently, though. The Protestant hankering to return to a past era, when the church controlled society, manifests as fundamentalism. A prime example of this is the Moral Majority movement in the United States, which evolved into the Christian Coalition. Under it, conservative Christians began to play a major role in politics. They twice helped secure the Presidency for Ronald Reagan, and continued to support the Republican Party after his departure. In return for their support, these fundamentalists expect Republican administrations to bring in legislation to enforce observance of their moralistic, so-called "Christian" values. They want abortion outlawed, prayers to be said in schools, and "decent," middle-class, values to be established. Neither they, nor the Republican party, however, take on the issues of structural social injustice which are plaguing America, and which Jesus and the old-testament prophets were so concerned about in their time. Ironically, it is liberals, who make much less of a show of being Christian, who promote these social justice issues through their own agencies and the Democrats. Implementing social justice through reform involves helping people who need it and want it; it is selfless service of the type Jesus commended. Implementing laws which punish people for so-called "moral crimes" is imposing a value system on others, and taking away their God-given free will. It is selfish and power seeking. Jesus clearly avoided doing it, and if his example means anything, Christians should too. Setting a good example, and having high expectations of others, as Jesus did, are far better ways of promoting right behavior.

Fundamentalism usually attracts the Christian spotlight, with its high political profile and tele-evangelists, but for every fundamentalist in the church there is also another caring, loving, tolerant Christian with a more liberal outlook. By and large this liberal outlook is reflected in the World Council of Churches. In this liberal Christianity, the separation of church and state is accepted, and energy is not spent trying to reverse it. Instead there is a concentration on helping the poor and dispossessed, properly caring for the world God entrusted to us, and trying to find common ground between believers of different denominations and faiths. Unfortunately, the historical problems of church and society have often caused these liberals to react to more conservative religion by being very rationalistic, often to the point of not believing in the miraculous, or the power of the Spirit in individual lives. At the same time Pentecostal Christians, with their personal faith in the saving power of the Spirit, often lean toward fundamentalism. This is the strange dilemma of modern Christianity, and it is tearing it apart. If only the concern for spirituality of the Pentecostal movement could be combined with the social concern, love and tolerance of the liberals, then Christianity could really begin to meet the needs of spiritual seekers in our society. I believe the tacit acceptance of many false doctrines and attitudes from the medieval church is preventing such a joining of the best with the best in the church. A cleansing must take place first, before healing is possible. Then the conservatives will be able to see that much that is traditional in the church is actually holding it back, and the liberals will be able to see that the corrupt and the miraculous aren't at all just one package, and can be separated. Until this cleansing takes place, the church in western countries will continue to stagnate, because it will keep on failing to meet the needs of discriminating people, and will keep on leading more emotional people down a path of selfishness.

There is a very good reason why the church has been so successful in Africa, when it has been languishing in western countries. African culture delights in the charismatic and ritualistic, and is at home with a conservative interpretation of the Bible. It also honors hierarchies and titles, and readily accepts strict discipline.[13] The church structure of our past suits most African societies much better than it now suits ours. Also, since the church is new in Africa, the dead weight of the past isn't holding it back in the same way it does in the West. Africans have been quick to adapt Christianity to their culture, and a wide variety of local churches have arisen, mostly emphasizing the Pentecostal experience of the power of the Spirit. There may be some lessons for the West in the way the church has succeeded in Africa, but it is unlikely to be as simple as that we should just imitate it; the differences between the two societies, and their past exposure to Christianity, must be taken into account.

The church in the West is dogged by its past, but it doesn't have to be forever, unfortunate as this past is. A twentieth century Indian saint, Sri Yukteswar, said this about what has gone before:

> Forget the past. The vanished lives of all men are dark with
> many shames. Human conduct is ever unreliable until anchored
> in the divine. Everything in the future will improve if you
> are making a spiritual effort now.[14]

It is advice the Western church can heed. But in order to make it possible for the church to forget the past, it needs to acknowledge with Albert Schweitzer that:

What has been passing for Christianity during these nineteen centuries is merely a beginning, full of weaknesses and mistakes, not a full-grown Christianity springing from the spirit of Jesus.

The wrongs of the past must be acknowledged, and the lessons learned from them. Then forgiveness can take place, the dross of the past can be left behind, and finally the church will be able to move on and grow in the true spirit of Jesus.

Part 2

Healing — Original Christianity at Last

Chapter 11

Confidence in the Bible

In looking to purge itself of the corruption and worldliness of its past, the church's greatest asset will be the Bible. Many critics of Christianity have assumed the flaws of the church are a reflection of flaws in the Bible. They have made the mistake of assuming Christianity is, as it claims to be, squarely based on the Bible. Christianity has, in fact, nearly always been out of step with its own Scriptures in important ways. In particular, it has never really understood the teachings of Jesus. This is, of course, deplorable, but looked at in another way, it is also a great blessing: it means the church has the Bible there to be its guide during any process of renewal it may undertake. If the church can bring itself into step with what its own Scriptures really are saying, rather than with what it imagines they are saying, then it can be transformed.

It is not always easy to interpret the Bible consistently and reasonably — to lift truth and wisdom from its pages. Nor is it, for many people, easy to be convinced that the highest truth is even to be consistently found in it, and that it is not full of errors, or punctuated by vital omissions. In attempting to assess the integrity of the Bible, we first have to be clear about what the Bible really is. There is no use in pretending it is something which it is not. What has emerged from our look into Ancient Judaism is that the Bible is not a complete or reliable history. What has also emerged, though, is that it was never primarily intended to be history. In the Bible, religious truths take precedence over historical facts, and it is reasonable that they should.[1] An historical novelist is not criticized for embellishing the facts of history if it enables the author to better convey the mood and feel of the story. Nor should the Bible authors be criticized for historical embellishments or inaccuracies, even though much of it is loosely based on Jewish history. Attempts to portray the Bible as accurate history are bound to fail, and bring it into unnecessary disrepute when it conflicts with archaeological and historical evidence.

It may be interesting to try and match the Bible with history, in order to determine the sorts of ways in which it is, and isn't, historically reliable. This knowledge makes the Bible a more useful historical source document than it would otherwise be. The Bible's authority, however, is not undermined by its shortcomings as history; it is a collection of spiritual books, written for a spiritual purpose, and its authority can only be judged by its spiritual integrity and power. Likewise, the Bible can't be taken as being scientifically authoritative, although it is remarkable how much sound science it contains, considering the scientific illiteracy of the ancient world.

Most importantly, though, it has to be realized that the Bible can't always be taken literally. Parables, moral tales, symbolism, and simplifications are often used to convey moral, spiritual and scientific ideas which were ahead of their time, and couldn't have been expressed accurately and understandably in a literal way. We have to be able to discern this when reading the Bible, and read it the right way. We should, as Jesus said, "Stop judging by mere appearances, and make a right judgment." (John 7:24). And like Paul, we should be able to realize that parts of the Bible can be taken figuratively:

> For it is written that Abraham had two sons, one by the slave woman and the other by the free woman...
>   These things may be taken figuratively, for the women represent two covenants.   (Galatians 4:22,24)

I believe the Bible is "inerrant," as fundamentalists claim, but only when it is seen for what it really is: a spiritual guide. It is certainly not an inerrant guide to the whole spectrum of human knowledge — it can never have been intended to have such a wide scope. Creation scientists court trouble by being too literal about the greatly simplified account of creation in Genesis. Critics of the Bible also make mistakes by taking symbolic statements and stories literally, and sometimes they can be laughable. Of course, some of these critics may be more poking fun at Christians who insist on taking the Bible literally, than actually criticizing the Bible's integrity. A good example of this is Jeanette Winterson's review of *The Book of J*, a recent translation of one of the Bible's oldest sources.

Before discussing what Winterson says, I would like to digress slightly to explain that modern study of the Pentateuch, the first five books of the Bible, shows it couldn't all have been written by Moses, as tradition asserts.[2] Research reveals there are, in fact, four main literary sources drawn together by an editor from after the exile in Babylon. There are two early sources, called "J" and "E," and two later sources, called the "Deuteronomic" and the "Priestly."[3] Much of Genesis (after the first chapter, which is from the Priestly source), and a fair bit of Exodus and Numbers, were written by J.[4] *The Book of J* is an attempt to separate this source from later additions.[5]

In her review of *The Book of J*, called "God the Sod," Jeanette Winterson claims that by normal Jewish or Christian standards, J's portrayal of Yahweh is blasphemous. The Church Father Origen, along with Philo, the Stoics and early Christians at Alexandria, took essentially the same view, that many Biblical texts are absurd or immoral if taken literally.[6] To justify her claim, Winterson discusses a number of J's descriptions of Yahweh's actions, starting with the "Fall":

> J's Yahweh is volatile and violent and manifestly unfair. When we read J's story of the expulsion from the garden of Eden, we find no sense of sin or a fall from grace. Rather, we find two curious children to whom the rules have not been properly explained.
>
> Along comes a serpent who is absolutely not Satan, but who has been around a bit, and naturally the three get together. Did Yahweh ever say "Don't go talking to strange snakes?" No. Neither did he say, "If you touch this tree, I'm throwing you out of our little home." The punishment is fantastically cruel and incommensurate with the offense...[7]

She goes on to ask,

> What can you do with a God who eats meat and no veg with

Abram at Mamre and then haggles with him down the road to
Sodom over the ethics of destroying the righteous with the
wicked? How galling too that it's not so much the buggery that
worries Yahweh, as the lack of hospitality shown in Sodom.
They are corrupt because they show contempt for everything
and everybody outside their own desires. Sin is not one of J's
concepts; contempt is, and Yahweh always punishes it.

Sexual prohibitions are not among J's concepts either.[7]

This last point can be demonstrated by looking at a number of
passages from J in the Bible. J uses what appears to be black
sexual humor in describing what happened in Sodom:

> They had not gone to bed when the house was surrounded by the
> men of the town, the men of Sodom both young and old, all the
> people without exception. Calling to Lot they said, "Where are
> the men who came to you tonight? Send them out to us so that we
> may abuse them."
>
> Lot came out to them at the door, and having closed the door
> behind him said, "I beg you, my brothers, do no such wicked thing.
> Listen, I have two daughters who are virgins. I am ready to send
> them out to you, to treat as it pleases you. But as for the men, do
> nothing to them, for they have come under the shadow of my
> roof." (Genesis 19:4–9, J.B.)

Yet despite Lot's willingness to allow his virgin daughters to be
raped to appease the crowd, and so protect his guests,[8]
Yahweh felt pity on him and led him to safety before Sodom
was destroyed. At the same time Yahweh was prepared to kill
up to nine just men in the process of destroying Sodom. What
kind of notion of God is this?

Shortly after escaping from Sodom, Lot's daughters con-
nived to get their father drunk and sleep with him, since there
weren't any other men around, and they wished to preserve
their family line. Both became pregnant by their father, yet attracted no blame or punishment from Yahweh (Gen 19:30–38).

When Abram went to live in Egypt during a famine, he
passed his wife, Sarai, off as his sister, since she was beautiful,
and he didn't want the Egyptians to kill him for his wife. Sarai
did, in the event, come to the notice of the Pharaoh, and was

taken into his palace. Abram was treated well for her sake, and given servants and other riches. Instead of punishing Abram, who perpetuated this deceit, Yahweh punished the innocent Pharaoh, who had no idea Sarai was already married, by inflicting severe plagues on him and his household. (Gen 12:10–20)

Yet Yahweh also punished the Israelites, when they offended him, as when Onan refused to cooperate with Judah's wishes:

> Judah took a wife for his firstborn Er, and her name was Tamar. But Er, Judah's firstborn, offended Yahweh greatly, so Yahweh brought about his death. Then Judah said to Onan, "Take your brother's wife, and do your duty as her brother-in-law, to produce a child for your brother." But Onan, knowing the child would not be his, spilt his seed on the ground every time he slept with his brother's wife, to avoid providing a child for his brother. What he did was offensive to Yahweh, so he brought about his death also. Then Judah said to his daughter-in-law Tamar, "return home as a widow to your father, and wait for my son Shelah to grow up," for he was thinking, "he must not die like his brothers..."
> (Genesis 38:6–11, J.B.)

Judah was afraid Yahweh would kill his last remaining son merely for being too young to provide a child for Tamar! One could hardly blame him: Yahweh could be seen to be rather capricious at times. Nowhere is this more apparent than when Yahweh decided, for no very good reason, to murder his newly appointed prophet Moses, but backed down when Moses' courageous and loyal wife, Zipporah, stood up to him and saw him off:

> On the journey, when Moses had halted for the night, Yahweh came to meet him and tried to kill him. At once Zipporah, taking up a flint, cut off her son's foreskin and with it touched the genitals of Moses. "Truly, you are a bridegroom of blood to me!" she said. And Yahweh let him live. (Exodus 4:24–26, J.B.)

Of course, if you claim these episodes shouldn't be literally taken as reflecting on the character of God, but rather reflect on the primitive Israelites' prurience and limited understanding of God, as revealed in their early myth, then you also have to admit that much else in the Bible can't necessarily be taken to be literally true. Christians can't have it both ways: insist on "creation science" and "original sin," and you have to accept "God the Sod" too. In fact, it is reasonable to take all these as examples of the unsophistication of the early Jews. As has been mentioned, a number of the early Church Fathers including Origen took the view that many Bible texts would be immoral if taken literally. Consequently, the practice of treating parts of the Bible, especially the Pentateuch, as allegory, has become an integral part of much Christian theology. Even the Hellenistic Jews often allegorized the writings attributed to Moses, in order to make sense of them.[9] A prime example of the early recognition of the inadequacy of much of the Yahwist material is the "Genesis Apocryphon" from the Dead Sea Scrolls, which retells the story of Abram and Sarai in Egypt in a way which rectifies its moral deficiencies.[10]

Why, then, is this "mythical" material in this sacred book, if it isn't the last word in truth? One very good reason, it seems to me, is that it shows, along with later material, the gradual evolution of the Jewish conception of God, from the God of Moses who, though often protective, was also often vengeful and capricious, through to the God of justice of the Prophets, and finally to the God of love Jesus knew and taught about. We have seen that the Yahwist material, written by J, at times seems almost to be poking fun at the early Mosaic view of God. Perhaps this is because this material was written, as some suggest, well after the time of Moses, in the 800's B.C., after the reign of King Solomon, and maybe even after the calling of Elijah.[11] At this time, the Jews' conception of God would have moved a long way toward the just and consistent God of the Prophets. From this perspective, and in the sophisticated court of the kings of Judah, it would be understandable that J, and even those who passed the stories on to him (or her[12]), might have taken a gently satirical view of these quaint old stories of their ancestors' experiences with God. Of course, despite this changing perception of God, there is no suggestion that God himself changed: the fascinating thing about the Old Testament is that it shows how the Israelites' conception of the Divine gradually evolved into a fuller understanding, as God progressively revealed himself to them.

To "allegorize" the Yahwist material, rather than seeing it simply as a very early account of even earlier primitive beliefs, seems to me to be merely an attempt to disguise its moral weaknesses, deny the gradual evolution of the Israelites' understanding of God, and make it into something it was never intended to be. To say morally weak sections are not complex allegory is not, of course, to say there is no symbolism or figurative language anywhere in J. Symbolism and simple allegory are typical of early religious writings, and there are plenty of examples of them in J.

From the book of Ruth onward, the notion of God being violent and capricious is largely left behind, and the Bible increasingly commands respect for its high moral tone. The Jews' conception of God had advanced to the point were they could clearly perceive much of His wisdom and righteousness. This perception was later crowned by Jesus, who showed us the love of our heavenly Father (our "Dad"), who cares for us personally. Jesus also taught how we can come to know this personal parent God, and live in the kingdom of heaven with Him.

So, this is what the Bible is: a collection of spiritual books about the history of the Jews' relationship with God. And when we read it we recognize there is much in it to admire and live our lives by — much that is widely seen across human society as being true and important to happiness and well-being. But there is also a lot of contentious material in the Bible, and a host of seeming contradictions. Many are left wondering whether the Bible has come down to us accurately through nearly two thousand years, especially considering how worldly, power seeking and corrupt the church was for much of this time. Perhaps later additions by a corrupt church are the cause of the contradictions in the Bible? And if so, how can we tell what is genuine and what is not? And what important teachings have been deleted from the Bible, or never included in the first place? These are good questions, and they need to be satisfactorily answered if we are to have confidence in the Bible.

First, let's look at the question of later alterations to the Bible. From as early as the ninth century, scholars have been on the look-out for just such changes. At that time the emperor Charlemagne gave Alcuin the task of revising the Latin Bible. The Carolingian Bible, used during the dark ages, had picked up numerous errors, many probably from mistakes in copying, but some obviously deliberate changes. Jerome had gone to great pains, in the fifth century, to produce the most accurate Latin Bible he could, the Vulgate. He spent much of his life at the task. Now Alcuin removed the accumulated errors of the dark ages and restored the Vulgate to its original purity. One deliberate addition removed by Alcuin was the well known "Johanine Comma," where the words: "in heaven, the Father, the Word, and the Holy Ghost: and these three are one." were added to 1 John 5:7 (along with a connecting phrase in the next verse), in order to claim the Bible text directly supports the doctrine of the Trinity. This insert can still be found in the King James Version of the Bible, although it has been properly removed from more modern translations.

In the fifteenth century, the meticulous Latin scholar Lorenzo Valla exposed a number of spurious Christian texts, such as the long-accepted and popular correspondence between St Paul and Seneca, and the celebrated *Donation of Constantine*, supposedly an edict in which that emperor granted the Roman popes control over the Church and Christendom. In the *Adnotationes*, Valla compared the New Testament Vulgate with a Greek original and made long lists of errors in translation which had slipped past Jerome. This was the most thorough scrutiny the Bible had come under since Jerome himself. During Valla's own lifetime his work had little impact, but sixty-five years later, when printing was well established in Europe, the manuscript of *Anotationes* was discovered in a Belgian abbey, and published (in 1516). It became an inspiration to a new generation of scholars who were re-examining the Bible in preparation for translating it into their own languages.[13]

The King James (Authorized) Version of 1611 follows the Greek of Erasmus's hastily compiled New Testament, later reverently referred to as the "Received Text." In the light of the many further New Testament manuscripts which have been discovered since then, and their analysis by the technique of Textural Criticism, the "Received Text" has been found to contain hundreds of errors, including some important ones, and is no longer generally considered to be reliable. Generations of study and critical research, based on a wide variety of early manuscripts, have gone into preparing the Greek texts used for modern translations. This task was made much harder by the fact that no original New Testament manuscripts have survived. Our knowledge of the gospels, for instance, depends on several hundred full texts from before 1000 A.D., and eighty fragmentary texts from before 400 A.D. This compares very well, however, with many documents from the ancient world which we regard as authoritative. The *Annals* of Tacitus, for instance, which we rely on for much of our information about the Roman emperors of Jesus' century, are known from only a single thirteenth century manuscript. We have to trust that it was accurately copied from its original.[14] With New Testament material, by contrast, there are multiple lines of copying from different parts of Europe and the Mediterranean, including much earlier manuscripts. Copying errors or alterations in one line are exposed though comparison with other lines. What this adds up to is that we can be next to certain the modern Greek New Testament texts we have very closely resemble the first and second century originals.

Next we need to consider whether the right books were selected for the New Testament in the first place. In the chapter on the early church, we saw how St Paul's letters tie in well with the gospel teachings of Jesus if they are read with a knowledge of the history and cultural movements of the time. But do the four canonical gospels, not written until at least a generation after Jesus died, accurately capture Jesus' teachings? There are, after all, dozens of apocryphal gospels, many of which give different perspectives on Jesus' teachings. This question is the subject of Ian Wilson's book *Are these the Words of Jesus?*, which carefully searches apocryphal sources for sayings of Jesus which might be genuine. Wilson does sift out quite a few new sayings of Jesus.[15] His overall impression, though, which is well backed-up by his material, is that these additional sayings do not significantly add to what is already there in the Bible:

> Instead what we have, and always have had, of Jesus is rather like a hologram: even if it were smashed to pieces and individual fragments lost, those that remained would still convey the picture of the whole.[16]

Although there are minor differences between the gospels, mainly in the circumstances of Jesus' life, the four Bible gospels support each other well in the areas of the character and teachings of Jesus, and strongly testify to Jesus' being a real person. As Ian Wilson puts it:

> ...more important than the sheer profusion and antiquity of the documentation, is the fact that such an individual, consistent, and striking personality emerges from the pages of the four gospels, despite their differing authorship. If there had not been a real-life Jesus of Nazareth that sparked off all this, we should have to look for someone else, equally remarkable.[17]

In recent years, much attention has been given to the "Gnostic gospels" found among the texts unearthed at Nag Hammadi in Egypt in 1945. They challenge Christianity with a number of concepts the orthodox consider heretical. Yet many of these concepts are present in the canonical New Testament as well, though perhaps not so prominently. Take the concept of *gnosis* itself: it means knowing through observation or experience, and the Gnostics claimed people could know God through deep inner intuitive experience.[18] Orthodox Christianity through the ages may not have liked this idea, nevertheless Jesus and Paul both taught it, and the record of these teachings is in the Bible. Jesus said,

"The kingdom of God does not come visibly, nor will the people

say, Here is is,' or 'There it is,' because the kingdom of God
is within you."   (Luke 17:20–21)

and:

"I will ask the Father, and he will give you another Counselor
to be with you forever—the Spirit of truth. The world cannot
accept him, because it neither sees him nor knows him. But you
know him, for he lives with you and will be in you."
                                   (John 14:16–17)

Paul wrote:

...God...made his light shine in our hearts to give us the light
of knowledge of the glory of God. (2 Corinthians 4:6)

And the "knowledge" mentioned is the word *gnosis* in the
Greek.

Another Gnostic concept long repugnant to orthodox Christianity was that they possessed a secret teaching, consisting of
the same mysteries Jesus shared with his disciples but didn't
reveal to outsiders. That Jesus had such teachings is clear from
Mark's gospel:

"The secret of the kingdom of God has been given to you. But
to those on the outside everything is said in parables so that,
'they may be ever seeing but never perceiving,
      and ever hearing but never understanding;
   otherwise they might turn and be forgiven!'" (Mark 4:11)

That Paul was also in possession of secret teachings not to be
revealed to all, is equally clear:

We do, however, speak a message of wisdom among the mature,
but not the wisdom of this age or of the rulers of this age, who
are coming to nothing. No, we speak of God's secret wisdom, a
wisdom that has been hidden and that God destined for our glory
before time began.   (1 Cor 2:6–7)

Gnostics also claimed that following the crucifixion Christ
continued to reveal himself to some disciples, giving them,
through visions, new knowledge of divine mysteries.[19] Though
orthodox Christianity denied this, Paul himself described such

an experience. So as not to boast too much about himself (2 Cor 12–5), Paul put the experience into the third person, but there seems little doubt he is referring to himself. But even if he isn't, he still clearly approves of the vision. He said,

> I know a man in Christ, who fourteen years ago was caught up to the third heaven. Whether it was in the body or out of the body I do not know — God knows. And I know that this man...was caught up to paradise. He heard inexpressible things, things that man is not permitted to tell.   (2 Cor 12:2–4)

Many orthodox Biblical scholars, from Rudolph Bultmann onward, have insisted Paul does not mean what he says in this passage, and argue that Paul does not claim to have a secret tradition. Apparently such a claim would make Paul sound too "gnostic." Professor Robin Scroggs and Elaine Pagels take the opposite view, pointing out, as I just have, that Paul clearly does say he has secret wisdom (1 Cor 2:6–7). Gnostic Christians in the early church also knew this. The much reviled Gnostic poet Valentinus even claimed to have learned Paul's secret teaching from Theudas, one of Paul's own disciples.[20]

Another Gnostic belief was that there is no great chasm between people and God, needing to be bridged by priests, as the orthodox in the early church soon reverted to claiming. Gnostics claimed they were all equally sons of God with Jesus, and claimed to know God through the inner self, considering the self and the divine identical.[21] If by this they meant that "the kingdom of God is within you" — that man is inherently divine and only needs to mature into the realization of it to become one with the Father the way Jesus is — then both Jesus and Paul support them. Not only does it say in Psalms,

> "I said, 'You are "gods"; you are all sons of the Most High,'"
> (Psalm 82:6)

but Jesus also used this to defend himself against Jewish charges of blasphemy for claiming to be one with God. He didn't defend himself by saying he was different from his accusers; rather, he pointed out that the Scriptures say they too are gods, so why are they accusing him of blasphemy, especially as he was doing God's work? (John 10:34–36) Jesus also indicated that his disciples could reach equality with him, when he said,

> "The disciple is not above his master: but everyone that is perfect shall be as his master." (Luke 6:40 AV)

and,

> "Be perfect therefore, as your heavenly Father is perfect." (Matt 5:48)

In his letter to the Romans Paul says,

> The Spirit himself testifies with our spirit that we are God's children. Now if we are children then we are heirs—heirs of God and co-heirs with Christ. (Rom 8:16–17)

and in Galations he adds,

> ...as long as the heir is a child, he is no different from a slave, although he owns the whole estate. He is subject to guardians and trustees until the time set by his father. So also, when we were children, we were in slavery under the basic principles of the world. But when the time had fully come, God sent his Son, born of a woman, born under law, to redeem those under law, that we might receive the full rights as sons. Because you are sons, God sent the spirit of his Son into our hearts. (Gal 4:1–6)

So we can see that four of the most universal of the "heretical" Gnostic beliefs are, in fact, affirmed by the Bible. And, of course, the Gnostics considered themselves Christians and held most of their beliefs in common with the orthodox. There were many groups of Gnostics, though, and some did have extreme beliefs which appear to be foreign to Jesus' teachings. Some, for instance, were misogynists, and attributed anti-feminist sayings to Jesus, which are totally out of character for him.[22] Others believed the God of the Old Testament is evil, and the world contains evil because he created it.[23] Nevertheless, it is clear that the most common Gnostic beliefs already had their basis in the Bible the orthodox accepted. This is one good reason why the Bible doesn't suffer from not having these Gnostic gospels included in it, even though some of these extra gospels are useful in highlighting genuine areas of belief which have been rejected by orthodox Christianity. There are other good reasons, though, for not including the Gnostic gospels in the Bible. Some Gnostics openly acknowledged they derived their "gospels" from their own "gnosis" or experience, rather than from reports of what Jesus actually taught.[24] Most of the Gnostic gospels reflect the fact that they are inventions of this type: the character of Jesus in them is inconsistent and weak, and doesn't at all match the Jesus revealed in the Bible. Take this example from the "gospel" of Philip, written by Valentinus:

> [The Lord loved] Mary Magdalen...more than [all] the disciples [and used to] kiss her [often] on her [...] The rest of [the disciples...] They said to him, "Why do you love her more than all of us?" The Savior answered and said to them, "Why do I not love you like her? When a blind man and one who sees are both together in darkness, they are no different from one another. When the light comes, then he who sees will see the light, and he who is blind will remain in darkness." (Philip 64:2–9)[25]

And then there are the anti-feminist sayings ascribed to Jesus in the "Dialogue of the Saviour" and the "Gospel of the Egyptians." These include:

> The Lord said, "Pray in the place where there is no woman."
> ("Dialogue" 91)

and:

> The Savior himself said, "I came to destroy the works of the female." (Gospel of the Egyptians (not from Nag Hammadi))[26]

For Jesus to be so partial or so prejudiced, just doesn't fit with what we know of him from other sources. These writings are unlikely to be genuine records of what Jesus said.

Among the Nag Hammadi texts, though, there is one document which stands out from the rest, and has authentic features. It is the Gospel of Thomas. Not only does its portrayal of Jesus line up with that in the canonical gospels, but many of its sayings and stories coincide as well. In addition to this, a part of this gospel, which, like all the Nag Hammadi texts, is in Coptic, has an equivalent in a fragment of Greek manuscript found at Oxyrhynchus. This fragment contains about forty short lines of text, more than enough to clearly identify it as being from the same gospel. Comparison between the two, however, reveals something very disappointing: it shows the Coptic translation has been altered to make it coincide with Gnostic belief. In the space of just forty lines, three distinct changes have been made, and two of these have been made in the direction of known Gnostic belief. One of them is a deletion of a reference to the resurrection, presumably done because the Gnostics believed in the survival of the spirit rather than the resurrection of the body. Saying 5 of the Coptic text ends with: "There is nothing hidden which will not become manifest." The Greek version from Oxyrhynchus, however, has in addition: "There is nothing buried which will not..." And a grave wrapping from Oxyrhynchus from a few centuries later completes the saying: "Jesus says, 'There is nothing buried which will not be raised.'" The Coptic translation of the gospel of Thomas has left this line out. Unfortunately there is no way of knowing how many other changes were made, and what they might be. Consequently, despite its many genuine features, this text must be considered unreliable.[27] It is quite likely the Nag Hammadi Gnostics were among the more extreme Gnostics. The presence of many "subjective" gospels and pagan manuscripts in the find suggests this.[28] And, of course, their dishonesty in tampering with the Gospel of Thomas adds weight to the supposition.

If a complete Greek text of the gospel of Thomas were to be found, free of Gnostic tampering, it would surely be worthy of consideration for inclusion into the Bible. The same would be true of the Gospel of the Hebrews, which a number of the early church fathers quoted from, and which contains, even from these quotes, a number of genuine sounding stories and teachings of Jesus not found in the canonical gospels.[29] Either of these would be a celebrated archaeological find. At this point, though, we don't have them, and there are no apocryphal gospels we have texts for which warrant such serious consideration. Whether the gospels of Thomas and the Hebrews were available to the church fathers who compiled the

Bible isn't known. It is quite likely, though, that they didn't have these books, for neither of them appear on the *Decretum Gelasianum*, a "List of Books to be Accepted and Not to be Accepted" drawn up by the church in the late fifth century.[30] Fortunately, the teachings of Jesus do not seem to be very much affected by the lack of these books. Certainly, neither the fragments we have of the Gospel of the Hebrews, nor the Gnostic Gospel of Thomas, contain anything which significantly changes the nature of Jesus' teaching. We can be confident the four gospels we have are an accurate, representative, and reasonably complete selection of the teachings of Jesus.

But even if it is conceded that the Bible contains an accurate record of the teachings of Jesus, this still doesn't say anything about the ultimate truth and worthiness of these teachings. Most would agree there are many very worthy things said by Jesus in the gospels. Many, however, would definitely not agree that everything said in them is worth believing in. In defense of their position they would point out that Jesus contradicts himself a number of times, and makes many contentious and seemingly unreasonable statements. Bertrand Russell points out some of these his essay "Why I am not a Christian":

> I do not think that Christ was the best and wisest of men,
> although I grant Him a very high degree of moral goodness...
> There is one very serious defect to my mind in Christ's moral
> character, and that is that he believed in hell. I do not myself
> feel that any person who is really profoundly humane can believe
> in everlasting punishment...There is, of course, the familiar
> text about the sin against the Holy Ghost: "Whosover speaketh
> against the Holy Ghost it shall not be forgiven him neither in
> this world nor in the world to come." That text has caused an
> unspeakable amount of misery in the world, for all sorts of
> people have imagined that they have committed the sin against
> the Holy Ghost, and thought that it would not be forgiven them
> either in this world or in the world to come. I really do not think
> that a person with a proper degree of kindliness in his nature
> would have put fears and terrors of that sort into the world.[31]

Russell is reflecting the feelings of millions of people who have rejected the church because they can't stomach a supposedly just and loving God who would punish people forever for a few short years of not loving Him, and wanting to do things their own way. Neither could I stomach such a God. It is only because I know there is no such thing as everlasting punishment in hell, that I can love God. But if there is no eternal hell, why did Jesus go on about it so much? This is a big question, one a whole chapter will be devoted to, and one which is too involved to thoroughly go into here. The short answer, though, is that Jesus did not, in fact, ever say anyone would have everlasting punishment in hell after death. But if this is the situation, how can the Bible be an accurate record of Jesus' teachings when it portrays him as saying there is such a hell?

Actually, I didn't get as far as demonstrating the accuracy of the Bible's portrayal of Jesus. I showed only that the Greek texts modern Bible translations are made from appear authentic. And, indeed, on going back to the Greek, the concept of hell disappears—all that is left is a garbage tip. Hell is an error in translation, and quite possibly a deliberate one, foisted on the world by a corrupt medieval church intent on using fear to control people.

There are two different words which Jesus used, and two different words in the Greek, which have been translated into one word, "hell," in medieval and modern Bibles. Only when these two words, otherwise unconnected, are translated as one word, does the concept of everlasting punishment in hell become possible. In the Greek the two words are *Gehenna* and *Hades*. Whenever Jesus talked about the "eternal fire of hell," he referred to the "Valley of Hinnom," *Gehenna* in the Greek. The Valley of Hinnom was the garbage tip just outside the walls of Jerusalem, where there was a huge garbage fire which never went out. It was literally an eternal fire, and its heat and sulfurous fumes, combined with the stench of rotting garbage, would no doubt have made Gehenna a very unpleasant place to be. It was probably the most unpleasant place anyone of the time knew of, so Jesus used this wasteland as a metaphor for an awful-feeling corrosive state of mind ("living hell," we might call it). Jesus used it in a number of his teachings, such as when he warned of the folly of getting angry and saying abusive things to people:

> "...anyone who says, 'You fool!' will be in danger of the
> fire of hell."   (Matt 5:22)

Never was Jesus' use of the word *Gehenna* associated with punishment after death. On the one occasion where Jesus did talk about someone being punished after death for the evil life he had lived, in the story of "the rich man and Lazarus" (Luke 16:19–31), Jesus talked of the rich man being in *Hades*, not in *Gehenna*, and although the point is driven home, in this story, that the rich man cannot escape his punishment, it is never said that this punishment is to be forever. *Hades* means "the place of departed souls," and this is where everlasting punishment would have to be, if it were anywhere. Yet Jesus never talked about *Hades* as being a place of eternal punishment. Jesus, quite simply, did not teach about hell as we know it. Everlasting hell is a sadistic concept dreamed up by the medieval church to enable it to control people through fear, and given that it is not true, it is a terrible defamation of the otherwise good names of God and Jesus.

In point of fact, most modern Bible translations go a long way toward correcting the "hell" problem. In the Old Testament, *Sheol* is no longer translated as "hell," but as "the grave" or something similar. In the New Testament, only *Gehenna* is still consistently translated as "hell." In the Jerusalem Bible *Hades* is left as "Hades," and *Tartarus* (the deepest depths of Hades) is translated as the "underworld." In the NIV, however, *Tartarus* remains as "hell," and *Hades* is still translated as "hell" in the story of the rich man and Lazarus, even though in all the other nine times it is used in the New Testament, in Matthew, Luke, Acts, and Revelations, it is left as "Hades" or translated as "the grave." This is clearly a bowing to traditional Christian doctrine by the editors of the NIV, at the expense of the truth, and puts a cloud over what is otherwise a wonderfully readable and reasonably accurate translation. I hope that when the falseness of "eternal hell" becomes more widely acknowledged in the church, *Gehenna* will be translated in a different way, perhaps as "living hell," to acknowledge that Jesus was using it as a reference to the here-and-now, and not to the afterlife. Although, from an objective point of view, everlasting hell can't easily be read into modern Bibles, we continue to see it there, because we are used to seeing it from the King James Version, and attitudes change slowly.

Translating the ancient Bible languages into modern tongues is not an easy task. This is partly because the ancient idiom was very different to the modern one. Word-for-word translation is frequently impossible, and often the translator has to understand a phrase or sentence in the Greek, then cast it into English (or another modern language) in a way that preserves the meaning and reads well. Often the order of the words has to be totally changed, and a different number of words used. This means a translation will be affected, at least to some extent, by the understanding and beliefs of the translators. Bible translators, when reaching for a meaning, use their knowledge of Christianity, including traditional church doctrine, as a guide. This needs to be kept in mind when reading the Bible, especially as church doctrine is far from being firmly based on the Bible. The bias of a particular translation can be offset by reading key passages in a number of different translations, which, as many will have noticed, often vary considerably from each other. A still-better way is to learn the Greek alphabet and study these key passages in Greek in an interlinear Greek-English New Testament. Although slow at first, it is not hard to do. The fact that interlinear New Testaments are so popular, and priests and clergy nearly always learn Greek at theological college, shows there is already a widespread recognition of the need to go back to the Greek to accurately interpret New Testament Scriptures.

Errors in translation have caused more problems than just the "hell" one, although it is by far the most damaging. A number of the apparent contradictions in the Bible are also due to translation problems, often quite subtle ones, which are resolved when one or both of the conflicting passages are more precisely or more sensitively translated. For instance, in some versions of the Bible Jesus appears to thoroughly contradict himself over the question of whether he has a secret teaching. He says in Mark,

> "The secret of the kingdom of God has been given to you. But to those on the outside everything is said in parables..." (Mark 4:11)

then in John he says to the high priest,

> "I have spoken openly to the world. I always taught in syna-gogues or at the temple, where all the Jews come together. I said nothing in secret. Why question me? Ask those who heard me. Surely they know what I said."   (John 18:20–21)

A quick look at the two passages in Greek in an interlinear New Testament reveals that the word "secret" in these two passages is translated from two different Greek words. In Mark the secret is a *mysterion*, from which the word "mystery" comes. The King James version actually translates it as "mys-tery," but this is not quite right either. Its meaning is actually "a shut mouth — not told, due to silence imposed by initiation into religious rites." In this passage, "The secret of" might be better translated as "Initiation into."

In John the secret is *kryptos*, from which the word "cryptic" comes. It means "hidden" or "concealed" in a more normal sense. Jesus is saying there is no concealed meaning in what he has been saying in the temple and synagogues (no subversive political message, for instance). And when Jesus said, "I always taught in synagogues or the temple," this cannot be taken to mean he never taught anywhere else, for everyone knew he taught out in the country in Galilee as well. This is obviously an idiom meaning "I am always teaching in a syna-gogue or the temple" (i.e. "often" teaching there). The King James Version captures this meaning reasonably well with, "I ever taught in the synagogue..." As for teaching in parables, this would not have been considered concealment, as parables were a common literary form in ancient Israel. Yet Jesus was something less than "open" with the world at large, for he did have a secret teaching, which for good reasons, he didn't share with everyone. Yet he did speak plainly to the public, and since the Greek word translated here as "openly" actually means "plainly," it would be better rendered that way.

More accurate translations of these verses, which at first sight appeared to contract each other, might be:

> "Initiation into the kingdom of God has been given to you. But to those on the outside everything is said in parables…" (Mark 4:11)

and,

> "I have spoken plainly to the world. I am always teaching in synagogues or at the temple, where all the Jews come together, and nothing I have said contains any hidden meanings. Why question me? Ask those who heard me. They know what I said."
> (John 18:20–21)

This example shows how much is involved in correctly translating passages in the Bible. It also shows how some apparent contradictions can be resolved by improving the translation.

Other contradictions and seemingly unreasonable statements remain, though, which are not just a product of faulty translation. Sometimes these are there to spur us on to dig for a deeper meaning, but sometimes they are a result of our looking at Jesus with pre-conceived notions about his character. Jesus' example was clearly that there were no outsiders to him, and that all people, Jews and Gentiles alike have an equal place in God's kingdom. The parable of the Good Samaritan (Luke 10:29–37) illustrates this, as does Jesus' great commission to his disciples: "Therefore go and make disciples of all nations…" (Matt 28:19) In the light of this, his conversation with the Canaanite woman seems most extraordinary:

> A Canaanite woman from that vicinity came to him, crying out, "Lord, Son of David, have mercy on me! My daughter is suffering terribly from demon possession."
> Jesus did not answer a word. So his disciples came to him and urged him, "Send her away, for she keeps crying out after us."
> He answered, "I was sent only to the lost sheep of Israel."

> The woman came up and knelt before him. "Lord, help me!" she
> said.
> He replied, "It is not right to take the children's bread and
> toss it to their dogs."
> "Yes, Lord," she said, "but even the dogs eat the crumbs that
> fall from their masters' table."
> Then Jesus answered, "Woman, you have great faith! Your
> request is granted." And her daughter was healed from that very
> hour.   (Matt 15:21–28)

What are we to make of Jesus' response in this incident? To call
people dogs is a highly offensive insult in the East. Could Jesus
really have insulted this poor woman who had asked for his
help, knowing she would take it without a word, in return for
the mere chance of him healing her daughter? It seems a cruel
and demeaning thing for him to have done. The answer to this
dilemma is, however, not in any shortcoming of Jesus' character, but in our own preconceived notions about his character.
We never think of Jesus having a sense of humor, or of him
being quite so human as to make a joke at his disciples' expense
as a gentle way of correcting their poor behavior. Yet if we look
at this passage with the possibility that Jesus is "taking the
Mickey out of" his disciples for snubbing this poor woman so
cruelly, and doing it in such a way as to show the woman he
rejects the snub, and is siding with her, then we can see Jesus
responding in the kindest possible way. Jesus can't seriously be
saying, "I was sent only to the lost sheep of Israel," as this
directly contradicts his saying, "I have other sheep that are not
of this fold. I must bring them also." (John 10:16). Jesus is
actually being facetious, saying, "So, I was sent only to the lost
sheep of Israel!" in order to point out to his disciples both their
error and his disapproval of their snub. When the woman came
and knelt at his feet, Jesus would have exchanged a look with
her which said something like, "We know what they are
thinking!" He then spelt out what their thoughts were: "It is
not right to take the children's bread and toss it to their dogs!"
With a quick wit, the woman replied in like humor, though
very humbly and poignantly: "Yes Lord, but even the dogs eat

the crumbs that fall from their masters' table." By this time, I think the disciples would have been thoroughly ashamed of themselves. Jesus, having made this woman feel good about her request, of course went on to heal her daughter. Read in this light, the story becomes one of the most touching illustrations of Jesus' kindness and understanding. Once this story is understood for what it is, it can of course be better translated: no Bible I have seen has it right.

Another example of Jesus' humanness emerges when he is invited by the Pharisee Simon into his home to have a meal with him. The Jerusalem Bible says he "took his place at the table," The NIV says he "reclined at the table," and the King James Version says he "sat down to meat." This is remarkable, considering the Greek makes no mention of a "place," a "table," "sitting" or "meat"! The Greek simply says he "lay down" or "reclined." The translators of all these versions seem to be assiduously avoiding what they believe is a portrayal of Jesus which is too relaxed and informal. They can't believe Jesus would have gone into the house of a friend and just layed down on the floor and relaxed while waiting for dinner to be served. Yet apparently this is what Jesus did. What is more, we know Jesus must have been lying on his front or his side. We know this because the woman with the alabaster jar of ointment, hearing he was there, came in and:

> waited behind him at his feet, weeping, and her tears fell on
> his feet, and she wiped them away with her hair; then she
> covered his feet with kisses and anointed them with the
> ointment.   (Luke 7:38)

If Jesus were reclining, that is lying on his back, his feet would have been in front of him, not behind him, so he must have been lying on his front, or on his side with his knees bent. Of course Jesus wasn't being unduly familiar, or taking liberties, by lying on the floor, as it is made clear there were others lying there with him. It was obviously just the accepted practice of the times.

Having resurrected Jesus' kindness and common touch, let's return to the weightier question of the "unforgivable sin," mentioned by Bertrand Russell. Russell said of it:

> I really do not think a person with a proper degree of kindliness
> in his nature would have put fears and terrors of that sort into
> the world.[31]

So could Jesus really have meant what he appears to have when talking about the blasphemy against the Holy Spirit? Having discredited the idea that Jesus taught there is everlasting punishment in hell, the unforgivable sin teaching seems way out of line. Is it possible we are looking at this in the wrong way? There is a well-known drawing, illustrating how optical illusions can occur, which is seen as a wine glass by some people, and as two faces about to kiss by others. It depends on your way of looking at it, and what you expect to see. If, in reading the Bible, our expectation is governed by our prejudices, what people have said, or by traditional church doctrine, we can easily see the wrong thing. If, however, our expectation is guided by what is said elsewhere in the Bible, both in the immediate context and in related passages, and if we expect the Bible to be consistent, then we are more likely to see what is intended.

Looking from the perspective of a belief in everlasting punishment in hell, the concept of an unforgivable sin is quite reasonable. But if there is no everlasting punishment, how can there be an unforgivable sin? I believe God forgives us as soon as we show repentance. But, at the latest, when God's punishment ends, His forgiveness must come, for God's very unforgiveness would be a terrible punishment to anyone who loved Him. And how could it be in God's nature to be unforgiving? Amongst people, the holding of grudges is considered petty and childish. Could God be petty or childish? Such a notion would certainly never have been held by Jesus, and would probably never have even occurred to him. What other way is there, then, of looking at the "blasphemy against the Holy Spirit?"

Let's look at what Jesus actually said, in context, trying to put preconceived notions aside. He started by saying,

> "He who is not with me is against me, and he who does not gather with me scatters." (Matt 12:30)

He then went on to illustrate what he was working for, and what is necessary for us to be with him rather than against him, in the "unforgivable sin" passage:

> "And so I tell you, every sin and blasphemy will be forgiven men, but the blasphemy against the Spirit will not be forgiven. Anyone who speaks a word against the Son of Man will be forgiven, but anyone who speaks against the Holy Spirit will not be forgiven, either in this age or in the age to come."
> (Matt 12:31–32)

Jesus is saying he is not working for himself, but for the Holy Spirit, and if a person doesn't believe in him, he can still be on his side, "with him," provided he at least believes in the Holy Spirit. But if a person doesn't believe in the Holy Spirit, he will be against Jesus, scattering what he has gathered. It is characteristic of materialistic, worldly, people that they don't believe there is a spiritual side to life — they believe that only the material universe exists: *that* is speaking against the Holy Spirit. And in this denial of anything spiritual, it is impossible to make spiritual progress, and in fact, anyone in this state will be hindering those trying to enter the kingdom of God. This statement of Jesus', far from being extreme, is really a statement of respect and acceptance: he is saying that anyone who believes there is a spiritual side to life, beyond the material, is working with him, even though they may be falling short of the ideal (sinning) in many ways, even to the extent of not believing that God can, and has, incarnated as a fully human person (the Son of Man). All these other "sins" will be "forgiven" (i.e. tolerated or excused) in someone seeking God, but if a person doesn't believe in the Spirit, it is impossible for him to even begin to find God, because it is the Holy Spirit, working through our spirits, which tells of the things of God. As Paul said,

...if anyone does not have the Spirit of Christ, he does not belong to Christ...
The Spirit himself testifies with our spirit that we are God's children.	(Rom 8:9,16)

And as Jesus himself said,

"God is spirit, and his worshipers must worship in spirit and in truth."	(John 4:24)

So not believing in the Spirit cannot be excused: a person will never find God while he has this attitude, not in "this age or in the age to come." In using these words Jesus is emphasizing the universal and absolute truth of what he has said.

However, this is not to say that if someone at any stage doesn't believe in the Holy Spirit, he can't start believing in it, and can't ever be forgiven. If this were the case, no initially materialistic and worldly person could ever be saved! What Jesus means by saying "anyone who speaks against the Holy Spirit will not be forgiven" is that *while* you don't believe in the Holy Spirit, you can't be "forgiven," and be working with him, whereas you can begin to make progress toward the kingdom of heaven, and be on Jesus' side, while still falling short of the spiritual ideal (sinning) in any other way.

The word "forgiven" is an unfortunate translation here, as in normal usage, someone is not forgiven until they stop doing what ever is to be forgiven, and to say an action is "unforgivable" is to say it can't ever be forgiven, even after the person has stopped doing it. A translation which would match Jesus' obvious meaning much better than "forgiven," would be "excused" or "tolerated," as actions can be excused or tolerated while they are still being done, and to say they can't be excused or tolerated means the person must stop the action, but will be accepted again after they have stopped. Considering this, it is hardly surprising that the Greek word from which "forgiven" is translated has a very broad meaning, which easily encompasses other similar meanings such as "excused," "tolerated" or "allowed." The Greek word *aphiami* literally means to "send away," but in various applications is also used to mean: "set aside," "suffer," "let be," "let go" and "forsake."[32] From this the meaning "forgiven" is taken, but from "let be," "set aside" or "suffer," the meanings of "allowed," "tolerated" or "excused" can just as easily be inferred, with the advantage that they don't clash with the context, and don't defame the character of God in the way "forgiven" does. The ancient Jews and Greeks don't appear to have made the subtle distinction between "forgive" and "excuse." To them there was just one word, and sins were just "sent away." The sadistic concept of "unforgivability" probably never even occurred to them.

A better translation of this passage, including the lead-in verse, without which it can't be taken in context, might be:

> "He who is not with me is against me, and he who does not
> gather with me scatters. And so I tell you, every shortfall and
> idle word will be excused people, except for the denial of
> Spirit. Anyone who speaks against the Son of Man will be
> excused, but there will never be a time when speaking against
> the Holy Spirit will be excused."   (Matt 12:30–32)

I hope I have been able to convince you that many of the apparent inconsistencies, contradictions and unreasonable statements in the New Testament are either products of poor translation, or of us seeing what we expect to see rather than assessing a passage in its true context. It is interesting to note that the Bible is self-correcting, in the sense that if errors are introduced during translation it causes inconsistencies and contradictions to arise which point to how they should be corrected. When correctly translated, and wisely interpreted, the Bible should not contradict itself at all, and this fact can be used as a principle for properly translating it. This principle will often be used in the chapters to come.

One final cause of apparent contradictions in the Bible is tied up with the very nature of the book, and its mission. Many of its truths are not revealed to people who read it in an unthinking or prejudiced way. On a superficial level, it lays itself open to many different interpretations; if read in a quest for wisdom, though, it reveals its underlying unity, and its deep truths. The Bible had to be like this to survive nearly two thousand years of a corrupt church. The Bible is such that churches could interpret it in a way which made it seem to support their worldly agendas. But the Bible is also such that the seeker after wisdom will find wisdom in it, and the true seeker after God will find in it the keys to the kingdom of heaven.

The Bible goes further than just presenting us with the truth in a direct and straightforward way — which it often does — it also encourages us to exercise our own moral faculties, and develop our wisdom, in order to dig deep for what is most precious in life: the truth. Many issues are, in effect, debated in the Bible, leaving readers, in the last analysis, to make up their own minds. On the question of whether salvation depends on grace or good works, for instance, Jesus concentrates on the importance of good works, Paul on the necessity of faith, and James presents a very possible answer to the dilemma by maintaining it is not a question of "either or," but that both are required, and that,

> ...a person is justified by what he does, and not by faith alone.
> (James 2:24).

The Bible is a more profound book than it may seem at first sight. It is a precious jewel beyond price for the church and all humanity.

Chapter 12

Free Will or Fundamentalism

The whole drama of creation emerges from God making us in His image and giving us free will, so we can choose between the fascination of the material universe He gave us, and the bliss of being with Him. God's greatest joy comes when we choose Him, for there is only one thing He lacks, and only one thing we can give Him — our love. For God to find real joy in having the creatures He created choose to love Him, it has to be a real choice, free and uncoerced, with the alternative being attractive in its own right. God doesn't want us to choose Him by default, which we would do if the physical universe were a totally unattractive place. God provides us with a world with many good things in it, in much the same way as parents provide books, musical instruments, toys, and other good things for their children. Parents are content to let children be amused by these things in their leisure time, if that is their wish, but gain their greatest joy in parenthood when a child comes and says, "I like my train set, but right now I really just want to be with you." Parents all hope their children will want them more than the play things they have provided them with. And God, our heavenly Father — the ultimate parent — is just the same: He'll never ask for it, nor coerce us into it, but when we come to Him and say, "Thank you for this wonderful world you put me in, but these days, whenever I see its beauty, it just reminds me of You, and I long to be with You," we melt His heart. And when we prove we mean this, by patiently sitting there, meditating, waiting on Him, loving Him with all our heart by not wanting anything else nearly so much, loving Him with all our soul by identifying with Him only, loving Him with all our strength by directing all our attention to Him, and loving Him with all our mind by not thinking of anything else, then He will come to us as a deep peace and a great joy that will float us away to paradise.

"No eye has seen, no ear has heard,
no mind has conceived what God has prepared
for those who love him." (1 Cor 2:9 (Isaiah 64:4))

Jesus illustrated the joy God feels when a person lost in the world returns to Him, in the Parables of the Lost Sheep and the "Prodigal" Son:

"Suppose one of you has a hundred sheep and loses one of them. Does he not leave the ninety-nine in the open country and go after the lost sheep until he finds it? And when he finds it, he joyfully puts it on his shoulders and goes home. Then he calls his friends and neighbors together and says, 'Rejoice with me; I have found my lost sheep.' I tell you that in the same way there is more rejoicing in heaven over one sinner who repents than over ninety-nine righteous persons who do not need to repent...

Jesus continued: "There was a man who had two sons. The younger one said to his father, 'Father, give me my share of the estate.' So he divided his property between them.

"Not long after that, the younger son got together all he had, set off for a distant country and there squandered his wealth in wild living. After he had spent everything, there was a severe famine in that whole country, and he began to be in need. So he went and hired himself out to a citizen of that country, who sent him to his fields to feed pigs. He longed to fill his stomach with the pods that the pigs were eating, but no-one gave him anything.

"When he came to his senses, he said, 'How many of my father's hired men have food to spare, and here I am starving to death! I will set out and go back to my father and say to him: Father, I have sinned against heaven and against you. I am no longer worthy to be called your son; make me like one of your hired men.' So he got up and went to his father.

"But while he was still a long way off, his father saw him and was filled with compassion for him; he ran to his son, threw his arms around him and kissed him.

"The son said to him 'Father, I have sinned against heaven and against you. I am no longer worthy to be called your son.'

"But the father said to his servants, 'Quick! Bring the best robe and put it on him. Put a ring on his finger and sandals on his feet. Bring the fatted calf and kill it. Let's have a feast and celebrate. For this son of mine was dead and is alive again; he was lost and is found.' So they began to celebrate."

(Luke 15:4–7,11–24)

These stories come as close as words can to describing the boundless joy God feels when a once worldly person, of his or her own free will, repents and comes back home to Him. Note that the father in the parable did not prevent his son leaving him, and even gave him the means to do it, if that's what he wished to do. God has done the same thing by providing this magnificent world for us, where we can live independently of Him, if we wish to. Note also that the father didn't interfere with his son once he left home: it would have been easy for him to have sent out scouts to see how his son was, and to pay people to make his life a little easier, but he didn't do it; if he protected his son from the consequences of his actions he would never have been able to learn. God does the same thing with those who reject Him: He doesn't interfere in any way, coerce or punish — He totally respects people's freedom. But He does not protect them from the consequences of their actions either, because this would rob them of their opportunity to learn. God shows great restraint, but is rewarded when, one by one, his children come home to Him, and each time this happens there is a great celebration in heaven.

God doesn't follow us into our life apart from Him—He just waits patiently for us. He could, of course, see into our future if he wished, and know the exact moment we would return to Him. But I suspect He doesn't do that: for one thing, it would be intruding into our freedom, but more importantly, it would rob Him of the joy of being surprised by our return, as the father of the Lost Son was surprised. In this respect God is like a husband who knows where his wife is hiding his birthday present, and could easily find out what it is if he wanted to, but who restrains himself so as not to spoil the shared joy of the surprise on his birthday. Deep down, I feel certain that each time you truly give your love to God, you surprise and delight Him.

In the light of this importance of free will to God's plan, and the fact that He has given us dominion over the world, and doesn't interfere in it, I would like to discuss the attitudes and actions of some religious fundamentalists. Christianity, Judaism, Islam, and Hinduism all have their fundamentalists, and they operate in much the same way in each religion. They each claim they are returning to the "fundamentals" of their religion. Indeed, the use of the word "fundamentalist" to describe ultra-conservative, hard-line religious groups which refuse to accept new thinking, dates from the early twentieth century, when an American reaction against modernism and the "social gospel" led to the publication between 1910 and 1912 of a series of pamphlets called "The Fundamentals of the Faith," which described the basics of faith it believed Christians should return to.[1] Initially "fundamentalism" referred just to these reactionary Protestant Christians, but since then the term has taken on a wider meaning, and refers to groups in any religion, and at any time, who react against change and wish to return to the ways of the past. The predominant religion of the time these groups wish to return to can also be described as fundamentalist, as it is of the same quality as modern fundamentalism. In this wider sense, fundamentalism is a particular approach to religion which has always been present, at least to some extent, in every major religion. When I refer to fundamentalists or fundamentalism, it will always be in this wider sense of the word, which is also becoming the more common meaning these days. I am certainly not referring in particular to members of denominations who describe themselves as fundamentalists — although they often do fall within the wider category I will be discussing.

In Islam, the fundamentals which fundamentalists wish to return to are, by and large, the founding principles of their religion, as espoused by their prophet Muhammad. In Christianity, though, fundamentalists harken back to a time when the church controlled politics and society, and most of their doctrines are way out of line with the teachings of Jesus, as presented in the Bible. Fundamentalists of all religions want to legislate religious values, and through penal sanctions force everyone to comply with them. Islamic fundamentalism has led to the establishment of a number of "Islamic states," where the ideals of the Qur'an are enshrined in law, and deviation from them is punished in a draconian way. Hindu fundamentalists want India to be a Hindu state, and often use violence in pushing for this to be enacted through legislation. Some Christian fundamentalists just wish to retreat from what they see as the wickedness of the modern world, and bring their families up shielded from it. The domain of the power they wish to exert is limited to the family and the church, and they are happy with this, providing modern society doesn't impinge on their family and attempt to corrupt their children with permissive ways of living and liberal attitudes.[2] Others, though, especially when they feel they can succeed, or feel threatened by liberal society, bring whatever pressure they can on politicians to enshrine in law certain moral values they consider important. They wish to punish abortion and homosexuality by making them criminal offenses. They also wish to legislate to have prayers said in schools, want the Genesis story of creation to be given equal time with evolution in biology classes, and oppose any legislation which establishes equal rights for women.[3] Usually they lobby for just one or two causes at a time, but they have other "values" they plan to impose on society when they have the opportunity.

Christian fundamentalists, although they often claim to accept the separation of church and state, in fact usually have not accepted this separation in any more than its most minimal aspect. An example of this is a pastor refusing to actually endorse a political candidate, but nevertheless leaving his congregation in no doubt about whom he feels they should be voting for, by preaching about what policies are acceptable to the church. The separation of church and state properly involves the ideal that both church and state should wield their beneficial influence on society, but should do so separately and independently. Under this ideal, both the general values of society, through the schools and child welfare laws, and the church, through the family, should influence children, so the new generation can choose their own values from amongst those in these two, often slightly different, sources. Fundamentalists certainly do not accept this, or anything like it. They see it as the secular state interfering in their lives. Many wish, instead, to have their brand of Christianity dominate society, and want to return to the ways of the medieval world when the church reigned over society and used criminal sanctions to force its opinions and practices on all. These fundamentalists want to take away the freedom of choice God gave human beings, and force their own children, at least, and everyone, if possible, to do things their way. This is totally against the true spirit of Christianity. Jesus never suggested his teachings should be made compulsory by giving them legal sanction, and punishing those who disobey them. On the contrary, he told us to keep the state and the things of God separate, when he said,

"Give to Caesar what is Caesar's, and to God what is God's."
(Matt 22:21)

Jesus also said we should not interfere in judgment, because it is not our place. In the Parable of the Weeds, the man who had planted the good seed didn't allow his servants to pull out the weeds the enemy had sown amongst the crop. His reason was:

"'...while you are pulling the weeds, you may root up the wheat with them. Let both grow together until the harvest.'"
(Matt 13:29–30)

And Jesus' example, as in the case of the woman caught in adultery (John 8:3–11), and the Samaritan woman at the well (John 4:4–42), was not to punish moral offenders, nor even to judge them, but rather to treat them with the respect and dignity all deserve. Paul was also clearly opposed to the church interfering in society. He said,

What business is it of mine to judge those outside the church?
(1 Cor 5:12)

Law reformers often call moral offenses "victimless crimes." This is only partially true, of course. No-one is physically hurt or threatened, or robbed of possessions or rights, by them, and this is why enlightened societies can afford to let them go unpunished. Nevertheless, moral offenses —like adultery for instance — do have unfortunate effects on people other than those who perpetrate them, and society would be better off without them. But does this justify legal sanctions against them? Each day, lack of consideration causes a tremendous amount of pain and misery. Should we, then, prosecute people and send them to prison for being inconsiderate? Jesus taught purity through his example, and by encouraging people to feel good about themselves, so that in future they would value themselves enough to not continue doing wrong. The Samaritan woman at the well was certainly transformed by the respect and love Jesus showed her, and the way he valued her by giving her "living water" to drink, in discussing eternal truths with her. She responded by praising Jesus in her town in such glowing terms that many of them came to believe in him. This is the powerful way to change people; it is the way Jesus taught, and it is the way society is tending toward. Great men and women down through the ages have followed Jesus' example in this.

Jesus backed up this example with many teachings, among them the Parable of the Good Samaritan (Luke 10:25–37), and his teaching about showing a good example. He said,

> "…let your light shine before men, that they may see your good deeds and praise your Father in heaven." (Matt 5:16)

And Jesus chided his disciples for trying to dominate each other. He taught them a better way, saying,

> "You know that those who are regarded as rulers of the Gentiles lord it over them, and their high officials exercise authority over them. Not so with you. Instead, whoever wants to become great among you must be your servant, and whoever wants to be first must be slave of all. For even the Son of Man did not come to be served, but to serve, and to give his life as a ransom for many."
> (Mark 10:42–45)

With this in mind, I would like to suggest an alternative way for concerned Christians to approach one of the social issues I believe they genuinely care about—the abortion question. The fundamentalist approach of making abortion illegal takes away people's God-given freedom of choice in the matter, and makes many people resentful and determined to find a way around the law. Many resort to illegal abortions, which may damage their health, make them unable to have children in future, and bind them up in terrible unresolved feelings of guilt. This is no blessing for Christianity to be bestowing on society, and it is self-defeating, for not that many abortions are prevented, and people's determination to win the right for "abortion on demand" is fired up by it.

It would be better if through support, compassion, respect and love, people concerned about this issue were able to promote the conditions in which more women would feel happy about continuing with their pregnancies, and more people would be careful about birth control. There is virtue in people choosing to do something for good reasons; there is little or no virtue involved when people do something against their inclination merely to avoid punishment. Also, it is much easier to succeed with people's cooperation than it is to fight them all the way.

To adopt such an approach, one would have to start by respecting the right of women to have abortions if they want to. Some women don't really want to have an abortion, they just know they don't have the support they need, whether it be emotional or financial, to have a baby. A genuine offer of support could help women such as these to do what they really want to do—continue with their pregnancies and keep their babies. Other women, however, in other circumstances, just don't want to have a baby. Usually this is because it would upset the plans they have for their life. These women are not going to be swayed by offers of support, and their right to choose should be respected.

Such a real respect, rather than a mere mouthing of platitudes, would involve not judging in any way, shunning, or treating coolly, any woman who chose to have an abortion, or any person who counseled her over the matter. Such a respect would also involve not bringing pressure to bear on a woman or her family, and not pressing unsought-for advice on them. Demonstrating a lack of hypocrisy by being devoted to the concept of the sanctity of human life in general would also help those promoting the "right to life." This could be achieved by those opposing abortion also opposing capital punishment, private ownership of guns, and the use of military force by their country except in peace-keeping roles and the genuine defense of their own territory, and by them supporting the provision of adequate social welfare, without which the quality of life for many is very low. The "pro-life" lobby falls short in many of these respects at the moment.[4]

No method of birth control is completely reliable, and women who don't want to have a baby at a particular time have a right to use abortion for back-up birth control. The better the primary method of birth control, though, and the better a couple understand it, the lower the chance will be of its failing, and the lower the chance will be that a woman will ever need to consider the serious option, which very few women take lightly, of having an abortion. It follows that promoting effective birth control, and helping couples properly learn the often skilled techniques involved, will greatly reduce the number of abortions resorted to. This is particularly true of natural birth-control techniques, which, if they are to be reliable, are quite involved and scientific in their application. There is a lot of scope, in both Western and third-world countries, for improving people's understanding of how to effectively use birth control. Anyone who is genuinely concerned about lowering the incidence of abortion could have a big impact on abortion numbers by supporting, and being involved in, the upgrading of birth-control education in schools and amongst adults.

The other effective way of helping to reduce abortion numbers, is, as was mentioned before, to give practical support to women who want to keep their babies but are being forced into having abortions because they don't have the means to provide for a child. There are a lot of single women, and families, in this position. A woman may be worried about her ability to properly care for a baby, or the effect on her other children of having another mouth to feed. Or she may be young and un-married, and feel her dreams for her future will be ruined, and her life made miserable, by having to care for a baby she didn't plan to have yet. In short, many of the women who decide to have abortions would keep their babies if circumstances were different — if they had more support: financial, emotional and social.

What can be done here is to do the good deeds Jesus recommended. Take an interest in people. Welcome them into your circle, and your church. If they happen to be pregnant, stand by them, whether they are married or not. Praise them for having the courage to keep their baby in the face of dif-ficulties. Make things for the baby. Help with the birth, if they want you to. Mind their other children. Give or lend them things they need. Go shopping with them. Make sure they have the best financial, legal, medical, psychological and parenting advice. Remember that Jesus said,

"It is more blessed to give than to receive." (Acts 20:35)

And if a friend does decide to have an abortion, accept her right to choose, and acknowledge the difficulty of her decision. Show your unconditional love by sticking by her, even if you don't agree with her decision. Next time she becomes pregnant she may want to keep her baby, and your friendship and help may be the deciding factor in her feeling confident that she can support the baby and give it a good life.

The great nineteenth century English reformer, Lord Shaft-esbury, devoted his life to helping the poor and downtrodden. He sat in the House of Lords, had a number of times been offered a Cabinet post, and was considered a possible leader of the Conservative Party, yet he was often seen with the poor and homeless, and even seemed to prefer their company to that of his educated and socially-refined peers. He treated all with res-pect, even the prostitutes who walked the streets of London.[5]

I wonder how many socially concerned Christians are prepared to be like Lord Shaftesbury? It would be easy to be cynical about this, but I think the real answer is quite a few. Fundamentalists are very vocal, and they attract the support of those who want to do something to help. I believe, however, that much of this support would fall even more strongly behind a compassionate approach. There are a lot of Christians who subscribe to fundamentalist ideas just because they are being peddled around the churches, not because they are truly fundamentalists at heart.

Chapter 13

Money Changers in the Temple

Fundamentalists[1] often debase themselves and their churches in the pursuit of money. This is not a corruption of an otherwise spiritual way of doing things in these churches. Money mindedness and worldliness is built into the very structure of fundamentalism, and has been since the time of the witch trials, which were great money makers.[2] Free enterprise is highly valued, and church members are encouraged to use their initiative to go out into the world and make money, to the extent that this is held to be the best thing for Christian men to do with their lives. Although giving to the church is much encouraged, giving to charities and the poor is not. Nor do fundamentalist churches themselves very often give to the poor: their money goes almost exclusively to evangelizing, supporting campaigns of interference in politics, such as lobbying for anti-abortion laws, and supporting church-building missionaries in third world countries who do little to help the poor. Fundamentalist churches often strongly support the conservative side of politics, such as the Republicans in the U.S.A., and encourage their members to do likewise, as they perceive the conservatives are more open to supporting their political agenda of legislating moral values. This is despite the fact that those on the progressive side of politics, such as the Democrats, are much more dedicated to pursuing the structural social reform required to overcome injustice and poverty. Many fundamentalist churches even seek to vilify progressive politicians and governments, and persuade their congregations not to vote for them by accusing them of supporting a "conspiracy" to form a "world government" supposed to be associated with the "beast" of the book of Revelation. The fundamentalists get a certain amount of support for their political agenda from the conservatives, although not all business interests support them, by any means. John D. Rockefeller, who represents the established wealthy class in America, gave a large gift to the newly formed World Council of Churches — the fundamentalists' "great satan" — in the 1950's, and he is typical of much of the old wealth in being unsupportive of the New Christian Right.[3] The support the fundamentalists do get, though, is at a price. In addition to delivering a high proportion of Christian votes at election time, the price is that they do not criticize the exploitation of the poor which takes place under conservative governments, either explicitly, by speaking out against it, or implicitly, by helping the poor themselves. Instead, they must use their moral weight to help legitimize the exploitative social agenda of the conservatives. This is why fundamentalist churches rarely if ever criticize governments for failing to remedy poverty and injustice, whereas progressive churches which have accepted the separation of church and state often do speak out on social issues. The New Christian Right in America even proposed a reduction in welfare spending, in a country where welfare services were already in crisis due to inadequate funding.[4] Fundamentalists conveniently forget that God, through both the Old Testament prophets and Jesus, strongly spoke against injustice and the exploitation of the poor, and requires his people to help those less fortunate than themselves. Take as an example just these few verses from Isaiah, Job and Jeremiah:

> I will make justice the measuring line and
> righteousness the plumb line. (Isa 28:17)

> Seek justice, encourage the oppressed.
> Defend the cause of the fatherless,
>   plead the case of the widow. (Isa 1:17)

> The Lord enters into judgment against the elders
>   and leaders of his people:
> "It is you who have ruined my vineyard;
>   the plunder from the poor is in your houses.
> What do you mean by crushing my people
>   and grinding the faces of the poor?"
>   declares the Lord, the Lord Almighty. (Isa 3:14–15)

And he looked for justice, but saw bloodshed;
    for righteousness, but heard cries of distress. (Isa 5:7)

Yet the Lord longs to be gracious to you;
    he rises to show you compassion.
For the Lord is a God of justice.
    Blessed are all who wait for him! (Isa 30:18)

He repays a man for what he has done;
    he brings upon him what his conduct deserves.
It is unthinkable that God would do wrong,
    that the Almighty would pervert justice. (Job 34:11–12)

"Does it make you a king to have more and more cedar?
Did not your father have food and drink?
    He did what was right and just, and so all went well with him.
He defended the cause of the poor and needy, and so all went
well. Is that not what it means to know me?" declares the Lord.
                         (Jer 22:15–16)

Add to these what John the Baptist said:

"Produce fruit in keeping with repentance. And do not think
you can say to yourselves, 'We have Abraham as our father.'"
                         (Matt 3:8–9)

And Jesus saying,

"I tell you that the kingdom of God will be taken away from you
and given to a people who will produce its fruit." (Matt 21:43)

Finally, there are Jesus' words in the story of the Sheep and the
Goats, which explain what good fruit are required to enter the
kingdom of God:

"Then the King will say to those on his right, 'Come, you who are
blessed by my Father; take your inheritance, the kingdom prepared
for you since the creation of the world. For I was hungry and you
gave me something to eat, I was thirsty and you gave me something
to drink, I was a stranger and you invited me in, I needed
clothes and you clothed me, I was sick and you looked after me, I
was in prison and you came to visit me.'
    "Then the righteous will answer him, 'Lord, when did we see
you hungry and feed you, or thirsty and give you something to
drink? When did we see you a stranger and invite you in, or

needing clothes and clothe you? When did we see you sick or in prison and go to visit you?'

"The King will reply, 'I tell you the truth, whatever you did for one of the least of these brothers of mine, you did for me.'"

(Matt 25:34–40)

And who are Jesus' brothers? Everyone. Anyone you run across who needs your help. This is why Jesus' second great commandment was to "love your neighbor as yourself." The Story of the Good Samaritan is about a man who loved a stranger the way he should.

One of the pieces of financial cheese-paring the Republican Party indulged in after it gained control of Congress in 1994, in order to provide tax cuts for the wealthy in its "Contract with America," was to end funding to a $5 million program to teach illiterate prisoners how to read. On judgment day these Republicans may well be accused, and find themselves saying to Jesus, "When did we see you sick or in prison and not go to visit you?" We know what Jesus' reply would be.

The main way fundamentalist and other churches get wealthy is through tithing. In ancient Israel, those who could afford it gave one tenth of their income to the Levites for the support of this priestly tribe of men who served God and had no other source of income, and for them, in turn, to look after the poor (Dt 26:12). In addition to being an income for the priests and their assistants, it was also, in effect, a welfare scheme, as taxes levied by governments were for capital works, administrative and military expenses — not for caring for the poor. The tithe and taxes in those days would have added up to about the amount of tax we pay now. And, of course, most welfare programs are now funded from tax revenue. This means that much of what was then the tithe is now included in taxes, and those who evade tax, or use loopholes to "legally" avoid a large part of their tax, are, in effect, failing to tithe, and, as well as not doing their duty as citizens, are failing to do their part to help those in need. In the words of Isaiah, "the plunder from the poor is in [their] houses."

[handwritten marginal note, right margin:] So, what about your separation of church & state.

But what churches nowadays mean by tithing is that people should give one tenth of their pre-tax income to the church, in addition to whatever income tax they may or may not be paying. And fundamentalist churches, in particular, don't see the need to spend more than a very little of this, if any, on the poor. Tithing was also abused in ancient Israel, where the priests and Levites often grew rich while the poor starved. God did not accept this injustice then, and He will not accept it now.

The advantage of tithing is portrayed by the church in terms of the benefits to the giver, and the "law of giving" is widely quoted:

> Give and it will be given to you. A good measure, pressed down, shaken together and running over, will be poured into your lap.
> (Luke 6:38)

This is, of course, very true. It is, as Jesus said, "more blessed to give than to receive." Great blessings come from generous and thoughtful giving. Generous people rarely find they are in want themselves, and if they are a little poor, they usually have much greater blessings than mere material prosperity. And there are things other than money people can give generously of: time, expertise, consideration, care, love, patience, thoughtfulness, understanding, tolerance and forgiveness — to name just a few. Indeed, when money is given, much of the value of the gift is lost if thought isn't given to where the money will go. If the virtue of giving were just in sacrificing money, rather than in the good the gift can do, we could gain blessings from throwing hundred-dollar bills into a fire. Giving to an organization which is going to spend your money in an unworthy way is just as useless. When people entrust the gift of their tithe to a church which is itself grasping and un-giving, and isn't using the money unselfishly for the benefit of others, and the needy in particular, this is a waste of a holy opportunity to give, and the blessings will turn to dust. Jesus said of the Pharisees' tithing:

"Woe to you, teachers of the law and Pharisees, you hypocrites! You give a tenth of your spices — mint, dill and cummin. But you have neglected the more important matters of the law — justice, mercy and faithfulness." (Matt 23:23)

To help us assess the attitude toward giving a particular church has, we could well use the wider context of the "law of giving":

"Do not judge, and you will not be judged. Do not condemn, and you will not be condemned. Forgive, and you will be forgiven. Give and it will be given you. A good measure, pressed down, shaken together and running over, will be poured into your lap. For with the measure you use, it will be measured to you." (Luke 6:37–38)

Fundamentalist churches are good at judging society and condemning many of its groups, and maintain a very unforgiving attitude toward moral offenders. At the same time they give little to society, choosing instead to spend their money on promoting their own causes. Consequently they leave themselves open to being judged and condemned, receiving few blessings, and stewing in their own unforgiveness. This is one reason why these churches don't show much real growth, despite their high public profiles. Many people join these churches, but almost as many leave them again. Tithing to such churches is more than just a waste of money; it actually contributes to their evil: financial scandals involving fundamentalist churches are frequently reported in the news, and such scandals are just the tip of the iceberg of a malaise which runs much deeper.

Most real churches present a mixture of good and bad, a measure of fundamentalism moderated by a measure of genuine giving, which varies from church to church across the whole spectrum from good to bad. We can encourage the church we belong to not to become worldly by not giving to it in excess of its legitimate needs unless we are very sure the extra money is being used to help the poor. Instead there is the opportunity to give directly of our time and money to organizations like Oxfam, World Vision, and Community Aid Abroad, which specialize in efficiently and lovingly helping the poorest and most neglected people in the world get on their feet again.

There are a number of dubious money-making schemes associated with the fundamentalist churches, other than the way they solicit and spend their tithes. Generally, these schemes gain an air of legitimacy from the authority of the church, so are supported by the faithful. They range from network marketing schemes to life insurance rackets, and sometimes when congregations are fleeced particularly badly we hear about it in the news. Much worse than purely money making schemes, however, are schemes which combine interference in politics and society, and judgment and condemnation of people, with large-scale money making. Typical of this, in recent times, has been the "Satanic abuse industry."

The Satanic abuse scare started in the U.S.A. and spilled over to the U.K. and other countries. It was claimed Satanist groups and covens of witches existed in many places and were recruiting large numbers of young people and involving them in all sorts of evil practices, culminating in secret nocturnal meetings for the more advanced initiates, where abominable practices were taking place such as the ritualistic raping and sacrifice of young virgins on Satanic altars. It was also claimed children were widely involved in Satanic practices, and that these often involved their sexual abuse. Huge amounts of money were made by "survivors" publishing books confessing their evil pasts. However, the stories of these "survivors" have never been corroborated by hard evidence such as bodies. Moreover, psychological assessment of some of the "survivors" suggests they could well be suffering from delusions, and in a couple of celebrated cases their stories have been denied by members of their families who would have known if the things described had been happening.

The allegation that this Satanic abuse involved children attracted the attention of social workers, and some became convinced that Satanic abuse of children really was taking place. The investigation of a number of alleged cases led to many children being removed from their homes and inter-

viewed. Recordings show the interviewers asked leading questions of the children, and told them what they expected to
hear. This included interviewers specifically describing certain
acts of sexual abuse, and asking the children whether their
parents had done these to them. The video recordings clearly
show children initially just denying that these events had ever
taken place, but becoming distressed, and getting their backs
up, when the interviewers kept pressuring them to admit to
them. This is reminiscent of the inquisitorial techniques used in
witch trials of former centuries. After sixty cases of alleged
Satanic abuse in Britain, not a single conviction has resulted.
There is now a growing concern that genuine child abuse might
be going unnoticed as effort is directed toward Satanic abuse
allegations. There is a fear the child welfare system could be
being undermined by the "Satanic abuse" industry, which is
making fortunes for fundamentalist Christian "survivors"
through book sales.[5]

It needs to be said that nearly all the books which promote
the Satanist scare are bought by Christians, as the waves of
sensationalist gossip they generate spread through churches. As
a result, it is not just the deluded authors who are responsible
for this insidious craze, it is also the collective responsibility of
all those who read the books, endorse what they are saying,
and recommend them to others. One of these books did the
rounds of a church I used to attend, and I was given a copy to
read. Although I started reading it with an open mind, it didn't
have a "ring" of truth to it, and it soon became apparent what
rubbish it was. The Christian publishing and book marketing
industry also has a lot to answer for. These books are not
usually credible enough to be published by main-stream publishers, or much stocked by ordinary bookstores. Such third-rate
pieces of Christian propaganda are nearly always published by
Christian publishers and marketed through the Christian book-
stores which nearly every town seems to have at least one of.
This Christian publishing and book marketing industry is a
major part of the financial infrastructure of fundamentalism.

One of the things the Christian publishing industry is concerned with is "spreading the word" about Jesus. At first sight, this seems like a reasonable, and indeed a laudable, thing to be doing. After all, didn't Jesus say, "...be my witnesses" (Acts 1:8)? If we look at the whole of Jesus' statement, though, the emphasis is slightly different:

> "It is not for you to know the times or dates the Father has set by his own authority. But you will receive the power when the Holy Spirit comes on you; and you will be my witnesses in Jerusalem, and in all Judea and Samaria, and to the ends of the earth."   (Acts 1:7–8)

It is clear that no-one can just decide to be this sort of witness. Jesus is saying that after the power of the Holy Spirit comes on people, they will be his witnesses, without even trying to, even if they don't say a word. In addition, Jesus had earlier said to his disciples,

> "...let your light shine before men, that they may see your good deeds and praise your Father in heaven." (Matt 5:16)

This shows another way people can be witnesses: by doing good deeds; something people *can* choose to do. Again the emphasis is on *being* a witness, rather than "witnessing." If you radiate the presence of God's Spirit by doing good deeds, people will notice, and be drawn to God. Compared to this, mere words have little power to draw people.

I'm not saying there's no place for Christian books. Readable Bibles like the New International Version and the Jerusalem Bible make the Scriptures much more accessible, and so do a wide variety of accurate and intelligent commentaries. Such books are indispensable to Christians, and are also effective witnesses to the value of Christianity. Books are also a valuable means of communicating what people are thinking, doing, and have done, and the good deeds and spiritual power of many men and women shine forth from biographies. These books, including old favorites like the lives of the saints, and contemporary accounts like *I Dared to Call Him Father* by Bilquis Sheikh, have great power to draw people to God.

On the other hand, words are very much two-edged swords, and if used unwisely can do much damage to Christianity, especially when they are used to criticize society and vilify other religions. Jesus' brother James had this to say about the misuse of words:

> All kinds of animals, birds, reptiles and creatures of the sea
> are being tamed and have been tamed by man, but no man can tame
> the tongue. It is a restless evil, full of deadly poison.
> With the tongue we praise our Lord and Father, and with it we
> curse men, who have been made in God's likeness. Out of the same
> mouth come praise and cursing. My brothers, this should not be.
> Can both fresh water and salt water flow from the same spring?
> (James 3:7–11)

Books which judge and condemn, and seek to make Christianity tall by "chopping off the heads" of others, are a negative witness. They might be popular with some Christians themselves, but to those outside the church they merely confirm the opinion of readers that Christianity is tainted and corrupt. Few, if any, are converted by them, but by them many are hardened against Christianity. A particularly pernicious example of a so called Christian book which was popular around the churches, but which denigrates another religion in a long tirade of unsupported blasphemous statements against it, accusing it of being devil-worshiping and worse, is *The Death of a Yogi.*

Another unfortunate form of witness is the conditional love shown by many fundamentalists. Attend one of their churches, and they will love you copiously while you conform to their beliefs, but will quickly turn a cold shoulder as a punishment if you don't toe the line. And if you fail to repent, and continue to hold heretical beliefs, you will be "out on your ear" before you know it. The fruits of conditional friendship will turn sour in your mouth. They may not actually prevent you from going to their church, but they'll look straight through you like you're not there, and you'll never feel so lonely in your life. And they'll be unrelenting: you'll soon leave that church, even though there are a few who accept you — the rest will make it so miserable for you. I know this, for I've been through it, and

I've met other people who have been through it too, a number of whom have ended up in "New Age" organizations where they finally found acceptance. It's a common problem in the church. This "withdrawal of love" method of "discipline" was often also practiced in the old Soviet Union, where it was the method officially recommended by the Communist Party for disciplining children. I expect it was widely ignored by caring parents, but where it was used, it was a powerful method of molding children into conformist adults, due to the insecurity instilled by parents withdrawing their love as a punishment. There was nowhere else for the children and young adults treated this way to go, and everyone needs love and approval. Although withdrawal of love was effective in the Soviet Union, it is less so in the church, because people can always leave the church and go to some other organization where, at least, they will be accepted and loved for who they are. Conditional love is a very poor witness to God's love, which should shine through Christianity.

The best sort of witness is, as Jesus and James have said, people's redeemed lives, and the good works which come from them. An outstanding example is India's Mother Theresa; her Christ-like good works are legendary, and much admired outside the church. She has done immeasurable good, not only for the starving of Calcutta, but also for her church. Millions of people know through Mother Theresa what great goodness can come from Christianity. Christ-like actions are not limited to Christianity, of course. Anyone who has read or seen *Out of Africa* and remembers Karen Blixen prostrating herself at the feet of the new governor in a last-ditch, and successful, attempt to obtain land for her natives to live on, after she lost her farm to the bank when her crop went up in flames, knows what a Christ-like act is. And Mahatma Gandhi's non-violent dismantling of colonialism in India was one long string of Christ-like acts, from this century's best known Hindu. The Christian Martin Luther King Jr. did a similar thing in the U.S.A. for black Americans.

Not all Christ-like acts come from well-known figures, though. Many saints are known in this world only to those they help, and perhaps a few other people who are inspired by them. Jackie Pullinger is now well-known because of the books she has written, but I believe there must be hundreds of other Christians who have done similar good work amongst under-privileged people.

Jackie Pullinger went to live in the "Walled City" in Hong Kong to see what she could do about the heroin addiction and poverty which had stricken the place. After the social club she established there as an outreach had been broken into, the windows smashed, and the walls painted with excrement, Goko, the gang boss of the 14K Triad sent an emissary who said, "If anyone touches you again, we'll do them in." This reassured her a little. She later found out that when Goko told those of his followers who had trashed her club to go back and apologize to her, they were reluctant, saying,

"She'll never forgive us or welcome us back after what we did."
"She has to," Goko replied, "She's a Christian."

He had been waiting for someone to do what he knew Christians were supposed to be doing. As Jackie Pullinger put it, "He was watching to see if I measured up."[6]

All around us, people searching for a spiritual side to life are watching to see if Christians measure up. If we do measure up, they will follow us; if we don't, they will look elsewhere, because they intuitively know their spiritual welfare is too important to entrust to hypocrites. The Christian message is very well known, perhaps the best known message in the world. Just about everyone has heard of Jesus and the Gospel, to the extent that even a Triad gangster in the Walled City of Hong Kong has a good grasp of what Christianity is about. What most people haven't seen is Christians living Christ-like lives. Only when they experience the power of Christ will they be converted. It is time to stop spreading the word, and start living it. The example of our Christ-like lives is the only thing that can effectively witness to people. It follows that the advice of many evangelists to church members to get out and show their Christian colors by "witnessing" to people — that is telling them about how great it is to be a Christian — is very poor advice indeed. People in our society have heard about Jesus and Christianity *ad nauseam*, and many have experienced gross hypocrisy in Christians. Telling them about it all over again is only going to antagonize them. Most people in the West are well-educated, discriminating, and not easily fooled. The adage "once bitten twice shy" applies to many. Words will not convince them; only actions performed in Christ's wisdom and power can do so — actions like Jackie Pullinger's response to her club being vandalized:

> Unaware of Goko's expectations, my initial reaction had been to close the club and fly back to Kensington as a rejected martyr. "The Walled City Triads can play ping-pong elsewhere," I thought, hoping that would make them suffer. But the next night I opened up after all, having spent the day weeping and sweeping, scraping up sewage with a growing suspicion that I should be praising God in all circumstances, and that God would turn the situation around. I began to mutter "Praise God, praise God" as I swept.[7]

This was, of course, the turning point of her ministry in the Walled City.

The original Christ-like act was Jesus' decision to submit to crucifixion with the prayer,

> "My Father, if it is possible, may this cup be taken from me.
> Yet not as I will, but as you will."   (Matt 26:39)

What makes an act Christ-like is doing what God wants, not what we want. It is doing the right thing when the ego tells you to do just the opposite, and a hundred reasons for opting out present themselves ever so convincingly, but the still inner voice of your conscience says "swallow the bitter pill," and you do it. Then the bitterness turns sweet in your stomach, and your life and those of others are sweetened by God's indescribable love, and God's light burns a little brighter in the world because of your faith. Jackie Pullinger summed it up by saying,

What is important is that we be like Jesus, loving someone even
if he seems hopeless. We are going to try, whatever happens —
that is the heart of Christ.

It's not the words. It's the doing. I had to learn to share my
rice bowl with someone who had nothing to eat.[8]

But you don't have to go half way across the world to serve
God. I'd like to illustrate the good Christians can do just by
having a progressive, open-minded attitude and the courage of
their convictions, and helping those around them when they
can. This insight comes from the history of the Christian
missions to aboriginal Australians, which had its good and bad
sides, like similar missions to American and Canadian Indians.
Most of these missionaries were conservative people of their
day, as missionaries still are, and went along with the government's iniquitous "dormitory" policy of separating mixed-
blood aboriginal children from their families, and bringing
them up on missions like Mornington Island. On the other
hand, the more liberal missionaries and church leaders of the
early twentieth century were often the only whites the Aboriginals could relate to. They had a lot to do with preserving
aboriginal culture and dignity, and encouraged the use of their
traditional art in a Christian context. A. P. Elkin was a shining
example of this. The love and understanding of these few
liberals led to Christian beliefs being incorporated into the
aboriginal adjustment to the world of white people — made
necessary by earlier generations killing most of them to drive
them from their lands, and reducing the rest to slavery. These
liberals accepted that Aboriginals should be able to express
Christianity through their own song, dance and ritual. Today
nearly all Christians involved with aboriginal peoples believe
this. Even the pope has expressed the view. But once, not so
long ago, a few courageous liberals had to fight for it and, no
doubt, endure being called heretics by the conservative and
fearful of their time.

In our time, too, there is a lot of good to be done by taking
a fearlessly progressive stand in the way the church interacts

with our society and others, and by reaching out in love, compassion and tolerance, rather than judgment, even when this conflicts with the traditional ways of doing things in the church. We can be a part of a dynamic future, rather than a dead past, if we act in this courageous way. Most people don't have to go to Hong Kong or India to do this. More often than not, God selects work for you which is on your own doorstep. If you want to work for God, and are open to doing whatever is asked of you, He'll provide a job for you. And while you are working for God you don't need to worry about money, for Jesus promised those doing God's work would be looked after. This promise is the most important part of the Law of Giving:

"Do not store up for yourselves treasure on earth, where moth and rust destroy, and where thieves break in and steal. But store up for yourselves treasures in heaven, where neither moth nor rust destroy, and where thieves do not break in and steal. For where your treasure is, there your heart will be too.

"The eye is the lamp of your being. If your eye is single,[9] your whole being will shine with light. But if your eye is tainted, your whole being will be full of darkness. If then the light within you is darkness, how great is that darkness!

"No one can serve two masters. Either he will hate one and love the other, or he will be devoted to one and despise the other. You cannot serve both God and money.

"Therefore I say to you, do not be anxious about your life, what you will eat or what you will drink; or about your body, what you will wear. Is not life more important than food, and well being more important than clothes? Look at the birds of the air; they do not sow or reap or gather into barns, yet your heavenly Father feeds them. Are you not more valuable than they? Who by being anxious can add a single thing to his worth?

"And why worry about clothes? See how the lilies of the field grow. They do not labor or spin. Yet I tell you not even Solomon in all his glory was clothed like one of these. If this is how God clothes the grass of the field, which is here today and tomorrow is thrown into an oven, will he not much better clothe you, little faiths? So do not worry, saying, 'What shall we eat?' or 'what shall we drink?' or 'what shall we wear?' For people everywhere seek these things, and your heavenly Father knows you need them. But seek you first his kingdom and his righteousness, and all these things will be given to you as well." (Matt 6:19–33 AT)

These words of Jesus from the Sermon on the Mount contain the secret of living by faith. If year by year you try to live more and more by this teaching, your faith, the extent by which you live in the kingdom of heaven, will grow like the mustard seed:

"Though it is the smallest of your seeds, yet when it grows, it is the largest of the garden plants and becomes a tree, so that the birds of the air come and perch in its branches." (Matt 13:32)

Jesus said the kingdom of heaven is like that mustard seed.

Chapter 14

Playing God — Science, Progress and Fundamentalism

We live in an age when many babies spend part of their embryonic lives in a test tube, and where there are numerous ways in which science interferes to control and regulate the process of human reproduction. Scientists interfere to a much greater extent still in the reproduction of plants, animals and microorganisms, where genetic engineering has provided countless benefits for humankind, such as the mass production, at a reasonable price, of the insulin needed for diabetics. The genetics of human beings works in much the same way as that of all higher life, and many people are afraid that genetic engineering may soon be performed on human beings, with disastrous consequences. Christians regard human beings as the foremost creation of God, the one creation He made in His own image. Consequently, many of them consider interference in the human reproductive process to be an arrogant intrusion into God's domain, and are vehemently opposed to scientists "playing God."

Since God is defined as the creator of the universe and of life, when scientists create new things from the building blocks of matter, and especially new life forms from old, it does seem like they are "playing God." But is there anything wrong with this? We were made in God's image, but this doesn't mean we actually look like God; it means we have some of God's qualities and abilities, including the free will to choose what we want to do, and the ability and desire to create new things and new ways of living. Since God made us like Himself in these ways, is it any wonder we "play God" by creating things? To create is to use the talents God gave us; it is both inevitable and laudable that human beings should "play God" in this way.

The important thing is that people try to play God in as
God-like a way as possible, learning from how God creates,
and avoiding, as much as possible, doing things God does not
do, like upsetting the ecological balance of nature. Looked at in
this way, it is fundamentalists who more often play God in an
un-Godlike way, attempting to control people in a manner God
could do but doesn't, and in supporting and encouraging an
exploitation of the earth's resources which threatens to throw
nature out of balance. In this second respect, fundamentalists
invariably support big business rather than the conservation
movement, and this is tied in with their attempt to legislate
moral values through an alliance with the conservative side of
politics. Compared with this, the vast majority of scientists are
playing God in a sensitive and appropriate way, studying nature
carefully to see how God does things, and imitating Him as
closely as they can, with the considerable humility of the
"scientific method," which never considers a theory proven,
but rather always leaves it open to being disproved. The fundamentalist should remove the "plank" from his own eye before
attempting to remove the "speck" from the eye of the scientist.

The hypocrisy of religious opposition to Science can be
shown by looking back over its history, and seeing that it is
invariably the "new" which has been feared, much more than
any damage to the natural order. Two thousand five hundred
years ago, Lao Tse objected to roads, carriages and boats as
being unnatural, probably because he grew up in a village
which didn't have them, yet he accepted clothes and cooking,
which were a part of his childhood.[1] In more recent times the
umbrella was objected to by a clergyman when it was first
invented, on the grounds that God "sends the rain to fall on the
righteous and the unrighteous." (Matt 5:45) Bertrand Russell,
in his time, could say:

> Birth control is thought wicked by people who tolerate celibacy,
> because the former is a new violation of nature and the latter an
> ancient one.[2]

In our time, though, artificial birth control is totally accepted amongst Protestants, and also by many Roman Catholics who have grown up in a world containing it.

The church started off by fervently objecting to the Copernican model of the solar system, but has long since stopped considering the suggestion that the earth revolves around the sun a threat to Christianity. Catholics, along with the rest of the church, initially were implacably opposed to Darwin's Theory of Evolution, yet the Roman Catholic church, along with most Protestants, have for some time now totally accepted that God used Evolution to create life; only the highly vocal fundamentalist churches still oppose the Theory of Evolution. Christian opposition to science has, for the most part, just been conservatism, rather than being based on genuine concerns, and there is every reason to believe their opposition to current scientific endeavors is from the same mold. Certainly, the concept of people "playing God" is not a new one. Humans have always played God, with more or less success, and the inventions of the "God players" have nearly always been accepted by even the most conservative Christians once they have been around for a while. Christians should remember that Jesus was a great innovator, and encouraged us to seek out and accept the new along with what is already known to be true. He said,

"Therefore every teacher of the law who has been instructed about the kingdom of heaven is like the owner of a house who brings out of his storeroom new treasures as well as old."
(Matt 13:52)

In addition to their objection to scientists "playing God," many Christians are also concerned with the right to life of the embryos which are destroyed in the process of *in vitro* fertilization programs, both in research and in the actual application of the technique. Their argument is virtually the same one they use against abortion. Again, certain Christians want to impose their moral views on the rest of society. As we saw in previous chapters, Jesus advised against judging others, and Paul specifically warned his followers not to judge those outside the church. Whether embryos or fetuses have a "right" to life is a question for society in general to decide. In the past, in some countries like India, the right to life of the next generation was considered absolute, and for a woman to miss any opportunity to conceive was thought to be quite wicked. As a result women were married at the onset of puberty so their first ovulation would result in pregnancy, and after that every attempt was made to keep them continually pregnant until they died or reached menopause. In this way no potential life was denied its chance to exist. This is the logical conclusion of the "right to life" argument, but I don't suppose even the most fundamentalist Christians would want to go this far. At the moment the legal systems of most countries do not consider human life begins until birth: death certificates are not issued for miscarriages, and fetuses are not considered to be people in any area of the law.

It is by no means clear, either, that a barely fertilized embryo *should* have any more right to life than a separate ovum and sperm which are being kept apart by contraception or avoidance of sex, or even by two people not marrying who might. The argument depends on the assumption that the "soul" is incorporated, or created, in the embryo at the moment of conception, and is locked into that embryo, and there are a number of good reasons for believing this is not so. The first is that something like half of all pregnancies end in spontaneous abortions (miscarriages) in the first three months of pregnancy. To avoid a situation where half of all souls are snuffed out before they experience any living at all, the allocation of souls must work in a different way. Either God must be able to re-allocate souls whose embryo has failed to grow properly to a new embryo, or the allocation of souls must not finally take place until after the danger period of the first trimester, even though they may be provisionally associated with the embryo before that. Possibly both these mechanisms can operate. Significantly, the time of "quickening," just after the first trimester, is when most pregnant women first notice movement of the new life within them. It could be reasonable, then, to suppose that the soul might not become firmly established within its body until quickening. Another reason for supposing this is that there is every reason to believe the human soul needs a sophisticated body to exist in, with an advanced brain and nervous system. This sophisticated nervous system isn't present in the early embryo, but is beginning to be present by the time of quickening. As a result of these observations, I don't believe the "right to life" is a good argument against first trimester abortions or experiments with embryos, as I believe the souls attached, or potentially attached, to these embryos will achieve their right to life anyway, even if not in their body of first choice. In this case the question becomes one of when, and through which parents, a soul gains its body, not whether it gains one or not. The potential attachment of a soul to a physical existence may even begin before conception, to parents who are just thinking of having a child, or to a parent who is not even married. The soul has the right to "offer" itself to parents in this way; the parents have the right to accept or reject the offer, and, if they accept it, to have a say in its timing. They can do this through contraception, or if this fails, through abortion. No matter what one's own views on abortion may be, presuming to take away someone else's right of choice in the matter would be hypocritical. It would be trying to ensure God's giving of new life was not interfered with by interfering to thwart another even greater gift of God — the gift of free will He gave all people.

If Christians wish to see our society live by the principles Jesus advocated and lived by, they should not be pushing for more laws to punish people for using their free will. Rather, they should be advocating, and putting their vote toward, having fewer punitive sanctions, for, as we saw in Chapter 12, Jesus was clearly against punishment as a method of making people behave well. He taught, and showed through his example, far superior ways of insuring people live up to the goodness which is inherent in them. Over the last few centuries it has largely been the progressive free thinkers who have advocated Jesus' way of governing society, not Christians, and the stiffest opposition these reformers had to face, in the process of law reform, was always from the church.

Before leaving the topic of fundamentalism, I would like to address the question of how an organization becomes fundamentalist, and what keeps it that way. Organizations are very important to human beings, the most social of all animals. They enable us to share our endeavors with each other, and achieve things people working singly cannot do. One reason for this is that organizations, when working well, can utilize each member's strengths, while shielding, or compensating for, any weaknesses. Creativity is generally a solitary pursuit, but even here, organizations can shine by supporting their creative people and ensuring they can devote their time to being creative. Sometimes organizations create in groups, and produce results which bring to mind the Chinese saying that "a camel is a horse designed by a committee." There is no need for them to do this, though, unless, of course, they want a "camel." Because of the importance of organizations, it is vital they work well, and this is particularly true of churches, to which people's spiritual welfare is entrusted.

Looking at motives, people can be divided into those who seek to exploit the organizations they belong to for their own selfish ends, and those who are loyal to their organizations, seeing their own good in the overall good of the organization's work — the benefit to all its members, and to all it tries to help. Loyal members can be further classified into the "unquestioningly loyal," who are the backbone and muscles of an organization, and the "questioningly loyal," who, though much smaller in number, are the conscience and eyes of an organization. Neither of these two types of loyal member is better than the other — both are needed if an organization is to be vital and useful. What is important is that both are loyal, and both are tolerant in accepting the value to the organization of the other.

Some organizations are fundamentalist from the start. Others become that way, and it would appear that, in many if not most cases, this happens when an organization is hijacked by disloyal members who are in it, consciously or unconsciously, for their own selfish and egotistical ends — usually to satisfy their desires for material possessions and power over people. In a church, power over people is usually the main motive, although greed, as we have seen, is often present as well. Fundamentalist power seekers typically start the process of hijacking an organization by disparaging the loyalty of the "questioningly loyal" members who can see through their deceit. Fear is the friend of fundamentalism. If the power seekers can play on the fears of the more vulnerable of the "unquestioningly loyal" majority, and convince them that the questioners' criticisms of the organization in general, and of them in particular, are attacks on the organization, designed to weaken and eventually destroy it, then, if there are enough fearful members, they have won. The power seekers go on to bring into line or expel all the "questioners," and continue by promoting the supreme virtue of unquestioning loyalty to they, the new leaders. After this these worldly leaders are unopposed, and have a loyal and hard-working band of supporters to help them do whatever they wish. The megalomania that results leads these fundamentalist leaders to expand the realm of their power as far as they can go — to encompass the whole of society, if it were possible. This is exactly what Islam did in creating the most powerful empire the world had ever seen, within one hundred years of its foundation in the seventh century. It is also what the church did in medieval times, and, as we have seen, Augustine, and later Aquinas, were so enthusiastically accepted by the Vatican precisely because they advocated unquestioning obedience and loyalty to the church.

Whether an organization goes the road of fundamentalism, depends on the good will of the majority of the "unquestioningly loyal" members. Even in the best and most open organizations, there will always be some of these who are afraid that criticism will destroy their organization, and who think everyone should be as unquestioningly loyal as they are, and that people are disloyal if they ask questions.[3] If there is more than a small percentage of such fearful and dogmatic people in an organization, it will be in danger of falling into fundamentalism. On the other hand, if the large majority of members believe it is fair and reasonable for the leadership of the organization to be questioned at times, and be accountable for their actions, policies and beliefs, even if they themselves are not the ones to do the questioning, then the fate of fundamentalism will be avoided. The true fundamentalists in a stricken organization are the unscrupulous leaders themselves, and the "dogmatically loyal" followers. The ordinary "unquestioningly loyal" members, who would be prepared to accept criticism of the organization and its policies and doctrines from other members, are not fundamentalists at heart, even if they do belong to a fundamentalist organization and do "buy" many of its doctrines — they are just the hard-working majority in any organization, who get its day-to-day work done.

Fundamentalist organizations are often out of touch with reality, and when their pride leads to a fall, many of the "unquestioningly loyal" followers are forced to question why their organization failed. These members will, in future, be more likely to insist on being able to question their leaders, and on having some input into policy, and perhaps this is a way out of fundamentalism. An extreme example of this process is when, as has happened a number of times, a pastor persuades his congregation to sell their homes and retreat to a mountain top because he has told them the end of the world is approaching. When the supposed date of the end of the world passes and they are left with nothing, they begin to ask questions, especially if the pastor himself has been found to have kept his house, "just in case," and has absconded with much of their money. Less extreme examples are also commonly reported, such as pastors who preach against the low standard of public morality being caught in adultery themselves — being judged by the same "measure" they used to judge others (Luke 6:37–38). In a broader sense, the whole of western society has been caught out by the institutional nature of churches, become skeptical of them, and is staying away from them. Putting a new facade on the same old corrupt Christianity, based on fear but not on the Bible, will not work anymore. This is a major reason why church attendance has dropped so low. Deep-level reform of the church will be necessary before large numbers of discerning people in well-educated countries will return to Christianity.

Finally, in this chapter, I would like to take a quick look at the two great enemies fundamentalists perceive they have in society: the "conspiracy of secular humanism," and the "New Age Movement." In *The Rise and Fall of the New Christian Right* Steve Bruce shows how the fundamentalists of the New Christian Right identified "secularism" and "humanism" as being common features of most of the things they did not like. They then constructed this joint "secularity" and "humanism" into what appeared to be a coherent belief system, and attributed it to those who promoted ideals or behavior they rejected. "Secular humanism" provided a neat explanation, for them, of the many social changes they didn't like, and didn't want to understand. It also became an enemy they could fight against.[4] As Bruce points out, though, there is no secular humanist conspiracy, and one of the main reasons why the New Christian Right's Moral Majority movement failed is that it was fighting against a chimera. Ninety-seven percent of Americans believe in God, and the figure is almost as high in most countries, yet non-belief in God is just one of a long list of things fundamentalists say secular humanists conspire to believe in and impose on society.[5] The fundamentalists' profile of the secular humanist conspiracy is really just a list of things they don't like, and so extensive is their list, that virtually no-one can fully match the profile, and so be able to be considered a potential member of such a conspiracy.

In the late twentieth century, we have a vast array of options in our lives, which previous generations did not have, and much of secular and humanist thinking in an inevitable response to this smorgasbord of choices. Some instances of humanist thinking, however, are reactions against abuses of Christianity by the church in the past — reactions which perhaps went too far, in many cases rejecting altogether the validity of a spiritual approach to life. The return swing of the pendulum came with what has been called "New Age" thinking. This is a reaction against secular and humanist thinking by people who have been brought up in secular and humanist environments, who know the paucity of materialistic existence, and who want to return to a spiritual approach to life. There are thousands of New Age organizations, independently trying to find a way forward to a more spiritual life. In most cases, their members feel unable to return to the church, because of their awareness of its problems of lack of spirituality, exclusiveness, and use of fear to control people. As with "secular humanism," there is no such thing as a united "New Age Movement." New Age organizations vary from the high spiritual to the downright materialistic and exploitative, with everything in-between, and fundamentalists make themselves look silly when they target blanket judgments against the figment of their imaginations they call the "New Age Movement," which they would like to see as their enemy.

The church should rather see the wisdom of allowing itself to be informed by New Age thinking as to the spiritual needs and anxieties of our age, and thereby be able to determine the right direction for reform in the church. New Age thinking could be the church's ally rather than its enemy, as it represents a turning from materialism to spirituality, be it ever so shallow in some of its manifestations. The church would do well to work with the best New Age organizations, rather than against them, and confine its criticism, if it must criticize at all, to the most superstitious and exploitative New Age groups.

Chapter 15

Defaming the Name of God — Eternal Hell

While getting to know a neighbor of mine, we came to realize we had an interest in yoga and meditation in common. But when I used the word "God," as I frequently do, she became quite hostile. "I don't believe in God," she said. I asked her what she did believe in, and she responded with a sublime description of a cosmic power of love which she was aware of when she meditated, when she sat on the top of a hill at sunset, taking in the stillness and beauty around her. It was a personal power to her, and it made her joyful and inspired when she took the time to inwardly commune with it. I don't remember the exact words she used, but I do remember thinking it was an excellent description of God. I told her this, but she wasn't impressed. She explained that God was someone who made you feel guilty about sex, and who threatened to send you to burn forever in hell if you didn't do what He wanted. She said she was afraid of God until she realized He didn't exist. She'd spent years getting over her Christian upbringing, and wasn't going to get involved with all that again. She was even suspicious of my enthusiasm for God. Although she seemed to like me, she also appeared to be on guard against some hidden "nasty" which might pop up out of the woodwork as a consequence of my belief in God. I tried to explain that the church had given her a very unfortunate view of God, and that in reality the cosmic love she experienced was the essence of God, and was how I experienced Him. I may have sown some seeds, but they were not about to sprout in a hurry. I gained the distinct impression she resented having her very special and important cosmic power of love compared to something she loathed as much as "God."

This woman's attitude is not an uncommon one. I have met many people who find the concept of God distasteful, to the extent that they squirm at the very mention of the word, yet who lovingly help others, and are quite clearly looking for a spiritual side to life, even if they wouldn't use the word "spiritual" to describe it. How did these people come to gain this impression of God? How has much of society come to see Him as a kind of "anti-Santa Claus" — a mythological tyrant people are pressed into believing in during childhood, who watches over their every move, noting down any mistake for eventual punishment, and never letting them know whether they are doomed to burn in hell forever, or whether they have not yet been quite so bad that they might not just be allowed into heaven on sufferance? Fear is the watchword for this concept of God: fear you will earn eternal torture in hell if you have too much fun, or don't conform obediently to what those in authority expect of you.

How did the good name of God get defamed in this way? It almost seems superfluous to even ask this question. It is supremely obvious that the church has caused it — by preaching, over the centuries, of the sinfulness and shamefulness of sex, and of the wrath of God that results in eternal punishment in the fires of hell. A better question would be: "Why has the church defamed the good name of God in this way?" The short answer is that it was done to control people. The medieval church didn't care whether people were happy. It didn't even care what God wanted. It was just intent, in its megalomania, on controlling people, and making people bow down to worship it, and used whatever means it could to achieve this end. Although it used every physical threat and method of violence it could to enforce compliance, including the three degrees of torture and burning people alive at the stake, it found this was not enough. Not everybody could be controlled this way. Some preferred to die rather than sacrifice their integrity, putting their faith in a better life to come, either on this earth again or in heaven. The church also found it necessary to foster the belief that there was no second chance, and if you didn't do what the church said you would simply be condemned to everlasting punishment in hell when you died.

The modern church has retreated from this "hell-fire and brimstone" preaching to some extent. The wife of a Pentecostal pastor I know even went as far as to say that there is no place for hell-fire teaching in the modern church. Many modern Christians bask in teachings of God's love, and are rarely confronted with hell. Their attitude is often like that of a certain young woman, earlier this century, who wrote that, although her church believed in hell, she felt God really was friendly, and organized the world in such a way that things always worked out well in the end.[1]

But although the teaching about everlasting hell is not stressed, it has not been renounced by Christianity, and is still there in the background. This has two unfortunate consequences. Firstly, the impression of the public that the church believes in a God who punishes people forever in hell persists, even though the love of God is preached much more often than hell these days. Secondly, it leaves even the most forward-looking churches, where the love of God is held high, open to itinerant "hell-fire and brimstone" preachers coming in and sowing ghastly fears amongst their congregations. I was in a church where this happened. A visiting preacher played on the fact that we don't know when we might die: it could be next year. Then a little later in the sermon he said it could be next month. Each time he returned to the point, the time grew closer: it could be tomorrow, or in five minutes. Hadn't we better confess our sins and repent now, rather than run the risk of burning forever in hell? The normally happy and joyous congregation were greatly subdued after this service, and sour looks were on the faces of many.

I think many Christians would like not to have to believe in hell, but consider they must, because this traditional doctrine appears to be supported by a number of Jesus' teachings in the Bible. My aim, in this chapter, is to help remove this burden from Christianity, by demonstrating that the support for the doctrine of everlasting punishment in the Bible is only apparent —a result of wrong translations from the Greek into modern languages, compounded by misinterpretations based on looking at the Bible in the wrong way.

In Chapter 11 I pointed out that the word "hell," in the Gospels, is used to translate two different words Jesus used. In the Greek, these two words are *Gehenna* and *Hades*. *Gehenna* was the Greek word for the "Valley of (Ben) Hinnom," a deep ravine south of Jerusalem which was used as the city's garbage tip, and had been used in the past for child sacrifice. If you look at the map of Jerusalem in the back of most Bibles, you will see the Valley of Hinnom at the bottom of it. That this is what *Gehenna* was, and that Jesus was using it as a metaphor for something else is acknowledged by even the most conservative Christian authorities. Biblical Greek dictionaries define *Gehenna* as the valley of Hinnom, a valley near Jerusalem, used in a figurative way to refer to the place or state of everlasting punishment.[2] There is no evidence, though, that Jesus is using it figuratively to refer to a place of punishment after death, and it is much more reasonable to suppose he is referring to the corrosive state of mind people get into in the here-and-now when they sin. The main reason for my saying this is that Jesus never actually associates Gehenna with what happens after death, and on the one occasion where Jesus does talk about a place of punishment after death, in the story of The Rich Man and Lazarus (Luke 16:19–31), he calls it *Hades* (the underworld), not *Gehenna*. There is also no mention in this story of the Rich man's punishment being "eternal" or "forever," although it is made clear he can't avoid his punishment, and that he is in a fiery place of torment. This story does say there is an impassable "chasm" between heaven and Hades, which can't be crossed by those on either side. Some take this as indicating punishment in Hades is forever, however this just doesn't follow. There is also an impassable gulf between those serving a term in a maximum security prison and those outside. The prisoner can't get out (at least that's the intention), and members of the public can't get in; the best they can do is very occasionally talk to a prisoner distantly, through a wall of glass, or a grille, rather like Abraham talks to the rich man in the story. This doesn't mean the prisoner will not be let out at the end of his term, though.

The presence of fire and torment are the only two "hellish" attributes *Gehenna* and *Hades* have in common, except for the fact that medieval, and some modern, Bibles translate both words as "hell." There is, however, one reassuring thing both have in common, and that is that there is no suggestion that the torment of either is an everlasting state. Having established this for *Hades*, let's look at *Gehenna*. Most of the time Jesus simply refers to Gehenna without further describing it, as his listeners would have known what a hot, stinking wasteland it was — he didn't need to elaborate on it. On one occasion, though, Jesus did say,

> "If your hand causes you to sin, cut it off. It is better for you to enter life maimed than with two hands to go into hell [Gehenna], where the fire never goes out." (Mark 9:43)

The fire never going out has been taken to mean that punishment there is forever. However, there is a more mundane explanation for it. In fact, this merely accords with what is known of the Valley of Hinnom, that it had a garbage fire which literally never went out, from one year's end to the next. There is no suggestion that peoples' "punishment" in the state of mind figuratively referred to as *Gehenna* never ends, although the comparison with a place where the fire never goes out could be being used to reinforce the message that misery is unending while you remain immersed in sin. In relation to the other part of this passage, Jesus is not literally advocating that we cut off our hands if they offend us. There isn't any physical part of our body which causes us to sin and live in the garbage tip of misery. Rather it is what our selfish motivations and bad habits cause us do with our hands which make us miserable, and it is these motivations and habits Jesus is advising us to cut away, even if at first we might feel "maimed," not our whole selves, without them. The reward is "life" in the kingdom of God.

The here-and-now nature of Gehenna comes out clearly in this passage, and, as we shall see, this is true of all Jesus' references to Gehenna. In the Sermon on the Mount, Jesus says,

"You have heard that it was said to people long ago, 'Do not murder, and anyone who murders will be subject to judgment. But I tell you that anyone who is angry with his brother will be subject to judgment. Again, anyone who says to his brother, 'Raca,' is answerable to the Sanhedrin. But anyone who says, 'You fool!' will be in danger of the fire of hell [Gehenna]."

(Matt 5:21–22)

Here Jesus draws two parallel comparisons between acts which bring a legal penalty, and behavior which, although not illegal, brings unfortunate consequences to the doer. The Greek word translated as "judgment" is *crisis*, which has the basic meaning of "separation." The modern words "criminal" and "criterion" both come from it; a criminal is someone who is separated from society, and a criterion is a basis for separating things. Judgment is just one possible meaning of this word, which like many Greek words has a wide range of meaning, depending on context: in some contexts it simply means separation, with no sense of it being imposed as a judgment, and in these cases the translation as "judgment" is inappropriate. Murder would, of course, have been judged, and the most severe kind of separation was imposed on those found guilty of it: separation from their life through capital punishment. Jesus is saying getting angry with your brother is also a thing to be avoided, as this too leads to a type of separation, although not such a drastic one. Anger brings isolation from your fellow human beings, and separation from the peace of God's presence. Anyone used to living in harmony with friends, and dwelling in God's peace, who has given way to anger, can testify to this. I can myself. Days can pass before you regain that "peace of God which passes all understanding," even after you have thoroughly repented of the anger, and the barriers created between you and the person you were angry with can last for years, and even be permanent. This is what Jesus is warning of here. He reinforces this with the parallel illustration of someone saying "Raca" to his brother. Saying this particular word (which may mean something like "empty head") was an offense punishable by the Sanhedrin, the Jewish court. But Jesus points out that saying anything nasty to someone else, such as calling them a fool, is to be avoided, even if there is no law against it, because it will set fire to your happiness and peace of mind, and land you in that mental garbage tip of misery Jesus likened to Gehenna. Jesus certainly seems to be talking about the here-and-now, on-this-earth, consequences of these actions, rather than any after-death punishment. He makes it abundantly clear that this is in fact what he is doing, when he immediately follows these illustrations with advice about the importance of being reconciled with people so you can pray well, and so you can avoid the retaliation which can come when people hate you—both here-and-now concerns:

> "Therefore, if you are offering your gift at the altar and there remember that your brother has something against you, leave your gift there in front of the altar. First go and be reconciled to your brother; then come and offer your gift.
> "Settle matters quickly with your adversary who is taking you to court. Do it while you are still with him on the way, or he may hand you over to the judge, and the judge may hand you over to the officer, and you may be thrown into prison. I tell you the truth, you will not get out until you have paid the last penny." (Matt 5:23–26)

Jesus goes on to say,

> "You have heard that it was said, 'Do not commit adultery.' But I tell you that anyone who looks at a woman lustfully has already committed adultery with her in his heart. If your right eye causes you to sin, gouge it out and throw it away. It is better for you to lose one part of your body than for your whole body to be thrown into hell [Gehenna]. And if your right hand causes you to sin, cut it off and throw it away. It is better to lose one part of your body than for your whole body to go into hell [Gehenna]." (Matt 5:27–30)

This is similar to the reference to Gehenna we looked at in the book of Mark, though this talks about your "eye" causing you to sin as well as your "hand." In fact the Mark passage goes on to talk about the "eye," and even the "foot," leading you into sin — I just didn't quote all of it. Whereas the "hand" and the "foot" refer to motivations and habits which can lead us astray, the "eye" refers to the power of the senses to do so, and lead us into a life of depravity and misery. Again, Jesus is not suggesting bodily mutilation, as, after all, even a blind man can fall prey to lust. What he is admonishing us to "gouge out" is the lust itself: the extension of our senses and imaginations out into temptation in the world. Rather we should withdraw our senses into the peace within ourselves, and find the incomparable joy of seeking the kingdom of God "within." The twentieth century Indian saint, Sri Yukteswar, had advice for his disciples which aptly illustrates this teaching of Jesus:

> "Do not allow yourself to be thrashed by the provoking whip of a beautiful face. How can sense slaves enjoy the world? Its subtle flavors escape them...All nice discriminations are lost to the man of elemental lusts...
>
> "Conserve your powers. Be like the capacious ocean, absorbing quietly all the tributary rivers of the senses...Roam in the world as a lion of self-control; don't let the frogs of sense weakness kick you around."[3]

Further on in Matthew Jesus says,

> "Do not be afraid of those who kill the body but cannot kill the soul. Rather be afraid of the One who can destroy both soul and body in hell [Gehenna]. Are not two sparrows sold for a penny? Yet not one of them will fall to the ground apart from the will of your Father. And even the very hairs of your head are numbered. So do not be afraid; you are worth more than many sparrows.   (Matt 10:28–31)

Here he is alluding to the fact that the depravity of living in a worldly way, in hell, rather than relying on God for our needs, destroys both the serenity of the soul, and the health of the body.

Matthew 18:7–9 is another "if your eye causes you to sin" passage, this time almost an exact repeat of the passage in

Mark. Then, in attacking the pride and selfishness of the intelligentsia, Jesus says,

> "Woe to you, teachers of the law and Pharisees, you hypocrites!
> You travel over land and sea to win a single convert, and when
> he becomes one, you make him twice as much a son of hell
> [Gehenna] as you are." (Matt 23:14–15)

Since Jesus referred to these Pharisees as being "sons of Gehenna," it follows they were living in Gehenna, or one way or another were being molded by it during their lives here on earth. This could only be possible if Gehenna were a here-and-now state of mind engendered through worldliness, rather than a place or state of punishment after death. With this verse the argument against everlasting punishment in hell could rest its case. There are, however, a few more passages which need explaining, and a number of issues which must be addressed, if there is to be a consistent Biblical basis for not believing in everlasting punishment.

Jesus next mentions hell while continuing to speak against the teachers of the law and Pharisees:

> "You snakes! You brood of vipers! How will you escape being
> condemned to hell [Gehenna]?"   (Matt 23:33)

This verse is fairly neutral in terms of our discussion. If Gehenna were referring to a punishment after death, it would make sense. But it also makes sense with Gehenna being a here and now state of mind, and this interpretation has the advantage that it ties in well with the verses around it. The "brood of vipers" will be condemned to living a life of misery because of their inner "greed and self indulgence" (Matt 23:25). Jesus said of their inner state:

> "You are like whitewashed tombs, which look beautiful on the
> outside, but on the inside are full of dead men's bones and
> everything unclean."   (Matt 23:27)

The only reference to Gehenna in Luke (Luke 12:5), is an exact repeat of one we have already looked at, and John contains no reference to hell at all, either Gehenna or Hades. The last remaining reference to Gehenna is in the book of James:

> The tongue also is a fire, a world of evil among the parts of the body. It corrupts the whole person, sets the whole course of his life on fire, and is itself set on fire by hell [Gehenna].
> (James 3:6)

Here the tongue is seen as a metaphorical fire, which can set fire to and destroy the course of a person's life. James explains that the "hell" people live in is what sets fire to the tongue in this way, then the fiery tongue goes on to destroy the rest of their lives. This again confirms Gehenna operates in this life rather than after it. By contrast, James sees the tongues of those living in the kingdom of heaven in the here-and-now as spreading peace:

> But the wisdom which comes from heaven is first of all pure; then peace-loving, considerate, submissive, full of mercy and good fruit, impartial and sincere. Peacemakers who sow in peace raise a harvest of righteousness.   (James 3:17–18)

The list of New Testament references to hell is completed by a few references to *Hades* in the books of Matthew, Luke, Acts and Revelation, and one to *Tartarus*, the "deepest depths of Hades," in 2 Peter. None of these refers to *Hades* as a place of punishment, but rather as "the grave," the "underworld," or as an image of the destruction of a city or institution.[4] The King James Version has numerous references to "hell" in the Old Testament. They all come from the Hebrew *Sheol* which simply means "the grave," and this is how it is always translated in modern versions of the Bible. The last reference to *Hades* in Revelation does add something relevant, though, and is worth looking at:

> The sea gave up the dead that were in it, and death and Hades gave up the dead that were in them, and each person was judged according to what he had done. Then death and Hades were thrown into the lake of fire. The lake of fire is the second death.

If anyone's name was not written in the book of life, he was
thrown into the lake of fire.   (Rev 20:13–15)

This is part of John's richly symbolic vision of the "afterlife."
As with dreams, meanings have to be assigned to its symbols
before an interpretation can be made. A later chapter will be
largely devoted to this book. For now, what is of interest is the
assertion, in this passage, that Hades is a temporary abode, that
it gives up its dead before judgment, and that those whose
names are not written in the book of life do not return to it,
but rather are thrown into the "lake of fire." There is no
statement, however, that human beings are thrown into this
lake of fire forever, in contrast to the "devil," the "beast" and
the "false prophet" which are specifically consigned there for
all time:

> And the devil, who deceived them, was thrown into the lake of
> burning sulfur, where the beast and the false prophet had been
> thrown. They will be tormented day and night for ever and ever.
>   (Rev 20:10)

These three creatures, in this symbolic context, are archetypes
of three faces of evil: the devil is temptation, the beast is
worldliness, and the false prophet is deceitfulness. None of
these can ever be a part of the holiness of heaven. Human
beings, on the other hand, can choose, if they wish, to renounce these evils and seek God. Until such time as they do,
however, they too will be confined to the realm where evil can
exist, symbolized by the "lake of fire" in John's vision, and
have to contend with its torments — a second death which is
not necessary if people have chosen God.

     Jesus also described a "judgment day," and ascribed a simi-
lar fate to those who hadn't done the right thing during their
time on earth:

> "Then [the King] will say to those on his left, 'Depart from me,
> you who are cursed, into the eternal fire prepared for the devil
> and his angels. For I was hungry and you gave me nothing to eat,
> I was thirsty and you gave me nothing to drink, I was a stranger
> and you did not invite me in, I needed clothes and you did not

clothe me, I was sick and in prison and you did not look after me.'

"They also will answer, 'Lord, when did we see you hungry or thirsty, a stranger needing clothes or sick or in prison, and did not help you?'

"He will reply, 'I tell you the truth, whatever you did not do for one of the least of these, you did not do for me.'

"Then they will go away to eternal punishment, but the righteous to eternal life." (Matt 25:41–46)

The "eternal fire prepared for the devil and his angels" sounds like the "lake of fire" of Revelation. And here at last is an actual reference to certain people, those who don't help their neighbors when they need help, being sent to eternal punishment. It is the only one in the whole Bible. Does this mean we have, finally, to concede that there is everlasting punishment? Not necessarily. The King James Version renders the last of these verses as:

And these shall go away into everlasting punishment: but the righteous into life eternal. (Matt 25:46 A.V.)

It translates the Greek word *aionion* first as "everlasting," then as "eternal," as if the words were exactly synonymous. But both the NIV and the Jerusalem Bible translate both occurrences as "eternal." In modern English "eternal" does have a slightly different meaning from "everlasting," and the fact that modern versions substitute "eternal" for "everlasting" is the clue to a deceitful translation having taken place. When looked up in Greek dictionaries, the noun *aion*, from which the adjective derives, is found to properly mean just an "age," a "particular amount of time,"[5] or a "long period of about a lifetime,"[6] and only by extension to mean "in perpetuity." The English word "aeon" comes from this Greek root. So what Jesus is saying here is that when people die and are judged, those who haven't helped their neighbors who needed help will go away to a "long period" of punishment, of about a lifetime perhaps, whereas the righteous who have helped those in need will go to "an age" of "life" in the "kingdom prepared for

[them] since the creation of the world." (Matt 25:34) That only a period of "life" is referred to here in no way implies an end to existence after this period, or that those who "overcome" don't finally go to heaven forever. This will be further discussed in the next chapter.

Since an "extension" meaning of *aion* as "in perpetuity" is claimed by Christian scholars, it is just possible, looking at this passage in isolation, that Jesus meant that certain people would be punished forever, but it is much more reasonable to assume Jesus was referring to the proper meaning of "an age" or "particular period," and was rather saying that a period of punishment was set aside for people who did the wrong thing. It becomes even more reasonable to assume this proper meaning when the many references in the Bible to God's mercy, compassion, justice, and patient desire to see everyone saved, are taken into account. Consider just a few of them:

> ...the Lord longs to be gracious to you;
>   he rises to show you compassion.
> For the Lord is a God of justice.
>   Blessed are all who wait for him! (Isaiah 30:18)

If a man owns a hundred sheep, and one of them wanders away, will he not leave the ninety-nine on the hills and go to look for the one that wandered off? And if he finds it, I tell you the truth, he is happier about that one sheep than about the ninety nine that did not wander off. In the same way your Father is not willing that any of these little ones should be lost.   (Matt 18:12–14)

This is good, and pleases God our Savior, who wants all men to be saved and come to a knowledge of the truth. For there is one God, and one mediator between God and men, the man Jesus Christ, who gave himself as a ransom for all men.
(1 Timothy 2:3–6)

But do not forget this one thing, dear friends: With the Lord a day is like a thousand years, and a thousand years are like a day. The Lord is not slow in keeping his promise, as some understand slowness. He is patient with you, not wanting anyone to perish, but everyone to come to repentance.   (2 Peter 3:8–9)

This is a trustworthy saying that deserves full acceptance (and for

this we labor and strive), that we have put our hope in the living
God, who is the Savior of all men, and especially of those who
believe.   (1 Timothy 4:9–10)

It is clear from these quotes that Jesus, Paul and Peter taught
that God wants everyone to be saved, that Jesus gave himself as
a ransom for all men, not just some, and that God is patient in
waiting for all to come to repentance. In the light of this, to say
only some people will be saved is to say God is not omnipotent
and able to carry out His own wishes. This is quite a slander of
God's ability. I venture to suggest that, in reality, what God
wants, He gets. Of course, God made it hard for himself by
giving humans a totally independent free will. He must enjoy a
challenge. Some people can be particularly obdurate in holding
out against God's love, but God knows no-one can hold out for
ever, so with His infinite patience, He knows all will be saved
in the end. And when the very last soul is saved, rescued finally
from worldly delusions and vices, there will be an enormous
celebration in heaven.

There is a popular Christian song, "The Steadfast Love of
the Lord Never ceases," which talks of God's mercies never
coming to an end.[7] Are God's mercies never-ending, or are
His punishments never-ending? We should be able to see by
now that God only punishes people by making them face reality so they can learn from it; He is the ever-loving parent in
this. As Jesus said,

"Which of you, if his son asks for bread, will give him a stone?
Or if he asks for a fish, will give him a snake? If you, then,
though you are evil, know how to give good gifts to your
children, how much more will your Father in heaven give
good gifts to those who ask him!"   (Matt 7:9–11)

What parent would say to his child, "If you don't start behaving properly before a time I choose — and I'm not going to tell
you when it will be, it could be any time at all — then I'm going
to punish you in the most vicious way I possibly can: you will
be locked up and ignored, and every day your flesh will be
burned in a fire till you are in agony. And it will be too late

then to decide to be good, for even if you plead with me to forgive you, I will just go on punishing you like this forever and ever." Even just seriously threatening a child in such a monstrous way would be enough to make the child welfare authorities take interest; any attempt to implement it would certainly lead to the child being taken away from the parent. Yet the church has seriously tried to tell us that God could behave like this.

For a long time the church has presented a yawning credibility gap to the world. People simply do not believe God can commit people to everlasting punishment and also be merciful, just and loving. It doesn't make sense, and as long as Christians continue to insist it is so, discriminating people will increasingly reject the church. This issue has also divided the church from within, by making it difficult, if not impossible, for Christians to understand the nature of God's justice and love. Christians have had to say something like: "I know it sounds harsh, but it says there is everlasting punishment in the Bible, so we've just got to accept it; God's ways are beyond our understanding." I believe the vast majority of Christians are not sadists, and will be hugely relieved to know that everlasting punishment has just been read and translated into the Bible, and simply isn't there in the original Greek.

Chapter 16

Answering the Dilemmas — Reincarnation and Salvation

An immediate consequence of not believing in everlasting punishment in hell is that it raises a serious dilemma: where do the wicked go when they die? Most would agree that God cannot accept wicked, unrepentant people into heaven, so if there is no hell, where do they go? This dilemma would be a problem for anyone arguing that there is no hell at all, and makes it very reasonable to believe that there is, in fact, a place apart from heaven where the wicked go after death. God can't be considered unjust for rewarding the good and not rewarding the bad. In the previous chapter I did not take issue with the existence of a place of punishment after death, only with the nature of that punishment. It is only the suggestion that God punishes people *forever* that defames the good name of God. Just as a loving parent never gives up hope in a wayward child, and will always accept him back if he gives up his evil ways and seeks to do good things with his life, so God could never give up on any person. Not only does this make good sense, but, as we have seen in the previous chapter, there are many passages from the Bible which show this is indeed God's attitude — that He wants all to be saved, and is patient in waiting for it.

The real point of departure from traditional Christian doctrine suggested by this, is the idea that this life here on earth is not the only, or the last, opportunity for people to learn and grow, and have a change of heart and come to God. Traditionally, even amongst those Christians not believing in predestination, the end of this life has been seen as the end of all opportunity to improve, and the life after death is simply an everlasting reward or punishment for what has been done during one short lifetime. Of course, to those believing in predestination, there isn't even this opportunity to improve —

to them God is like a child who collects a bag of ants and divides them into two containers, says "these are going to be the good ants, and those are going to be the bad ants," and proceeds to give honey to the "good" ones, and one by one throw the "bad" ones on to the fire.

There are a number of Scriptures which suggest that this life is just a short episode in the total life of the soul, such as:

> What is your life? You are a mist that appears for a little
> while and then vanishes.   (James 4:14)

There are also Scriptures which indicate that the afterlife is not just a simple black and white dichotomy between heaven and hell, such as Jesus saying,

> "In my Father's house are many rooms; if it were not so I would
> have told you. I am going to prepare a place for you."
>   (John 14:2)

This suggests heaven accommodates the varying needs of many different sorts of people, presumably to meet their different needs for further development. That not all in heaven are judged to be equal is shown by Jesus saying he will "reward each person according to what he has done," (Matt 16:27), a teaching Paul also stressed by twice referring to it.[1] Jesus reinforced the concept by adding,

> "...whoever humbles himself like this child is the greatest in
> the kingdom of heaven."   (Matt 18:4)

The Roman Catholic Church concedes souls have further opportunities for redemption after death through its doctrine of purgatory. It greatly abused this doctrine, during the Middle Ages, by saying souls in Purgatory can do nothing to help themselves, and rely totally for their passage to heaven on the prayers and indulgences of those on earth. By payment of money to the church, people could supposedly buy redemption of sins for their relatives in purgatory. Each type of sin had a specified price in this accountancy of sin, and since most people had a good idea what misdeeds their parents might have committed, they could calculate what they would have to pay the church to gain their release from purgatory. The famous St Peter's Basilica in Rome, designed by Michelangelo, was paid for with money raised by indulgences, in a shameful deal: the pope granted the rights to the sale of all indulgences in Saxony to the Archbishop of Mainz, who had bought his office from the Church with a loan from money lenders. The deal struck was that half the money from the sales of the indulgences would be returned to Rome to pay for the building of St. Peters, while the other half would be used by the archbishop to repay his debt to the money lenders.[2] Luther didn't know of this particular deal, but abuses of the system of indulgences were widespread, and he and the Protestants were quite rightfully implacably opposed to them. And because indulgences were to secure the release of souls from purgatory, the Protestants threw purgatory out as well, and established a hard-line belief that once you died it was heaven or hell and that was it, forever. This was an understandable reaction, yet it could perhaps be said they "threw the baby out with the bath water." They could have retained purgatory as a place where people have a continuing opportunity to repent and come to God, while abandoning the ridiculous notion that its occupants can do nothing to help themselves, and depend solely upon the indulgences bought by people on earth. Or if they had to do away with purgatory, they could have proposed that hell itself was such a place of limited punishment and continuing opportunity to repent. Martin Luther didn't seem to be able to appreciate the justice which could be afforded by a place like that, which would give people a vastly extended time to come to God, despite the fact that he loathed the idea of everlasting punishment. He said,

> I did not love — nay I hated this just God who punishes sinners, and if not with silent blasphemy, at least with huge murmuring. I was indignant against God, as if it were really not enough that miserable sinners, eternally ruined by original sin, should be crushed with every kind of calamity through the law of the Ten Commandments...And so I raged with a savage and confounded conscience;[3]

Christians can acknowledge the justice, mercy and patience of God by conceding that opportunities must continue in the afterlife for people to repent and come to God. And we know from the Bible that these opportunities must be sufficient for God to achieve His wish that all be saved. Just what these opportunities are, though, is another matter, and with our limited earthly knowledge, we may never know the full picture. It is sufficient to acknowledge that there isn't everlasting punishment in hell, and that God is patient enough, in providing opportunities for repentance, to ensure all are eventually saved.

Having said this, a possibility worth investigating is that one of the ways God provides further opportunities for people to return to Him is through reincarnation. Since being in a material body on earth is one way we know of that God gives people the chance to overcome evil and come to repentance, it makes good sense that at least a large part of the extra opportunity God patiently gives those who need it, should be through additional lives on earth (or some other material planet). This is also a very prevalent belief. Apart from being a universal belief amongst Buddhists and Hindus, about twenty-five percent of Westerners now believe in reincarnation. This is comparable to the number of practicing Christians. Reincarnation is not a "way-out" idea anymore — it is fast becoming the norm. Because of this, Christians owe it to themselves to further investigate reincarnation, especially as for the first five centuries of its existence Christianity itself embraced the concept (see Chapters 6 and 8). Could it be that the corrupt medieval church dispensed with reincarnation in order to meet its own worldly ends, such as making hell appear more immediate, and a more useful means of terrifying people into submission?

Before we look to see whether the Bible supports the concept of reincarnation, we need to be clear about what it entails. Reincarnation is a complex and much misunderstood concept, with many implications for living, so it is important we spend some time becoming at least a little bit familiar with it. Without doing this we could see reincarnation in the Bible when it isn't really there, or miss it even though it's under our noses. Before we look, we must know what we are looking for. There are a number of variations of the belief in reincarnation, of course, and new ones are always possible. I will describe a sophisticated and widely held version of the belief, deriving from the Indian Yoga tradition. Although there are details of it which vary from group to group, it is very much the consensus belief of most people who have gone into it thoroughly.

Reincarnation is a belief that the soul, the individual self of a person, does not die when the body dies, but lives on for a while without a physical body in its "astral body," a body of light, until it becomes attached again to the physical body of a fetus during pregnancy. In this way a person may have many lifetimes in a physical body, possibly even thousands of them. Each soul will be predominantly male or female, but will spend some lifetimes in a body of the opposite sex. This helps account for the presence of effeminate men and rather masculine women. The circumstances into which a soul is born depends on its needs, and on its actions in previous lives. This is where the concept of *karma* comes in. The word *karma* means "work," in the sense of the things we choose to do, our works, and the Law of Karma is simply just the law of cause and effect. As Paul puts it in the Bible:

> Do not be deceived: God cannot be mocked. A man reaps what he sows. The one who sows to please his sinful nature, from that nature will reap destruction; the one who sows to please the Spirit, from the Spirit will reap eternal life.   (Galatians 6:7–8)

If you do evil things and create evil tendencies in yourself in one life, this "bad karma" will carry over into your next life, and you will eventually have to face the consequences of these actions, and work to overcome the bad tendencies you have created. Likewise, if you do good things you create good tendencies in yourself which will warrant being born into a better situation in your next life, where your good deeds will be rewarded, and where you can build on your goodness.

The point of having so many lives is so people can have the time to overcome their obsession with worldliness, and so they can enjoy and progressively work through all the relatively good things this earth has to offer, till they no longer attach importance to them, and only want to seek God. The good things of this world are like the toys a parent gives a child. A little boy may spend years being absolutely obsessed with toy cars, but the time comes when he grows out of them, and rarely if ever plays with them again. He then prefers to do more adult things with his parents, even though he still values his toy cars as gifts from his parents, and would think it was good if his younger brother played with them. In a similar way, God gave human beings a sex drive, and the capacity in members of the opposite sex to satisfy it. "What a toy!" you may say — well God is a rather superior parent. And sex is no more wrong for human beings than playing with toy cars is for little boys — we are meant to have our fill of it (though I believe it should be with moderation and responsibility, and within a committed relationship). But the time will come when each of us will grow out of sex, along with our obsessions for food and wine and the material possessions money can buy. These things are not wrong, but too great an obsession with them is immature. An immature child will be more interested in his toys than in relationships with people. As he grows in maturity he will become more interested in interacting with his parents and friends. His interest in toys will become secondary, and he will use them primarily as something to share with his friends. But until he has totally outgrown them toys will still be a part of his environment to some extent: he is still a child. This is the stage most of us are at in the drama of life. This material world is still our environment. Sex, food and material possessions are not as important to us as our relationships with other people and with God, and are seen more as something to share with other people than an end in themselves. And, like the child growing out of toys who spends more and more time doing adult things with his parents, we spend more and more time seeking a spiritual life with God. This is not a time to be rushed through. Some children seek to seem more adult than they are by pretending not to be the slightest bit interested in toys, but by doing so actually delay their growing up, and make themselves unhappy in the process. Likewise, some "super-spiritual" people believe they should not be interested in sex, and should fast all the time and give away their possessions, when in fact they are not ready to make these sacrifices, and inwardly resent making them. All they do is slow down their spiritual progress and make themselves miserable. They forget that a person can only progress from the point they are at, and it is impossible to make actual progress from a point they only imagine they are at. This often happens because people think they have only one lifetime to become perfect, and can see how slowly they are progressing. In the light of reincarnation they can be more patient, relaxed and realistic about their spiritual progress. Nevertheless, the time will come when each person will no longer be interested enough in worldly things even to want to come back to earth, and from this point on they will no longer reincarnate on the physical plane — on earth, or on any other physical planet. They will have died to worldly things and their old selves, and have been born again in the spirit. As Paul said,

> ...when perfection comes, the imperfect disappears. When I was a child, I talked like a child, I thought like a child, I reasoned like a child. When I became a man, I put childish ways behind me. Now we see but a poor reflection; then we shall see face to face.
> (I Cor 13:10–12)

When the Pharisee Nicodemus sought an explanation from Jesus for his miraculous powers, and his closeness to God, Jesus said,

> "I tell you the truth, unless a man is born again, he cannot see the kingdom of God."
> "How can a man be born again when he is old?" Nicodemus asked. "Surely he cannot enter a second time into his mother's womb to be born!"
> Jesus answered, "I tell you the truth, unless man is born of water and the Spirit, he cannot enter the kingdom of God. Flesh gives birth to flesh, but the Spirit gives birth to spirit. You should

not be surprised at my saying, 'You must be born again.' The wind blows wherever it pleases. You hear its sound, but you cannot tell where it comes from or where it is going. So it is with everyone born of the spirit." (John 3:3–8)

And those who have been born again in the spirit, when they die, will literally not be born again in a physical body, but in the spiritual realm, in a spiritual body, for, as Paul declared,

...flesh and blood cannot inherit the kingdom of God.
(1 Cor 15:50)

Once people have died to worldly ways, and been born again in spirit, they become a people apart, separate from the world and identified with God. This is a key to understanding this controversial passage from Hebrews:

Nor did [Christ] enter heaven to offer himself again and again, the way the high priest enters the Most Holy Place every year with blood that is not his own. Then Christ would have had to suffer many times since the creation of the world. But now he has appeared once and for all at the end of the ages to do away with sin by the sacrifice of himself. Just as man is destined to die once, and after that to face judgment, so Christ was sacrificed once to take away the sins of many people; and he will appear a second time, not to bear sin, but to bring salvation to those who are waiting for him. (Hebrews 9:25–28)

The comparison with Christ dying for our sin on the cross, shows that the death we are "destined to die once" is the death to our old sinful self. It cannot be talking about physical death, as is often supposed, as a reference to the death of the body would be right out of context here. It is, rather, the death Paul talks about in saying:

...we know that our old self was crucified with [Jesus] so that the body of sin might be rendered powerless, that we should no longer be slaves to sin. (Romans 6:6)

It is heartening to know that once we have made this transition, we will not revert to worldliness and have to die to it over and over again. The Hebrews passage, when interpreted as I suggest, says this. Paul also explains this as he continues, in verses the Hebrews passage may well be based on:

> Now if we died with Christ, we believe that we will also live with him. For we know that since Christ was raised from the dead, he cannot die again; death no longer has mastery over him. The death he died, he died to sin once for all; but the life he lives, he lives to God.
>
> In the same way, count yourselves dead to sin but alive to God in Christ Jesus.   (Romans 6:8–11)

The reference in the Hebrews passage to having to face "judgment" at this point is a little puzzling at first, until it is realized that this is an instance of the Greek word *crisis* being translated as "judgment," when its basic meaning of "separation" is more appropriate. The literal word-by-word translation of this verse from the Greek is:

> ...it is reserved to men once to die, and after this, separation.

So what is being said, in context, is that it is reserved for men to die once to their old selves, then forever be separate from worldliness, living a life apart, under God's guidance, waiting for their final separation from life on this earth (and God's "judgment" about how to best provide for them in heaven) when they next leave their body. Ironically, this one short verse, taken out of context, and inappropriately translated as it is, is used by many Christians to try to show there is no reincarnation. Taken in context, though, and in harmony with Romans 6, it actually fits in very well with the concept of reincarnation. This is a good example of how easy it is to misinterpret the Bible if passages from it are taken out of context, and in isolation from other similar passages in the Bible.

Many who have truly died to worldliness, and been born again in the Spirit, may still use their last years of earthly existence to work out a few remaining areas of physical karma, and satisfy a last few material desires, before leaving it behind forever. The way in which people cease incarnating on earth once they have finally outgrown earthly things is well described in this passage from Hebrews:

All these people were still living by faith when they died. They did not receive the things promised; they only saw them and welcomed them from a distance. And they admitted that they were aliens and strangers on earth. People who say such things show that they are looking for a country of their own. IF THEY HAD BEEN THINKING OF THE COUNTRY THEY HAD LEFT, THEY WOULD HAVE HAD OPPORTUNITY TO RETURN. Instead they were longing for a better country—a heavenly one. Therefore God is not ashamed to be called their God, for he has prepared a city for them. (Heb 11:13–16)

The sentence I have emphasized with capitals clearly indicates that people who die still hankering after the things of earth, will be given the opportunity to return to it. This is precisely what reincarnation is all about. This passage also says that people who consider themselves "aliens and strangers on earth" will have a city prepared for them by God. This ties in with Jesus saying,

"In my Father's house are many rooms; if it were not so I would have told you. I am going to prepare a place for you."
(John 14:2)

It is also exactly what believers in reincarnation say happens when all earthly desires and karma have been worked out, except that they call these heavenly cities "astral planes" (or in some cases "etheric planes"). They mean exactly the same thing, though; only the words differ.

According to reincarnation theory, people spend a number of incarnations in the astral plane working out astral karma— which is all those things, other than the physical, that people need to work through, with God's help, on their way to perfection. People in a heavenly city (the astral) don't have any problems with lust, gluttony or avarice, as these are obsessions with the physical, and they would still be incarnating on earth if they had not overcome them. They may still, however, have problems with anger, selfishness or pride, which can continue to exist outside the physical. There are supposed to be many levels in the astral, to appropriately accommodate all those moving into it, and through it. Those replete with saintly qualities, when they finally leave earth, go to a high astral plane, whereas those still harboring negative qualities like anger and selfishness go to a much lower astral plane suited to making its occupants aware of the folly of such attitudes. The high astral planes correspond to the Christian "heaven," the low ones to "hell," and the ones in between might be likened to "purgatory." In fact, many Catholics who are aware of what reincarnation is about have compared the astral to purgatory. Reincarnation theory says that between incarnations on earth all but the most brutish and unaware people, who just stay totally unconscious until being reborn, will spend a period of time in the astral, in a body of light. Whether they spend this time in heaven or hell, or somewhere in between, depends on how good they have been in their last life. To illustrate this, the rich man in Jesus' story of the Rich Man and Lazarus would have been in one of the lowest astral hells.

After working out all their astral karma, souls progress to the "causal" level, the realm of ideas and creativity, where only pure thought and love exist, unalloyed even by the energy of the astral. In the causal, people have tremendous scope to be creative in a God-like way, and are able to fully express and work out their desires to create through the power of love, understand the mysterious causes of things, and fathom the depths of love and wisdom which lie behind the miraculous.

Qualities of self-discipline, self-control, patience and love are gradually gained and added to by a person during all three levels of incarnation, and the undesirable qualities they replace are gradually seen to be destructive of happiness and eliminated. The all-important, God-like good qualities are well described by Paul in his celebrated passage on love:

> Love is patient, love is kind. It does not envy, it does not
> boast, it is not proud. It is not rude, it is not self-seeking,
> it is not easily angered, it keeps no record of wrongs. Love
> does not delight in evil but rejoices with the truth. It always
> protects, always trusts, always hopes, always perseveres.
>   Love never fails. But where there are prophecies, they will
> cease; where there are tongues, they will be stilled; where

there is knowledge, it will pass away. For we know in part and we prophesy in part, but when perfection comes, the imperfect disappears.   (1 Corinthians 13:4–10)

Jesus also talked about the importance of us becoming perfect. He said,

"Be perfect, therefore, as your heavenly Father is perfect."

(Matt 5:48)

When each person overcomes all the possibilities for evil in creation, and becomes the embodiment of this love Paul talked about, he or she will be perfect, and will incarnate no more, in the physical, astral or causal. As the Spirit revealed to John in Revelation,

Him that overcometh will I make a pillar in the temple of my God, and he shall go no more out.   (Rev 3:12 AV)

After reaching perfection, people spend all their time with God. All sense of ego and separation from God is dissolved away, although a sense of individuality remains, so each soul can enjoy the bliss of being with God.

Reincarnation involves an ever upward evolution of the soul, although sometimes two steps backward seem to be needed in order to make three steps forward, as when great hardships are endured by people in order to overcome wrong attitudes. For instance, a wealthy person who does nothing to help the poor around him, harboring the attitude that they are responsible for their own plight, and should help themselves, will almost certainly be born very poor in his next life, and suffer poverty's worst indignities, and its most gnawing pains of starvation and disease. He will learn, first hand, what poverty is, and how helpless are its victims, so that in future he will know how to show compassion for others. Those who are compassionate have probably all learned their compassion in this way, in previous lives. Such important lessons are learned at great expense, in order to emphasize the importance of the qualities of love, and not see them devalued. The drama of life is not for the faint hearted: scaling Mount Everest is nothing compared to it, but the rewards of climbing the world's highest mountain are also as nothing, compared to the rewards of overcoming in the drama of life — it is the ultimate endeavor. Jesus, through "the words of the Amen, the faithful and true witness, the ruler of God's creation" (Rev 3:14), said to John in Revelation,

> Those whom I love I rebuke and discipline, so be earnest and
> repent. Here I am! I stand at the door and knock. If anyone
> hears my voice and opens the door, I will go in and eat with
> him, and he with me.
>   To him who overcomes, I will give the right to sit with me
> on my throne, just as I overcame and sat down with my Father
> on his throne.   (Rev 3:19–21)

But although many lessons are learned in a hard way, which challenges the soul to strive for greatness, no-one can go backwards more than a certain amount: the worst they can do is stagnate. Reincarnation jokes talk about people being reborn as animals. Certain primitive forms of belief in reincarnation do propose this as a punishment for a bad life, and say it often happens. All the more developed forms of the belief, however, agree this is not so, and that although an animal's soul can advance to becoming human, once having been a human, a person cannot easily revert to being an animal. Some teachers say it can never happen. Others do say that on rare occasions a soul can revert to the body of a higher animal for a lifetime if they have accumulated a particularly large amount of bad karma. This is out of mercy, though, as animals can work off karma without creating any new karma. One of the passages from Hebrews we looked at earlier shows that this non-reversion is also the case when people "die" to this world, become a people apart, and prepare for transition to the astral. The passage (Heb 9:27) makes it clear this "death" only takes place once, and then the transition (termed a "separation" or "judgment") takes place. Although this is primarily a desired separation from the physical world, a judgment is also involved, as it must be decided which astral plane a person should go to. So there is, at this point, as at the end of every

life, a "day of judgment," and on that day we will all have to
account for our actions during our life.

It may seem that people have to earn their salvation in this
process of working through the three different levels of incarnation, and that faith doesn't play a part. This is not the case,
though. Without God's help, the law of cause and effect would
ensure that no-one could ever escape the "wheel of karma."
While working through the consequences of past causes, they
would be creating new causes all the time, which would have
their effects in the future. To aggravate the problem, new
tendencies would be created by any wrong actions amongst
these causes, which would lead to further wrong actions in the
future. It is an impossible task for people to work out all their
own karma, and God does not require it. If, through their own
efforts, people reach the point of "repentance," where they are
no longer interested in being worldly, but just want to please
God, and do His will rather than their own, then God inter-
venes. He provides, through his grace, ways of burning up the
tendencies to produce future wrong actions, the seeds of new
karma, and this allows any remaining karma to be quickly
worked through.[4] Once people have the desire to surrender to
God—once they begin to love God, and seek first His kingdom
and His righteousness, and do not worry about worldly concerns, but identify with the Spirit—they are born again into the
kingdom of God, and their redemption by His grace begins.

While I don't believe it is absolutely necessary for Christians to believe in it, reincarnation does have the power of
resolving many of the dilemmas which have arisen concerning
the goodness of God. And these are crucial dilemmas, which
have split the church from society, and paralysed the church.
The most important of them involve God's justice, mercy and
holiness. The first dilemma is "how can God be just, loving and
merciful if He punishes sinners forever?" This is resolved, of
course, in the only way possible, by showing from the Bible
that God doesn't, in fact, punish anyone forever (see chapter
15). This much Christians must now accept, or they will
defame their God in a particularly ugly way, without the ex-

cuse, which they had in the past, of believing the Bible said there was eternal punishment. This, however, raises the dilemma of what God does with wicked people when they die, if his mercy prevents Him sending them to everlasting Hell, and his holiness prevents Him accepting them into heaven. The best answer is, of course, that His patience enables Him to wait for even the most hardened sinners to come to repentance. The Bible clearly says this is what God wants, and that He is prepared to be patient to achieve this end (see Chapter 15). There is, however, another answer which some Christians, including Jehovah's Witnesses, put forward. They say that the "lake of fire" doesn't in fact involve punishment, but is merely death to the soul. Unregenerate souls are supposedly just snuffed out, out of "mercy," rather than be let suffer, like an injured animal is shot to put it out of its misery. Apart from it not being Biblical (the "lake of fire" clearly being described as a place of torment in Revelation, though not as a place people are sent to forever), the biggest problem with this is that it assumes taking away the existence of a human being, who unlike most animals is very aware of his existence, would not be cruel. In point of fact, more than anything else, people want to live forever, and most would prefer to exist in torment than not exist at all. This argument is analogous to saying capital punishment is merciful compared with life imprisonment, because it puts the criminal out of the misery of having to live in prison and contemplate his misdeeds. This is condescending, to say the least: ask prisoners on death row, and nearly all will tell you they would prefer prison to death. This concept of the souls of the wicked being just snuffed out is also contrary to God's clearly expressed desire that all people be saved. As a result, I think Christians really do need to accept that this dilemma of what God is to do with the wicked can only be resolved by allowing that God does have the patience to wait for even the worst of sinners to come to repentance. Having come this far, Christians can still, of course, reject reincarnation, and say God has some other place in the afterlife where sinners can exist till they repent. This I grant them. However, reincarnation is a very convincing mechanism for providing people with further opportunities to come to God, and it resolves one further dilemma regarding God's goodness, and explains some otherwise puzzling things about life.

A most important, and much debated, dilemma regarding God's goodness is the "problem of pain." Most people can accept that a limited amount of pain can be useful as a part of a learning process, but cannot see that a total earthly existence of pain and misery can be fair, or serve any good end. Yet this appears to happen to many people, while others live lives of luxury on earth. How could a just and merciful God organize the world this way? Looked at from the point of view of reincarnation, however, the dilemma disappears. If we live hundreds, or thousands, of lives on earth, each lifetime is just a mere day in the larger life of the soul. The compassion which might take a whole lifetime of suffering to learn, would be used again and again to do great good over many lifetimes, and its possessor would eventually bless the lifetime spent learning it as much as an upright and successful person would bless his parents for punishing him for the wrong things he did as a child, even though these punishments and lessons may have seemed painful and unreasonable to him at the time. And, of course, under reincarnation there are plenty of opportunities for all people, over their many lives, to take in their fill of the good things of planet earth.

Reincarnation is not an easy teaching, which tries to get around the difficulties of life, but it is a fair and realistic one. The notion that all you have to do is pledge your acceptance of Jesus as your saviour, then just wait around till you are zapped into perfection at the end of the world, while those who didn't pledge their acceptance of Jesus are roasted in the fires of hell, is, by comparison, an easy teaching, and a boring and unchallenging one as well.

Although it has been most important to resolve these dilemmas involving God's goodness, reincarnation's ability to solve some of the other puzzles of life is also of interest. Have you ever wondered, for instance, how you can be fast friends with some people you meet — it can seem like you've always known them — but that it takes a long time to get to know others? This is because you *have* always known some of the people you meet: they have been your friends in previous lives.

The theory is that groups of friends, relatives and marriage partners stay together through many incarnations, exploring different ways of relating to each other. And have you wondered how a young child, even a baby, gets his individuality, which is often quite distinct from his parents' — a particular nature he keeps all his life? And why do some people have a natural talent for a particular skill, whereas others have to spend years learning it? These are both easily explained by reincarnation. The personality of a baby is not something new; it has developed gradually, over many previous lives. Skills and talents too, are present because they are areas which have been concentrated on in past lives. Child prodigies are not that much more intelligent than other people, as is shown by their ordinary abilities in most areas of their lives. Their extraordinary talents are more than just a gift, they have also been developed over many lives. Mozart already had his musical ability when he was born; he just had to brush up on it a little, get his new body used to playing instruments and writing down notes, and he was up and away at the age of six, composing some of the most beautiful music the world has ever heard. Of course, most children do have a lot in common with their parents, and, apart from hereditary similarities, this is because when being reborn, souls are attracted to parents who can set them on the course in life they need to continue their development, and this usually means their parents will have many similar qualities to themselves.

The concept of reincarnation is a very foreign one to start with. I found it that way when I was first introduced to it, but I also found, as time went by, that many things in life made more sense when seen in the light of it. It took me six months of open-minded consideration to finally realize reincarnation had to be true. When you look at your relationships with your friends and family, think of reincarnation. When you look at

new born babies, and their differences, and the slowness with
which people change their ways, think of reincarnation. Some
alcoholics may change during one lifetime, but most don't.
Some people with angry dispositions may change, but most will
not. How are many people ever going to be able change
enough to be in a position where they can value good things,
and choose to love God, if they do not have more than one
lifetime to do it in?

Having looked in some detail at what reincarnation is, we
are in a position to further investigate what the Bible has to say
about it. A number of the key Biblical passages supporting
reincarnation have already been quoted, during the discussion
of the concept, but there is more of this evidence to consider.
The most well known is a series of passages which establish
that John the Baptist was a reincarnation of Elijah:

> "See, I will send my messenger, who will prepare the way before
> me. Then suddenly the LORD you are seeking will come to his
> temple; the messenger of the covenant, whom you desire, will
> come," says the LORD Almighty.   (Malachi 3:1)

> "See, I will send you the prophet Elijah before that great and
> dreadful day of the LORD comes."   (Malachi 4:5)

> But the angel said to him "do not be afraid, Zechariah; your wife
> Elizabeth will bear you a son, and you are to give him the name
> John...And he will go on before the Lord, in the spirit and power
> of Elijah...to make ready a people prepared for the Lord."
>   (Luke 1:13,17)

Then three times, that we know of, Jesus assured his disciples
that John the Baptist really was Elijah returned:

> "But I tell you, Elijah has come, and they have done to him
> everything they wished, just as it is written about him."
>   (Mark 9:13)

> "For all the prophets and the law prophesied until John. And if
> you are willing to accept it, he is the Elijah who was to come."
>   (Matt 11:13–14)

> "But I tell you, Elijah has already come, and they did not
> recognize him…" Then the disciples understood that he was
> talking to them about John the Baptist.   (Matt 17:12–13)

And it's not as if Elijah just came down from heaven and
appeared as a herald for Jesus: his spirit and power manifested
in a little baby, born in the normal way — just how reincarnation says souls return. Some Christians say this only shows
John the Baptist was a prophet like Elijah, with a similar spirit
and power. They are contradicting Jesus, however, who quite
clearly, in the above passages, says John the Baptist *is* Elijah,
and is not just like him. This could, of course, be a special case
of reincarnation, and by itself it doesn't prove that everybody
reincarnates. For what it is worth, though, Jesus' brother James
makes a point of Elijah not being a special case, when he says,

> Elijah was a man just like us.   (James 5:7)

And, as I have shown, this is not the only evidence for reincarnation in the Bible, and the other passages do not refer to
special cases, but are universal in their nature. That it was quite
usual to believe in reincarnation in Jesus' day is shown by this
passage from John:

> As he went along he saw a man blind from birth. His disciples
> asked him, "Rabbi, who sinned, this man or his parents, that he
> was born blind?"   (John 9:1–2)

If the man was being punished for his own sin, and he was born
blind, his sin must have been from a previous life — obviously
Jesus' disciples were familiar with the idea of reincarnation,
and it was quite acceptable to talk about it. In this case, Jesus'
disciples assumed a belief in reincarnation, and Jesus did not
correct the assumption, even though he went on to shift the
focus away from who was to blame for the man's blindness, to
how his healing would demonstrate the glory of God.

The story of The Sheep and the Goats, told by Jesus, also
assumes a belief in reincarnation. I showed, in the last chapter,
that at the end of the story, where it says the wicked "…will go
away to eternal punishment, but the righteous to eternal life,"

the Greek word translated as "eternal" actually means "a long period." If the wicked are not punished forever, but only for a long period, it seems the righteous must not be rewarded forever either, but only for a similarly long period of time. If there were no reincarnation, then the question of what happens to the righteous after this limited period of reward is left begging: do they just disappear into nothingness? With reincarnation, this doesn't present a problem, as both the wicked and the righteous will eventually incarnate again, on the earth, or in the astral, until they finally "overcome," and become pillars in the temple of God, after which they will "go no more out," (Rev 3:12) but will be with God forever.

Finally, there are these two intriguing statements from the Bible which presume a belief in reincarnation:

> Naked I came from my mother's womb, and naked I shall return there.   (Job 1:21)

and,

> ...when Melchizedek met Abraham, Levi was still in the body of his ancestor.   (Hebrews 7:10)

Both of these are very obscure and strange references if you don't believe in reincarnation. How can a man return to his mother's womb if not through rebirth into another body? Apparently Job, in Old Testament times, believed in reincarnation. And, apart from reincarnation, how could anyone have ever been in the body of their ancestor? This could just supposedly be taken as an obscure reference to Levi's "seed" being still back with his line of descent, a number of generations before he was born. With reincarnation, though, it quite literally makes sense: in an earlier incarnation, Levi's soul was living in the body of one of the ancestors of his current body.

What adds weight to all this evidence in the Bible for reincarnation, is that there is not one shred of sustainable evidence against it. This is, of course, what you would expect, if the Bible is not to contradict itself. The one passage Christians have tried to use to prove there is no reincarnation is the verse from Hebrews:

> Just as man is destined to die once, and after that to face
> judgment,...   (Heb 9:27)

I have already shown, however, that, taken in context, the word "death" in this passage must be referring to a death to sin and worldliness, and that the passage then ties in perfectly with the concept of reincarnation. All that is achieved by insisting this verse refers to the physical death of the body is to put it into conflict with its context, and make it contradict the host of evidence for reincarnation from many parts of the Bible, including some from the same book of Hebrews.

Despite this Biblical evidence for reincarnation, I am not saying all Christians need necessarily believe in it. I would rather wish to suggest that great advantages would come to the church by acknowledging a Biblical basis for reincarnation, and allowing Christians to believe in it if they wish to. I believe Christianity would be enormously re-vitalized by a return to the acceptance of this belief, and the open-minded tolerance it would show. This would not be a totally novel position for the church, either. Not only did the church in general accept reincarnation during its first five centuries, but some modern churches have again embraced it. Examples include the Liberal Catholic Church, and Self-Realization Fellowship Church.[5] I believe they are the way of the future.

Before leaving the topic of Reincarnation, I would like to elaborate a little on how this alternate view of the afterlife fits in with the important Christian concept of salvation. Martin Luther suffered much mental agony as a result of the Catholic church's doctrine that confessions and good works are required to avoid everlasting punishment in hell. He was constantly worried about whether he had committed a sin since his last confession, and whether he had done sufficient works to justify his entrance into heaven if he should die in the near future. His revelation that salvation does not depend on works, but is by faith alone, obtained from reading Paul's letters, freed him from a tremendous burden. Unfortunately, his belief that he was completely helpless to save himself, and that his faith, and hence his salvation, was totally the work of God, led him, quite logically, to a belief in the predestination of a fixed elect. If we can't do anything to bring about our salvation, and assume only some people can be saved, then God must choose who is saved and who isn't. As we have seen, Luther initially hated the idea of a God who eternally punished helpless sinners, but, in time, he seems to have accepted it. Perhaps this acceptance of God's apparent harshness in dealing with people became the cause of some of his own later hardness — his support for the eradication of heresy, the persecution of the Anabaptists, and the burning of witches, for instance. His attitude seems to have been that if it was all right for God to burn sinners who didn't know any better, then it was all right for him to do it too.

I go one step further than Luther in suggesting that we are not justified by works *or* by faith, but simply by the fact that God made us. Everyone will be saved eventually, and there is no everlasting hell. *When* we are saved, though, depends on the faith and the good works we can, with God's help, demonstrate. After the novelty of exploring the physical plane of existence wears off, it rapidly becomes a hell for those who don't seek God's help to transcend it. Not until people acknowledge their own inadequacy, can God reach down and help them prepare to move to His heavenly realm. Such is the drama of salvation. And such is God's grace.

Chapter 17

A New Age of Miracles — the Power of Love

What does believing in miracles mean? Traditionally it has just meant believing that Jesus performed miracles, and that God performs them sometimes, often in response to the needs of believers, or as an answer to prayer. It is fashionable among "liberal" Christians not to believe in miracles. Many of them do not even believe Jesus literally performed any miracles. Rather, they propose the miracle stories have important symbolic meanings, and that certain teachings are couched in this form to emphasize their importance. These liberals certainly do not believe miracles occur in the modern world. They consider hoping for miracles is just opting out, and that humankind has the ability, and the responsibility, to solve its own problems, and should set about doing so.

In recent years, though, an extra dimension to the question of miracles has emerged. Quite a few Eastern holy men, such as yogis and fakirs, have performed miracles, right in front of the eyes of many onlookers, proving that miracles are possible. Fire walkers have walked many meters in their bare feet across beds of red-hot coals, and not been burned. Sadhu Haridas permitted himself to be buried alive in a tightly sealed container, with barely enough air for an hour or so, and emerged, with no ill effects, six weeks later. The Indian spiritual leader Sai Baba has materialized gems and jewelry out of thin air for so many hundreds of people, on so many different occasions, that it would be churlish to deny he has the ability to do so. And there are many other published accounts of holy men from the Hindu tradition performing miracles, some of them science-defying feats of healing reminiscent of Jesus. Some of these may be false accounts, but others have been witnessed by so many people that they can't reasonably be denied. The message from this is that miracles are not just the preserve of God and

Jesus: many other people can work them, and if so, perhaps we are all potentially capable of doing so. Jesus certainly expected people other than himself to perform miracles. Referring to his miracles, he said,

> I tell you the truth, anyone who has faith in me will do what I have been doing. He will do even greater things than these, because I am going to the Father.   (John 14:12)

This belief that "anyone who has faith" can perform miracles, certainly has a wide following these days. It is even possible to buy a set of self-study books called *A Course in Miracles*,[1] which has been around for some time now, and is highly regarded by many people. We will look into how and why it is possible for ordinary people to perform miracles a little later. For the moment, though, let's look at the miracles of Jesus, in the light of this proof that miracles do occur, and are even quite common.

Barbara Thiering, of Sydney University, has recently made some exciting interpretations of Jesus' miracles, based on research she has done into the Dead Sea Scrolls.[2] She claims the Gospels were written to have two levels of meaning, so they could be interpreted using the "pesher" technique which was used by the Essenes to read another level of reading into parts of the Old Testament. By this technique, general teachings in the surface level of a writing were seen as containing pointers to a detailed and specific "secret" history which could be read by those who had the special knowledge needed to interpret it. She claims this is why Jesus said,

> "The secret of the kingdom of God has been given to you. But to those on the outside everything is said in parables…" (Mark 4:11)

Dr Thiering's interpretation of the miracle of turning water into wine is a good example of her "pesher" method of reading the Gospels. John the Baptist had a claim to be the high priest, the "light," for he was of priestly birth. Jesus, being from the line of David, was not of priestly caste. Nevertheless, he declared, "I am the light of the world," (John 8:12) and put on the white vestments of the high priest. Thiering suggests that by this, as well as by many of his other teachings, Jesus was saying the Jewish priesthood was unnecessary, that he was a high priest, and that every lay person is a priest in the eyes of God. From the Dead Sea Scrolls, we know the Essenes gave water baptism to low-grade members such as women, married men and gentiles, but that new wine (non-alcoholic), as a communal sacred drink, was reserved for full members only — the celibate monks and priests.[3] There were two levels of initiation, symbolized by water for baptism, and wine for communion. With this special knowledge, it is possible to see that by turning water into wine, Jesus was underscoring his teaching that all are equal in the sight of God, and heralding in a new situation where all worshipers would be priests, and all could take communion.[4] This is much more significant than merely helping out the host at a wedding banquet by providing him with wine. Whether or not Jesus literally performed this miracle is secondary to its crucial symbolic significance. John's Gospel actually calls this miracle a "sign," the first of a series of seven signs in this gospel. A sign must be pointing to something, and this explanation shows what the sign of turning water into wine refers to. Thiering says the series of seven signs is a carefully constructed record of a series of changes made by Jesus to the rules of the Essene community he initially belonged to — a record of his reform of the way religion was practiced.[5]

Thiering claims all Jesus' miracles have crucial symbolic meanings, and that his teachings are often couched in miracle stories to emphasize their importance, and provide a "pesher" structure to them, whereby the general public, children in religious understanding, have supernatural stories and parables to interest them and moral teachings to edify them, but those with special knowledge can read an important level of facts from the same stories, about what really happened to Jesus and his disciples, and about his important but controversial teachings. The surface meaning is not invalid as teaching, but the hidden meaning contains the true history, and the deeper teaching. As a result of this theory, and in the liberal tradition, Dr Thiering

claims the miracles didn't really happen at all. She backs this up
by pointing out that it is only in the Gospels that Jesus' miracles are referred to, these spectacular feats not being mentioned
in the rest of the New Testament, nor by historians of the time,
such as Josephus. She also believes that the actual performance
of spectacular miracles runs counter to the humble, gentle,
long-suffering nature of Jesus revealed in the New Testament.

Many Christians are appalled at this conclusion of Dr
Thiering's. They believe the miracles actually took place, so
reject her symbolic explanations, as they evidently consider that
to accept them is also to accept her view that the miracles
themselves never took place. There seems to be the assumption
here that one must wholly accept either one position or the
other. However, I believe there is a compromise position which
can accommodate the important claims of those on both sides
of this argument, and which may just come close to the truth.
Thiering's interpretation of much of the New Testament may
be far-fetched, but her explanations of some of Jesus' miracles
do demonstrate how they symbolically underscore his teachings. As a result, these miracle stories could still be seen to
make excellent sense even if there never were any supernatural
miracles. Her explanations don't preclude the miracles having
taken place, though. She even says, herself, referring to the two
levels of meaning of the "pesharim" in the Gospels, that the
surface meaning remains valid, and is not negated by the
symbolic meaning.[6] In this case the actual performance of a
miracle would have illustrated the teaching it symbolized, and
its importance. Can you imagine how striking it would have
been to Jesus' followers to have seen water turned into top
quality wine, when he had been teaching them that the
priesthood, which they were very aware was symbolized by
wine, belonged to them as much as to the traditional priests?
This demonstration would have given authority to Jesus' teaching, and real hope to people that they could in fact change into
priests, just as the water, which symbolized their baptism, had
changed into the wine they wished they could partake of. And,
indeed, creating that change in perception in people's hearts

was the more important miracle, the primary thing Jesus set out to achieve. Compared with this, changing the chemical composition of a few water molecules was of minor consequence. Other people have been able to perform supernatural miracles, including Sai Baba, and others, in our day, and a number of people in Palestine in the century leading up to Jesus' ministry, and just after it, such as the hasidim ("devout ones") Honi the Circle Drawer, and Hanina-ben-Dosa.[7] What set Jesus apart is the powerful way he used miracles as signs to the authority of his teaching.

Such a use of miracles also answers Dr Thiering's objection that it would be out of character for Jesus to perform miracles, because of his humility, and willingness to suffer. By using miracles to underscore his teachings, he was not performing them for his own benefit. He was not using miracles to show off and say, "Hey, look at this: I am the Messiah." And the only other posible motive for Jesus performing miracles was compassion for people's suffering. There is certainly no record of him performing them for his own benefit, or even of him taking credit for them. He always gave the credit for what he did to God, or with his healings, to the faith of the person being healed.

Since miracles are nowadays so common, it certainly seems reasonable to suppose Jesus had the power to perform them, and that he used them in a wise and loving way, to show compassion, and add impact to his teachings. We shouldn't, however, reject Barbara Thiering's objective work in discovering certain symbolic meanings in the Gospels, just because she, personally, doesn't see the need for Jesus to have made supernatural displays, and thinks it would have been childish for him to have done so. And we don't have to accept all of her "pesher" history of Jesus' life in order to accept the validity of some of what she says about miracles. It is quite possible that some of what she says is right, but that many of her "pesher" interpretations (such as that Jesus was both married and divorced) have been forced on to parts of the Gospels which were never written to contain such a "secret history." She

herself says the Essenes forced "pesher" interpretations on Old
Testament passages which were never written to contain an
extra level of meaning.[8] So it is reasonable to suppose she
could be doing the same herself with the Gospels. Nevertheless,
some of her symbolic explanations do seem plausible, and do
add weight to the important teachings of Jesus — teachings
which have wrought the really important miracles: the changes
of heart, mind and lifestyle in so many people in his time, and
down through the ages to the present. These are teachings
which have been devalued and distorted by the church in the
past, and, as a result, need to be concentrated upon if there is
to be renewal in the church.

And we shouldn't be surprised at the discovery of such
symbolic meanings in the Gospels, for, as we have already seen,
it seems likely the Bible would not have survived medieval
times if its most spiritual and controversial teachings were
openly expressed. Foresight of the corruption of the church
may well have been a reason, along with the sensitive political
climate of the time, for many passages in the Bible being coded
in such a way that they could be superficially interpreted in a
worldly way, but would reveal their deep teaching and true
wisdom to genuine truth seekers. This structure of the Bible is
one of the most impressive things about it. Although it has led
certain people to point out many apparent inconsistencies in
the Bible, in reality it means the Bible is much more perfect
than it could ever have been if it had been more superficially
"correct." What use would the Bible have been to us if it had
not survived the middle ages intact?

Having established a framework within which it is possible
to tentatively accept both Dr Thiering's "pesher" reading of the
symbolic meaning of Jesus' miracles, and the likelihood that
most of the miracles really were performed as well, let's look at
some more of these fascinating interpretations. The fourth in
the series of seven signs in John's Gospel is the miracle of the
loaves and fishes, where the five thousand were fed. According
to Barbara Thiering, the story is about the first ordination of
Christian ministers. The loaves were Levites, assistant priests,

who traditionally helped in the temples and gave out the holy loaves. The Levites were members of a special tribe, born into this role, but Jesus was giving their power to ordinary lay people who didn't have this privileged birth. This allowing of ordinary married men to give out the sacred loaves at the communal meal was, in effect, an ordination of ministers. In this way the five loaves expanded into hundreds of loaves — hundreds of ordained ministers who were able to go out and spiritually feed the masses of people. The two fish were gentile monks, who gave their blessings to the "unclean" married men, who were then, in turn, able to go out and pass on the blessings to the masses. Gentile monks were called fish for two reasons. Firstly, as a play on the two Hebrew letters *daleth* and *gimel*. The letters of the alphabet had a symbolism to the Jews: gimel referred to the celibate, and daleth to the unclean or gentile, so together they referred to a gentile monk. When placed together, however, the two letters spelt *darg* which meant "fish." Secondly, they were baptized by being made to swim through salt water to a ship, which stood for Noah's ark. After they were hauled on board, the ship sailed up to a dock from which the baptized ascended on to the dry land of salvation. Straight after this story in John's Gospel, Jesus is said to have walked on water. This can also be explained as a part of the salvation rite. The priest who was to do the baptism had to get on to the boat, but, unlike the initiates, he wasn't required to swim to it. He walked out to it along a jetty. This probably led to a saying that a "priest walks on water." So by "walking on water," whether he was literally doing so, or whether he was just walking out on a jetty to baptize people, Jesus was claiming to be a priest, though not born of the priestly line. As with the loaves and fishes, and the turning of water into wine, Jesus was saying that ordinary lay people, not born into the priestly tribes, can be priests.[9] Together with Jesus saying a separate class of priests is unnecessary, these ceremonial illustrations of the teaching must have given it tremendous weight and authority, and established it as an absolutely central and vital part of Jesus' new way.

Understanding Essene traditions also casts an interesting light on the story of the raising of Lazarus, the last of the seven signs of John's Gospel. According to Thiering, joining an Essene monastic community was thought of as giving "life," and excommunication from it was thought of as "dying." So much was this so, that an excommunicated Essene was dressed in grave clothes and left in a burial cave for a few days, before being sent out into the world. In this context, "Raising from the dead" meant a person's excommunication being lifted, and their being allowed back into the community. Considering this, Jesus raising Lazarus from the dead could mean that he lifted Lazarus' excommunication from the Essene community, and invited him to become his disciple. If this were so, it could explain the consternation which was caused by the raising of Lazarus, a totally different reaction to that caused by his healing miracles.[10] It was at this point that the Pharisees and chief priests were said to have plotted to kill Jesus. In lifting an excommunication, Jesus would have committed an act of political defiance against the Essenes, which would have undermined their authority, and unsettled many of the most powerful Jews, as well as the Roman government of the province.

If Jesus planned to perform particular miracles to emphasize and symbolize certain teachings, then he imposed the "pesher" structure on the Gospels, rather than the Gospel writers having done it. The "pesher" structure of the Gospels then merely reflects the "pesher" nature of Jesus' ministry. The Gospel writers must, of course, have been aware of the symbolism of the miracles, in order to properly convey it, and this means they would have been able to use this "pesher" method themselves to emphasize, yet conceal, by couching in miracle stories, certain other important incidents such as the raising of Lazarus, and possibly the virgin birth, which didn't involve miracles in the first place. There would have needed to be a reason for doing this, though. With the raising of Lazarus, it could have been that persecution of early Christians arose from telling the political story of Jesus' lifting of an official excommunication, so it became necessary to convey it in the "pesher" way, as the story of the raising of a man who became sick and died, or not convey it at all. The times the first Christians lived in were certainly politically sensitive ones, so it would not be surprising if problems such as this arose.

Whether the story of the virgin birth is based on an actual physical miracle or not has long been the subject of speculation. Considering the modern evidence that supernatural miracles are possible, Mary being a virgin in the modern sense of the word when Jesus was conceived must remain a possibility, and arguably even a probability. After all, if you know these sorts of miracles are possible, and are often associated with spiritual leaders like Jesus, and if the Gospel records say there was a miracle, why question it? There are, however, at least two other possibilities which make sense of the situation, and are worth looking at. There is also an overriding symbolic signifi- cance to Mary being a "virgin," which is central to Christianity, and far outweighs any question of what sort of virgin she was.

Josephus described the marriage customs of the Essenes in some detail in his book *The Jewish War*. From this and from her understanding of the Dead Sea Scrolls, Barbara Thiering has constructed an explanation for the "virgin conception" of Jesus. Although the highest Essenes had no sex at all, certain members of their communities had to marry to continue family lines, and father the next generation. As a result, men from the second order did marry, and periodically left their monasteries to live with their wives. Women in such marriages had the status of nuns, and the name for a nun in the Hellenistic world was a "virgin" (as in the Roman Vestal Virgins). The word had the alternative meanings of a woman who was physically a virgin, or a dedicated woman. These marriages went through three stages. First was their vow of dedication, when they were physically virgin. Then, after a period, they were betrothed to their future husbands. During this time they were to stay apart as long as they could, as to the Essenes sex was sinful, and should be avoided for as long as possible. After such a long betrothal, there was a wedding, then sex began, if it hadn't already, along with a three-year trial marriage to determine whether the wife could bear children. If during the three years the wife became pregnant, and was still pregnant after three months, there was a second wedding, which marked the couples' commitment to stay together for life. Thiering says the situation surrounding Jesus' conception would have been something like this: Mary and Joseph were betrothed according to these rules of the Essenes, but during the betrothal period they came together prematurely. Mary conceived, and because she still legally had the status of a virgin, it could be said as a play on words that a virgin had conceived.[11]

Although this is a reasonably plausible and rational explanation of what might have happened, there are a couple of problems with it. The first is that although it explains how Mary might have been called a virgin when she conceived Jesus, it doesn't explain other details of the nativity story. Take this part of Matthew's account for instance:

> This is how the birth of Jesus Christ came about. His mother
> Mary was pledged to be married to Joseph, but before they came
> together, she was found to be with child through the Holy
> Spirit. Because Joseph her husband was a righteous man and did
> not want to expose her to public disgrace, he had in mind to
> divorce her quietly.   (Matt 1:18–19)

Contrary to Thiering's supposition, this directly says Mary and Joseph had not come together yet, and Joseph's reaction is certainly that of a man who knew he wasn't the father. Either Thiering is saying the Gospel accounts are just plain wrong, or she is saying this miracle story is a "pesher" like the other miracle stories, and that there is a specific history to be read from the nativity story, using her technique, which is significantly different from the surface appearance of the story. As far as I know, she hasn't published a "pesher" reading of the story of the virgin conception which goes beyond saying that Jesus' birth resulted from a perfectly natural and normal conception, and that the point of the "pesher" was merely to cover this up and make Jesus seem more God-like to the Greeks, who's mythology contains instances of gods being born as a result of virgin births. This would seem to be a very different, and a rather lame and pointless, use of the "pesher" technique, as previously discussed, and an unnecessary one. It would neither be an underscoring of a teaching (like the turning of the water into wine), nor an event which needed to be concealed to avoid persecution (like the Raising of Lazarus). Nor would it explain Joseph's knowing he wasn't the father. As a result, I can only conclude that the nativity story is either not written with a "pesher" structure, but is a straight-forward literal account of what happened, or that, if it is a "pesher," then there must be more to the true story than the merely normal conception Thiering suggests — something that could not have been told openly, for instance, and would need to have been held back from the general teaching for some good reason, such as to avoid the persecution which could have resulted from the political sensitivity of the true situation: something, for instance, like the situation behind the story of the raising of Lazarus.

Although I have no way of knowing whether it is actually the case, I can think of one scenario for the conception of Jesus which might not have been possible to talk about openly without attracting severe reprisals from Herod, and later from the Roman authorities, and which would have meant the story would have to have been conveyed in the "pesher" way, or not at all. For those who need to have a rational explanation, and can't accept the miraculous in this case, this seems to be the explanation which best fits the facts as they are known. The Jewish sacred books of the *Talmud* repeatedly impute that Jesus was the illegitimate son of a Roman soldier called Pantera, who is known to have existed.[12] John's Gospel also hints that there were Jews who accused Jesus of being illegitimate. It records that the Jewish elders protested to Jesus: "*We* are not illegitimate children." (John 8:41, italics mine) Someone then followed this with what appears to be a facetious aping of what he imagined Jesus may have said of himself: "The only father *we* have is God himself." (John 8:41, italics mine) The implication that Mary had an affair with a Roman soldier while betrothed to Joseph is, of course, insulting, and beneath contempt. Mary is certainly portrayed as an upright woman, and as a parent of an incarnation of God, responsible for his early education, must indeed have been. What would have been much more likely, if there is any truth in the Talmud's claim, and considering the sorts of violence which occur in countries subject to military conquest, is that Mary was a victim of rape in war. Palestine was conquered by the Romans in 63 B.C., and up until after Jesus was born, Judaea was governed by a puppet of Rome, King Herod, who closely collaborated with Rome and its army in military ventures, and often brutally put down Jewish nationalist insurrections. If this were the case, Mary would not have *chosen* to have any sexual relations at this time, so in a very real sense, in the moral sense, she would still have been a virgin, even though she had conceived a child. This would nicely explain Joseph's initial attitude of wanting to divorce Mary quietly, and his change of heart, after coming to realize, with the aid of a dream, that she was really not the slightest bit at fault, and that the soul of the child to be born, the real person, would be fathered through the Holy Spirit, and have nothing to do with the Roman soldier. And Mary, too, had such a dream. Jesus himself later conveyed this truth, in saying,

"Flesh gives birth to flesh, but the Spirit gives birth to Spirit"..."The Spirit gives life; the flesh counts for nothing." (John 3:6, 6:63)

This would be a very difficult situation for any parents, and, when you think about it, this is just about the only light parents could put on it in order to feel happy about keeping a child conceived in such circumstances. In this case Mary and Joseph would have adjusted to an awful situation in the best and most loving way possible, and shown for all time the miracle of how love can conquer even the worst of evils, and turn around even the most bitter circumstances.

This explanation would also nicely explain why the story of Jesus' conception needed to be told in a "pesher" way, as the story of a supernatural virgin conception. Any public claim that Mary had been raped by a Roman soldier would have invited

retribution against her and her family and friends. This
not have been the first time this crime had been comm
against Jews, and they would have been very aware of the fo
of angering the Romans with such accusations — they had to
live with the Roman presence. Yet her family and friends, and
later the Christians, would have been keen to assert her
innocence and purity, and so would have claimed that even
though she had conceived a child she was still a virgin. And
they would have got away with this, as it was not a specific
accusation against the Romans.

The question remains, though, of how God could have
been a party to such violence on the occasion of bringing His
son into the world. The only way to make sense of this would
be to realize that God is not responsible for the evil actions of
human beings: he has given us free will so we can choose
between good and bad actions. The very essence of the badness
in bad actions is that innocent people are hurt, so if God very
often intervened to prevent innocent people being hurt, he
would be preventing people with bad motives choosing to do
the wrong thing, and as a result there would be no consequences flowing from these actions which would help them
to change their motives for the better in the future. Having
given people free will, God doesn't make a mockery of it by
interfering with it. At first sight this system of God's might
seem rather flawed, with most of the benefit appearing to go to
those who do wrong. If, however, we consider that there is an
opportunity to overcome, even in the worst situations we face,
that if faced in the right way "there are no such things as
obstacles, only opportunities," and that through the trials of
life we learn to be strong, patient and forgiving, then we can
see the system is more balanced, and has more merit than we
might first have thought. And maybe the greatest benefits go to
those who need it most, rather than to those who behave best.
If we see God as a reformer of people, rather than a punisher
of sins, then this makes sense. I believe that if we knew enough
of God's ways we would realize that we do, in fact, live in the
best of all possible universes.

ough God can't much interfere to prevent
ithout eroding our free will, He can help by
rength to endure their hardships and grow
em. He can also help by compensating
.oving Him, are open to his gifts. And what
could God give a virtuous woman who loved Him,
and who had been terribly wronged in a crime of violence, than
the honor of being the mother of His divine son, who He was
sending into the world as a savior? How better could He have
turned her sorrow into joy? By doing this He would also have
reinforced, in the most emphatic way, the truth that innocent
victims of crimes are not defiled by them. If Mary was raped,
then she was no more defiled by it than Jesus was by being
crucified: in this case both were innocent victims of the most
terrible crimes of violence, and both overcame them through
their great power of love and forgiveness, and in the process
showed the world that even the worst crimes against the body
need have no power over the spirit.

Whether or not this is the truth behind the "virgin conception," it illustrates some important truths. One of these is that
in modern times, as in ancient ones, there can be no better way
of treating the victims of crimes than to consider they are not
defiled by them, even though they may be badly hurt by them,
and that this is true even to the extent that a virgin who is
raped and conceives a child should still be considered a virgin,
until such time as she chooses to have sex.

Irrespective of how one explains the virgin "birth" of Jesus,
its symbolic importance is the same, and, I believe, transcends
all divisiveness. It is this. In the Jewish world of Jesus' time, the
concept of "virgin birth" was well known and widespread, due
to its strong presence in Greek and Persian mythology.[13] What
a "virgin birth" signified in this mythology was the birth of the
spiritual man out of the animal man: a process of being born
again. In this rebirth the begetter was the spirit, not a human
father, and this was why it was called a "virgin" birth. It was a
spiritual transformation from a human to a divine state. The

writer of John's Gospel was aware of, and subscribed to, this concept of the "virgin birth" of people in general. He said,

> Yet to all who received him, to those who believed in his name, he gave the right to become children of God—children born not of natural descent, nor of human decision or a husband's will, but born of God. (John 1:12–13)

This is exactly the Greek concept of the virgin birth. No doubt the concept was widely understood at the time. In this context, the fact that Jesus' "virgin birth" corresponded with his actual physical birth, implied that he was already, at birth, a son of God, born of God. In this way, the virgin birth symbolizes that the birth of Jesus was a descent of God into human form. As John says, in the very next verse: "The word became flesh and lived for a while among us." (John 1:14) This is, of course, the central fact of Christianity. And, by being born of a virgin, Jesus highlighted, and drew attention to, this key fact—the fact that he did not become a child of God during his lifetime, as we through him have the right to do, but that he was already a child of God when he was born. This is the transcending symbolism of the virgin birth to Jesus' life.

There is also an inner symbolism to the virgin birth, applying to everyone, which a number of spiritual teachers have been advocating recently. Marianne Williamson, in *A Return To Love*, puts it beautifully:

> The meaning of Christmas is the birth of a new self, mothered by our humanness and fathered by God. Mary symbolizes the feminine within us all, who is impregnated by spirit. Her function is to say yes, I will, I receive, I will not abort this process, I accept with humility my holy function. The child born from this mystical conception is the Christ within us all.
>
> The angels awakened Mary in the middle of the night and told her to meet them on the roof. "The middle of the night" symbolizes our darkness, our confusion, our despair. "Come onto the roof" means turn off the television, sober up, read better books, meditate, and pray. The angels are the thoughts of God. We can only hear them in a pure mental atmosphere.

Most of us have heard the angels beckon us to the rooftop
already. Otherwise we would not be reading books like this one.
What happens at this point is that we are given the opportunity,
the challenge, to accept God's spirit, to allow His seed into
our mystical body...We shall, if we agree to, allow our hearts
to be a womb for the Christ child...

"There is no room here," said the innkeeper to Joseph. The
"inn" is our intellect. There is little if any room there for the
things of the spirit. But that doesn't matter because God doesn't
need it. All he needs is a little space in the manger, just a little
willingness on our part in order for Him to be born on earth.
There, "surrounded by animals," at one with our natural human
self, we give birth to the One who rules the universe.[14]

Having taken a brief look at the significance of some of
Jesus' miracles, I'd like to return to the phenomenon of miracles in our time, and to how more and more people are
appropriating the ability, that we all potentially have, to be
miracle workers. We have seen a number of times through our
discussion of Jesus' works that the greatest miracles of all
occurred when he was able to change people's attitudes from
fearful, restricting ones, to loving, hopeful ones. Even when he
healed, Jesus attributed the miracle to a loving and hopeful
state of mind — the faith of the healed person. In the modern
revival of miracle working, love, in the sense of reaching out to
be a part of the oneness of everything, is considered to be the
power behind miracles. *A Course in Miracles* says that miracles
occur spontaneously as outworkings of love.[15]

Marianne Williamson, writing about *A Course in Miracles*,
explains that miracles result from a change in attitude from fear
to love, and that this doesn't directly change things on a physical level, but, rather, solves problems by changing our consciousness of them.[16] In the early years of our childhood we
lived in love, and our lives were full of enchantment, but as we
grew older we learned to fear. We soon found out about
sickness, guilt, loneliness and anxiety, and learned that life was
about struggling to win, competing for a share of scarce
resources, achieving good grades, and making money. Getting

ahead became more important than love, and in the battle for success we learned that we are never quite good enough just as we are, and always have to strive to be better. In this state of mind we don't believe in miracles — they just seem to be imaginary mystical nonsense, even though they are only a shift in perception away from us.[17] Sadly, this shift in perception often has to wait till our lives are so ruled by fear that we are in despair, and can finally overcome our ego and ask God for help. Then we find that surrendering to God allows us to let go and just accept everyone and everything around us. We can then feel a part of everything — that we belong here in this universe, and that we can accept and love ourselves. In this state of loving acceptance we find happiness, even if our outer circumstances don't change.

This attitude of reaching out in love does begin to change even outer things, though. When we surrender our thoughts to God, and are willing to see things differently, God gives us back a new vision of unity which miraculously transforms our lives. The reason for this is that the outer, objective, story of our lives is just an illusion, a veil hiding the real world of consciousness in which God lives, and in which we are all one with Him. The outer life is, in reality, just a dream, and often a bad one. A miracle doesn't work by changing specific details of the dream, it works by waking us up, showing us it is a dream, and enabling us to influence the whole theme of its future unfolding (as we do while waking up from sleep in "lucid" dreaming). Once we find inner peace and oneness with all creation, our outer life becomes harmonious and prosperous too. As Jesus said in the Sermon on the Mount:

> "Do not worry about your life, what you will eat or drink; or about your body, what you will wear...your heavenly Father knows that you need [these things]. But seek first his kingdom, and his righteousness, and all these things will be given to you as well."
>
> (Matt 6:25,33)

If you ask God what He wants you to do, and see your joy in doing His will rather than your own, then miracles will start working in your life, as they did in Jesus'. It is a gradual process, though. You have to become purified by God—He has to work a miracle in you — before you can handle a great measure of His power. And your level of consciousness has to gradually grow. But if you let go of fear and start loving everyone, and do expect miracles, you will find that they will soon start happening. In this state of grace it is wise to not let your right hand know what your left is doing, for if you become egotistically attached to whatever ability to perform miracles you are given, you will soon lose that ability.

The willingness to forgive is a major attribute of a miracle worker. This willingness comes when we decide to think only loving thoughts, and forget all fearful, reproachful and hurtful ones.[18] You really have to "forgive and forget"; if you say you forgive but continue to dwell on a wrong done to you, then you judge the person who wronged you, and you haven't really forgiven him at all. The same is true in forgiving yourself for your past wrongdoing. If you let the hurts of the past go, as if they never existed, and refuse to be worried about the future, you will find unexpected depths of happiness within. Miracle workers live with God at the point where eternity meets time: in the present.

Above all, though, miracles are a function of our love and caring for people, and for the world we live in, for love is a reaching out for unity with others, and ultimately, with God. Miracles are manifestations of this love in action, and when there is love they happen automatically. Anyone can be a miracle worker, if they really want to love and give and grow in the service of God and their fellow human beings. *A Course in Miracles* says: "Child of God, you were created to create the good, the beautiful and the holy."[19] And Jesus said,

> I tell you the truth, anyone who has faith in me will do what I
> have been doing. He will do even greater things than these,
> because I am going to the Father.   (John 14:12)

We live in a new age of miracles, where love's power to work miracles is being increasingly recognized.

Chapter 18

One Shepherd, one Flock — Approaching
Other Religions

In its first three hundred years Christianity co-existed with a number of other religions, including Judaism, the Graeco-Roman polytheism, and the Alexandrian Egyptian religion. To some extent it both influenced these religions and was influenced by them. After becoming the state religion of the Roman Empire, though, Christianity became increasingly isolated from other religions. First it was isolated by its official status, and then, with the fall of the Roman Empire, by the dark ages. After this, for many hundreds of years, Christianity was confined to Western Europe by the superior culture and power of the Islamic empire. The Christian response was just to fight the Muslim enemy through crusades, and there was little understanding of their religion. The "Song of Roland" reveals the utter ignorance of Islam in the eleventh century: in it Muslims are portrayed as polytheistic pagans, worshiping three great idols called Mahmoud, Termagent and Apolyon,[1] where in fact, as is widely know today, Islam is the most monotheistic of all religions. The church's totally exclusive attitude at this time is summed up by the declaration of the Council of Florence in the fifteenth century, that:

> ...no one remaining outside the Catholic Church, not just pagans,
> but also Jews or heretics or schismatics, can become partakers
> of eternal life; but they will go to the everlasting fire which was
> prepared for the devil and his angels, unless before the end of
> life they are joined to the church.[2]

The Protestant missionary equivalent until recent times has been that there is no salvation outside Christianity, and many still hold to this view.

When Western Europe broke free of Muslim shackles and expanded by sea into the Americas and Asia, it took its narrow and exclusive Christianity with it. Missionary efforts, from then until now, have, with a few notable exceptions, ranged from the arrogant to the barbaric. A Franciscan friar, accompanying the Conquistadors to Peru, offered the defeated Incas the choice of being converted to Christianity or being killed. When their king refused to be converted, his hands were cut off, and the offer was repeated: "Be baptised and you will go to heaven." Again the king refused, saying, "If I went to heaven I might meet a second Christian like you."[3] Although there has been a lot less of this sort of violence in missionary effort in the last couple of centuries, it has still been characterized by arrogance. The exclusive assumption that there is no salvation outside Christianity stood behind nearly all missionary activity, right down to the present time.

Only in the twentieth century, when the failure of missionaries to make a significant impact on the Muslim, Buddhist and Hindu world has become obvious, have some Christians begun to question this exclusivism. Christianity has certainly been successful in displacing primitive animist religions in Africa, America and parts of Asia, but then so have the other main religions. Buddhism and Islam, in particular, have been strong missionary religions, and Hinduism, though it has never been a proselytizing religion, has spread its influence widely along India's trade routes. Places as far from India as Bali are Hindu to this day. What is more, in the twentieth century, Hindu emissaries to the U.S.A. and other Western countries have had an enormous impact, winning millions of admirers and followers from the educated and discerning elite of the West. Many Westerners have been attracted by these Hindu teachers because of their lack of arrogance, their love of Christ's teachings, and their desire to point out the fundamental similarities between Hinduism and Christianity, rather than dwelling on superficial differences. Swami Vivekananda and Paramahansa Yogananda come to mind as two of the greatest of these apostles of unity.

In terms of predominance, there is a "stalemate" between the four main world religions. All have made some inroads into the others, but all are still standing strongly, and don't even look like being displaced. It really does challenge the exclusive claims of any of them. Christians have to come to grips with the fact that their traditional missionary policy of "converting the pagan" just hasn't worked against the other main religions. Although about a quarter of the world's population is nominally Christian, and the number of Christians is slowly rising, the proportion of Christians in the world is actually declining, as the population rapidly grows.[4] Canon Max Warren, as General Secretary in London of the Church Missionary Society, summed the situation up nicely with this obituary for traditional mission policy:

> We have marched around alien Jerichos the requisite number of times. We have sounded the trumpets. And the walls have not collapsed.[5]

Karl Rahner points out that the continuing existence of other major religions after two thousand years of Christianity must be "the greatest scandal and the greatest vexation" Christianity has had to face.[6] If Christianity really is the absolute religion, intended for the salvation of all people, and no other religion can also fulfill this role, then surely it should by now be recognized as such by the world in general? At the very least it should be growing rather than shrinking.

An increasing number of liberal theologians are coming to explore the possibility that perhaps people from other religions can come to know God and partake in His salvation, and that perhaps the religions they are so faithful to might just be of some help in the process. Nevertheless, the church still comes out with statements, like the claim from the United Church of Canada's commission on faith, that "Without the particular knowledge of God in Jesus Christ, men do not really know God at all."[7] There is an increasing recognition of the arrogance of such claims, whether or not they are true. Wilfred Cantwell Smith points this out, and goes on to say,

...except at the cost of insensitivity or delinquence, it is morally not possible actually to go out into the world and say to devout, intelligent, fellow human beings: "We are saved and you are damned," or, "We believe that we know God, and we are right; you believe that you know God, and you are totally wrong."

This is intolerable from merely human standards. It is doubly so from Christian ones. Any position that antagonizes and alienates rather than reconciles, that is arrogant rather than humble, that promotes segregation rather than brotherhood, that is unlovely, is *ipso facto* un-Christian.[8]

And in fact, many missionaries, when they go out into the field, find this is the reality within which they work. I attended an Assemblies of God service where one of their missionaries from Asia was reporting on his work. To the congregation he spoke of the growth of his church and of the enormous need for Christianity in the country he was working in — just what they wanted to hear. Afterwards, however, when I spoke to him privately, I heard quite a different story. Recalling the opinion of my father, who had worked in South-East Asia for five years, that a person could be both a Buddhist and a Christian at the same time, I was determined to challenge this missionary, who worked in a Buddhist country, with the idea. To my considerable surprise, he absolutely agreed, and said he had partaken in many discussions with Buddhist monks, and had come to the conclusion that there wasn't much, if anything, in the central core of Buddhist teaching which he, as a Christian, couldn't go along with. In his view, the teachings and saving power of Jesus could be accepted by Buddhists without them needing to renounce their own religion. He said his dialogue with Buddhism started when a number of their monks came to call on him and greet him. Their politeness and gentleness impressed him, and he returned their visit. During the course of a number of these visits, both he and the Buddhist monks were able to learn a lot about each other's religions. The missionary said he greatly valued the good will and understanding this exchange had promoted. Of course, he couldn't have talked about this to the predominately fundamentalist congregations of the Assemblies of God churches he addressed, for they wouldn't have wanted to hear it, and his missionary work was funded by their financial support. He was supposed to be over there doing battle with the heathen, and rescuing souls from the evil embrace of Buddhism.

The conversations this missionary had with these Buddhist monks, and the friendships which grew up with them as a result, is the sort of dialogue that is beginning to occur in place of the traditional evangelizing which has so miserably failed, and something quite remarkable is happening through it. The knowledge gained from this dialogue is showing that other people's faith is not as different from our own as we were brought up to suppose. To demonstrate this, consider the prayers used by the faithful of the world's other main religions. Here is a part of a typical Jewish prayer:

> With great love have You loved us, O Lord our God, and with
> exceeding compassion have You pitied us. Our Father and King,
> our fathers trusted in You, and You taught them the laws of
> life: be gracious also to us, and teach us.[9]

Muslims worship God as the maker of heaven and earth, the sovereign Lord of the Universe, before whom all should bow in absolute submission. He is seen as all powerful, all holy, all wise, and all merciful. Here is a part of a Muslim prayer:

> Praise be to God, Lord of creation,
> Source of all livelihood, who orders the morning.
> Lord of majesty and honor, of grace and beneficence.
> He who is so far that he may not be seen
>   and so near that he witnesses the secret things.
> Blessed be He and for ever exalted.[10]

The large majority of Hindus who follow the *bhakti* or devotional approach worship God as the "ultimate Lord of all, infinite divine Life known under many aspects and names."[11] This is a typical Hindu hymn of praise:

> O save me, save me, Mightiest,
>   Save me and set me free.

O let the love that fills my breast
   Cling to thee lovingly.

Grant me to taste how sweet thou art;
   Grant me but this, I pray,
And never shall my love depart
   Or turn from thee away.

Then I thy name shall magnify
   And tell thy praise abroad,
For very love and gladness I
   Shall dance before my God.[12]

How similar these are to our own Christian prayers. The theologian John Hick has pointed out that:

When you visit the various non-Christian places of worship in one of our big cities you discover — possibly with a shock of surprise — that...the same kind of thing is taking place in them as in a Christian church. That is to say, human beings are coming together to open their minds to a higher reality, which is thought of as the personal creator and Lord of the universe, and as making vital moral demands upon the lives of men and women.[13]

Many Christians believe followers of other religions are not worshipping the same God they are, but these prayers, and this observation about their worship, certainly make it seem like they are worshipping the same God. How many Gods are there who are personal creators and Lords of the universe, and who reach down in mercy to redeem human beings? "Only one!" Christians are quick to answer, and Jews, Muslims and Hindus are in total agreement. Those of other religions must, then, be worshipping the same God as Christians do. The worst that can be said is that they have a wrong conception of this God, and worship Him incorrectly. Yet when we take the trouble to find out about their worship, and take into account the cultural differences, it seems so like Christian worship. And which Christian, this side of the grave, can claim to have such an accurate and complete conception of the infinite God, as to be able to judge the conceptions of other religions to be wrong, when there is so much overlap between their views and our own? John Hick's conclusion is that there must be:

> ...but one God, who is maker and lord of all; that in his infinite fullness and richness of being he exceeds all our human attempts to grasp him in thought; and that the devout in the various great world religions are in fact worshipping that one God, but through different, overlapping concepts or mental images of him.[14]

Dialogue with other religions is what brings Christians to this humble and unifying position. So important is this dialogue, that even such a relatively conservative theologian as Paul Tillich has been able to say that the emphasis of Christian interaction with other religions should be:

> ...not conversion, but dialogue. It would be a tremendous step forward if Christianity were to accept this![15]

One of the main qualities which the other world religions share with Christianity is diversity. Knowing this is a key to understanding them. Just as Christianity has many denominations and sects, so have Hinduism, Buddhism, Islam and Judaism. Many Christian sects border onto the idiot fringe, yet it would be unfair to judge Christianity as a whole by them. In the same way, it is unreasonable to judge other religions by their extreme manifestations. Yet Christians have so often done just this. They have observed groups of illiterate, superstitious, Hindus worshipping various stone images, and come to the conclusion that Hinduism is idolatrous and polytheistic. The reality is that the Hindu scriptures and enlightened Hindu practice have been monotheistic since the earliest times. We would wish our own religion to be judged by its best, rather than its most mediocre, or even its worst, manifestations. We should, consequently, do the same by other religions. In the first chapter of *The Religions of Man*, Huston Smith talks about why he has taken the approach in his book of letting "the best in each religion come through."[16] He says,

> This book is not a balanced view of its subject. The warning is important. I wince to think of the shock if the reader were to

close the chapter on Hinduism and step directly into the Hinduism described by Nehru as "a religion that enslaves you": her Kali Temple in Calcutta, the curse of her caste system, her two million cows revered to the point of nuisance, her fakirs deliberately offering their bodies as living sacrifices to bedbugs. Or what if he were to find himself in the streets of the leading city of Bali with one of its two movie houses named the Vishnu-Hollywood after the second god in the Hindu trinity and book-stores doing brisk business in KLASIK COMIKS in which Hindu gods and goddesses mow down hosts of unsightly demons with cosmic ray guns? I know the contrast. I feel it vividly between what I have written of Taoism and the Taoism that surrounded me during the years of my youth in China: its almost complete submergence in augury, necromancy, and superstition. It is like the contrast between the Silent Christ and the Grand Inquisitor, between the Sermon on the Mount and the wars of Christendom, between the stillness of Bethlehem and department stores blaring "Silent Night" in the rush of Christmas shopping. The full story of religion is not rose-colored. It is not all insight and inspiration. It is often crude; charity and wisdom are often rare, and the net expressions bizarre when not revolting. A balanced view of man's religions would record its perversions as well as its glories. It would include human sacrifice and scapegoating, fanaticism and persecution, the Christian Crusades and the holy wars of Islam. It would include witch hunts in Massachusetts, monkey trials in Tennessee, and snake worship in the Ozarks—the list would have no end.

...This is a book about values. Probably as much bad music as good has been written in the course of human history, but we do not ask that a course in music appreciation give it equal space. Time being limited, we expect no apology for spending it with the best. I have taken a similar position with regard to religion.[17]

Although one of my purposes in this book is to encourage reform in the Christian church, I believe other religions are clearly in as much need of reform as Christianity. One of the great advantages of dialogue between religions is that the best in any religion is often what overlaps with other religions—as it is the truth which has come from God—and dialogue high-lights this, in sharp contrast to the sham and worldliness religions carry around as excess baggage. Dialogue is an impetus to reform, enabling religions to judge themselves by each other, inspire each other, and reinforce in each other the truths they hold in common. The thing which impressed me, when I began to study Hinduism in some depth, is the extent of the underlying unity between the Hindu scriptures and the Bible, considering the enormous cultural differences. This struck me as being like two independent witnesses at a trial giving consistent testimonies about a crime, leading to an iron-clad conviction. For the first time, after this, I really believed what the Bible was saying.

After realizing, through open-minded investigation and dialogue, the similarities with other religions, both in worship and in concept of God, the huge problem many Christians face is over the question of salvation: it has been hard for Christians to let go of the idea that there is no salvation outside Christianity. Yet it has also become hard to believe that God could ignore, and let slide into damnation, all those people in other religions who piously and lovingly worship Him to the best of their ability, in ways which have been discovered to often be very similar to Christian worship. Most modern theologians have tried to resolve this dilemma by conceding that God's saving power must be universal, and extend to all human beings, whatever their religion, while still holding that Christianity plays a vital role in their salvation, whether they know it or not. This position is termed "Christian inclusivism" to distinguish it from the traditional exclusive approach. Bible passages have been found to show that those outside the Judeao-Christian tradition have been, and will be, saved. It has been noted that the covenant with Noah embraced all human beings, indeed all creation, and that psalmists and prophets of later times often referred to it. And it was not only the Jews who were delivered in an exodus. Through the prophet Amos, God declared,

> "Did I not bring Israel up from Egypt,
> the Philistines from Caphtor
> and the Arameans from Kir?" (Amos 9:7)

Isaiah said,

> In that day Israel will be the third, along with Egypt
> and Assyria, a blessing on the earth. The LORD
> Almighty will bless them, saying, "Blessed be Egypt
> my people, Assyria my handywork, and Israel my
> inheritance."   (Isaiah 19:24–25)

And through Malachi God said,

> "My name will be great among the nations, from the rising
> to the setting of the sun. In every place incense and pure
> offering will be brought to my name…But you profane
> it…"   (Malachi 1:11–12)

Perhaps Jesus was echoing this when he said to the centurion,

> "…many will come from the east and the west, and will take
> their places at the feast with Abraham, Isaac and Jacob in the
> kingdom of heaven. But the subjects of the kingdom will be
> thrown outside, into the darkness, where there will be
> weeping and gnashing of teeth."   (Matt 8:11–12)

Paul points out in Romans that God's nature is made known to
all people:

> …since what may be known about God is plain to them,
> because God has made it plain to them. For since the creation
> of the world God's invisible qualities — his eternal power and
> divine nature — have been clearly seen, being understood from
> what has been made, so that men are without any excuse.
>   (Romans 1:19–20)

Paul also makes it clear that those who do not have the "law"
can be saved without it:

> For it is not those who hear the law who are righteous in God's
> sight, but it is those who obey the law who will be declared
> righteous. (Indeed, when Gentiles, who do not have the law, do
> by nature things required by the law, they are a law for them-
> selves, even though they do not have the law, since they show
> that the requirements of the law are written on their hearts,
> their consciences also bearing witness, and their thoughts now
> accusing, now even defending them.)   (Romans 2:13–15)

Both Jesus and John the Baptist, likewise stressed that it is not what tradition people come from which is important, but the fruitfulness of their lives:

> "Produce fruit in keeping with repentance. And do not think you can say to yourselves, 'We have Abraham as our father'…The axe is already at the root of the trees, and every tree that does not produce good fruit will be cut down and thrown into the fire."
>
> (Matt 3:8–10)

So much for the doctrine that: "there is no salvation outside Christianity." It is one of the many Christian doctrines which are right out of step with the Bible.

The "inclusive" position that God's saving power extends to people of all religions, but that Christianity still occupies a prime and essential place in salvation, has led to some ingenious theories. There is the idea that people from other religions can be saved by their own "implicit" faith, whereas "explicit" faith is only possible in Christianity; that a "baptism of desire" (for God) can suffice if literal baptism is not available; and that the church is latent in other religions, but has only become manifest in Christianity. Then there is the suggestion that men can only come to God through Christ, but those who don't encounter him in this life will do so in the life to come. And there is Karl Rahner's notion that the faithful of other religions are "anonymous Christians." An approach closer to the old exclusivism is Karl Bath's notion that Christianity is not really a religion at all, but a revelation which judges and supersedes all religions. All these approaches are attempts to allow for the salvation of non-Christians, without fully abandoning the doctrine that only Christians can be saved. This reserving of a special place for Christianity seems, at the very least, to be rather contrived. John Hick has made a penetrating analysis of it in claiming the "inclusive" position is a transition state in which Christians are saying that devout non-Christians are really, in a metaphysical sense, Christians without knowing it.[18] He goes on to say that although the non-theologian might think this is double-talk, it is intended to be a charitable extension of grace to people who used to be seen as beyond the pale:

> ...a psychological bridge between the no longer acceptable older view and the new view which is emerging. But sooner or later we have to get off the bridge on to the other side. We have to make what might be called a Copernican revolution in our theology of Religions.
>   ...the old Ptolemaic astronomy held that the earth is the center of the solar system, and that all the other heavenly bodies revolve around it. And when it was realized that this theory did not fit the observed facts, particularly the wandering movements of the planets, epicycles were added, circles revolving on circles to complicate the theory and bring it nearer to the facts. By analogy the "no salvation outside Christianity" doctrine is theologically Ptolemaic. Christianity is seen as the center of the universe of faiths, and all other religions are regarded as revolving around it, and as being graded in value according to their distance from it. And the theories of implicit faith, baptism by desire, anonymous Christianity, the latent Church, the "ordinary" and "extraordinary" ways of salvation, and the claim that the Christian religion is not a religion whereas all the others are, are so many epicycles added to this Ptolemaic theology to try to accommodate our growing knowledge of other faiths and our awareness of the true piety and devotion which they sustain.[19]

He goes on to point out that this type of stand could be taken by any of the major religions, but that:

> ...it can only serve as an interim position whilst we prepare our minds for a Copernican revolution. Copernicus realized that it is the sun, and not the earth, that is at the center, and that all the heavenly bodies, including our own earth, revolve around it. And we have to realize that the universe of faiths centers on *God*, and not upon Christianity or upon any other religion. He is the sun, the originative source of light and life, whom all the religions reflect in their own different ways.[20]

This seems to be an enlightened and reasonable way of looking at the religions of the world. One apparent problem with it, though, is the highly exclusive claims most religions make — claims, indeed, which appear to lie at their very center of meaning. St Peter says of Christ that:

> Salvation is found in no-one else, for there is no other name under heaven given to men by which we must be saved.   (Acts 4:12)

And Jesus says of himself:

> "I am the way and the truth and the life. No-one comes to the Father except through me. If you really knew me, you would know my father as well."   (John 14:6–7)

In the Bhagavad Gita, Lord Krishna, similarly, says:

> "I am the goal of the wise, and I am the way." "I am the end of the path, the witness, the Lord, the sustainer."[21]

Can both Christ and Krishna be right? I believe they can, but not if each is considered to be a mere historical man. Christianity has had a tendency to see Jesus' saving power as being solely in the historical sacrifice of his human body on the cross at Calvary, and to see that saving power preserved only in the historical church, which is seen as being his mystical "body." This is rather an obtuse interpretation, which suits apologists for an "exclusive" or "inclusive" church, but is not well based on the Bible. The Bible, in fact, makes it clear that Jesus is an "incarnation" of the "Word," or "Christ," which has existed since before the world was made, and will never cease to exist. John's Gospel opens with the statements:

> In the beginning was the Word, and the Word was with God, and the Word was God. He was with God in the beginning.
> Through him all things were made; without him nothing was made that has been made. In him was life, and that life was the light of men.   (John 1:1–4)

and,

> The word became flesh and lived for a while among us. We have seen his glory, the glory of the one and only Son, who came from the Father, full of grace and truth.   (John 1:14)

At different times, Jesus refers both to this universal Christ nature, and to his limited human nature. When the rich young man referred to Jesus as "Good Teacher," Jesus replied,

> "Why do you call me good?" "No-one is good — except God
> alone."   (Mark 10:18)

He also said, "By myself I can do nothing." (John 5:30) By this he was pointing out that it was only by being a channel for God's spirit that he was able to do what he did. So totally was he able to be this channel, though, that God's nature *was* his nature, and he was able to say,

> "...learn and understand that the Father is in me, and
> I am in the Father," and,

> "...before Abraham was born I am!"   (John 10:38, 8:58)

Jesus' statement that, "I am the way and the truth and the life. No-one comes to the Father except through me," is another of these universal statements Jesus made about his Christ nature. It is possible, and indeed traditional, to put a limited interpretation on it and say it means you have to have heard of, and believe in Jesus the man to be saved, and as the Christian church, since Jesus' death, has been his "mystical body," no-one can come to God the Father except through Christianity. It is, however, also possible, and more reasonable, to give this statement the universal interpretation that whenever and wherever people come to God the Father, it is through the one and the same power and wisdom that is incarnate in Jesus, and that there is no other way for this to be achieved. This interpretation receives support from St Paul, in his letter to the Corinthians. Referring to Christ universally as "the power of God and the wisdom of God" (1 Cor 1:24), he says,

> ...our forefathers were all under the cloud and...they all
> passed through the sea. They were all baptized into Moses in
> the cloud and in the sea. They all ate the same spiritual food,
> and drank the same spiritual drink; for they drank from the
> spiritual rock that accompanied them, and that rock was Christ.
>   (1 Cor 10:1–4)

The Israelites of Moses' time had not heard of Jesus, they plainly didn't belong to the Christian church, and Jesus had not yet died for the sins of the world, yet Christ was the "spiritual rock" from which they drank. Consequently it must also be possible for people in other religions, who likewise are outside the Christian tradition, to drink from this "spiritual rock" and receive their salvation through Christ. And to do so they need not have heard of Jesus, nor need they even know that the power through which, by grace, they come to God, was incarnate at some time as Jesus of Nazareth. All they need to do is love God, love their neighbors as themselves, and drink of that spiritual rock, the spring of living water which is Christ, which can be known by all people simply by them turning their consciousness inward, away from the world, to the "kingdom of heaven" which "is within." There they will be guided by the "spirit of truth" which Christ asks God to send in place of his physical presence (John 14: 16–17). So the universal Christ is not just the prerogative of Christianity; he is at the center of all religions, though they may have different names for their experience of him.

It is also not unreasonable to suppose that this universal Christ could incarnate as a human being more than once, and that Lord Krishna, for instance, could have, as the Hindu's claim, been such an incarnation. Christianity quotes the Bible as saying Jesus is the "one and only Son" or "Only Begotten" of God, but forgets that Christ was this "Only Begotten" of God from before the beginning of time, long before he incarnated as Jesus, and nowhere does the Bible claim Jesus was the only incarnation of the only Son of God. Jesus never referred to his "second coming" (which would have implied he was in his first), it is only others who have done so; Jesus rather referred to himself "coming again," and gave a strong hint that he had already, or would in future, manifest to people of other religious traditions when he said,

> "I have other sheep that are not of this fold. I must bring them also. They too will hear my voice, and there shall be one flock and one shepherd."   (John 10:16 AT)

Hinduism, which has never been as exclusive as Christianity, accepts the fact that there have been, and will be, multiple incarnations of God, and welcomes the truth revealed by all of them. They call such an incarnation an *avatar*, which means "a descent of God to earth in the form of a human being," precisely the Christian conception of what Jesus was. The Hindu theory is that in times of spiritual decay, an avatar is born to relight the spiritual flame in people's hearts, and show them the way to God. In the Bhagavad Gita, Lord Krishna says:

> When Goodness grows weak,
> When evil increases,
> I make myself a body.
>
> In every age I come back
> To deliver the holy,
> To destroy the sin of the sinner,
> To establish righteousness.[22]

By living example, such an Incarnation shows humankind how to be perfect, even as the Father in heaven is perfect. In doing this the avatar really does become "the way and the truth and the life." The "Word" manifesting as the Holy Spirit can also show this way and truth and life, but amongst men, only an avatar can do so. Each avatar is a different soul, and comes in a different body, but each is an Incarnation of the same Spirit, which is the Word, the Only Begotten of God. As Swami Prabhavananda puts it in *The Sermon of the Mount according to Vedanta*:

> He who came as Sri Krishna, and as Buddha, came again as Christ, and as other avatars; he merely chose a different dress. To suit the particular needs of successive ages, with each coming, God reveals a new and characteristic presentation of the eternal truth of religion.[23]

The birth of an avatar is radically different from the birth of an ordinary person. As Jesus said,

> "You are from below; I am from above. You are of this world;
> I am not of this world."   (John 8:23)

The Hindu view is that ordinary souls are born as a consequence of their karma, but that an avatar has become perfect, and no longer has any need to incarnate on the physical plane. He chooses to do so out of compassion for humanity, and love of serving God. A twentieth-century avatar, Paramahansa Yogananda, explains his mission well in this passage from his poem "God's Boatman":

> I want to ply my boat, many times,
> Across the gulf-after-death,
> And return to earth's shores
> From my home in heaven.
> I want to load my boat
> With those waiting, thirsty ones
> Who are left behind,
> And carry them by the opal pool
> Of iridescent joy
> Where my Father distributes
> His all-desire-quenching liquid peace.
>
> Oh, I will come again and again!
> Crossing a million crags of suffering,
> With bleeding feet, I will come—
> If need be, a trillion times—
> So long as I know
> One stray brother is left behind.[24]

Although not strictly necessary for everyone, the blessings and teachings of the avatars are of an immense help to people who are striving Godward. As Lord Krishna says in the Bhagavad Gita:

> He who knows the nature
> Of my task and my holy birth
> Is not reborn
> When he leaves this body:
> He comes to me.[25]

This is similar to these words about Jesus in John's Gospel:

> Yet to all who received him, to those who believed in his name,
> he gave the right to become children of God—children born not

of natural descent, not of human decision or a husband's will,
but born of God.   (John 1:12–13)

The fact that both Christianity and Hinduism are centered
around the knowledge that God can, and has, incarnated in
human form to bring salvation to humankind, makes them very
much sister religions. It also makes it very sad that there is so
much misunderstanding between them, when they are essentially so similar. There is, however, a growing realization of the
basic oneness of Christianity and Hinduism among enlightened
theologians and teachers in both religions. Perhaps the time is
not far away when Jesus' vision of unity among the world's
religions will come to pass, when there really *shall* be "one
flock and one shepherd." (John 10:16) There are already a
number of world-wide religious movements which combine the
essential truths of Hinduism and Christianity. The Theoso-
phical Society, founded by Westerners who went to India, and
the Vedanta Society and Self-Realization Fellowship, both
founded by Indians who went to live in America, are some
examples of highly successful religious organizations based on
this premise. The "Aims and Ideals" of Self-Realization Fellowship, founded by Paramahansa Yogananda, clearly illustrate this
approach. Some of these aims are:

> To reveal the complete harmony and basic oneness of original
> Christianity as taught by Jesus Christ and original Yoga as taught
> by Bhagavan Krishna; and to show that these principles of truth
> are the common scientific foundation of all true religions.

> To point out the one divine highway to which all paths of
> true religious beliefs eventually lead: the highway of daily,
> scientific, devotional meditation on God.

> To encourage "plain living and high thinking"; and to spread a
> spirit of brotherhood among all peoples by teaching the eternal
> basis of their unity: kinship with God.

> To unite science and religion through realization of the unity
> of their underlying principles.

> To advocate cultural and spiritual understanding between East
> and West, and the exchange of their finest distinctive features.

To serve mankind as one's larger Self.[26]

A detailed comparison of Hindu and Christian Scriptures is beyond the scope of this chapter, but, in addition to those already remarked upon, I will mention just two more notable comparisons. John's Gospel begins with:

> In the beginning was the Word, and the Word was with God, and the Word was God.   (John 1:1)

The Vedas, the most ancient Scriptures in the world, put it with uncanny similarity:

> In the beginning was the Lord of Creatures; second to him was the Word...The Word was verily Brahman.[27]

The other comparison is of creation accounts. The Bible begins with the words:

> In the beginning God created the heavens and the earth. Now the earth was formless and empty, and darkness was hovering over the waters.
> And God said, "Let there be light," and there was light. God saw that the light was good...   (Genesis 1:1–2)

The "Creation Hymn" from the Rig Veda uses some similar images:

> Before the creation of this universe,
> There was neither being nor not-being,
> Neither sky nor the heavens beyond...
> There was only water unfathomably deep.
>
> There was neither death nor immortality,
> Nor demarcation between night and day,
> That One alone breathed in its own bliss,
> And by its own power, in spite of the absolute vacuum.
> Nothing else was there.
>
> In the beginning there was darkness everywhere,
> Enveloping the waters.
> All that existed was void and formless.
> Then, by the power of thought alone,
> That One gave birth to itself.

The first born was the Creative Energy,
The primordial seed of the mind.
It is through this energy that seers,
After long searching in the inmost chambers of their hearts,
Discovered the Supreme Spirit
Which joins the seen with the unseen.

This self-shining Spirit was everywhere,
In and through the universe; above and below it.
Primal seeds were sprouting, mighty forces moving,
Pulsation below, pure energy above.

Who here knows? Who can say for sure?
When it began and from where it came — this creation?...
He who watches everything from the highest heaven,
Only He knows — or perhaps even He does not know![28]

It almost seems as if the Genesis account is a terse summary of the Vedic hymn. Could this, perhaps, be its origin?

Both Western and Indian scholarship long considered the composers of the Vedas to be ritualistic worshipers of many gods, and claimed that monotheism didn't strongly emerge in Hinduism until the time the Upanishads were composed, at about 500 B.C. Modern scholarship has now challenged this, and shown that the Vedas are consistently monotheistic, right back to the most ancient times. What were once thought to be polytheistic gods, have been shown to be either names for God, or personifications of forces of nature. This verse from the Rig Veda is one of many which demonstrate this:

Seers call that One Supreme Reality, our Sovereign Guide,
by various names — such as, Indra, Mitra, Varuna, Agni,
Garutman the heavenly bird of beauteous plumage, Yama
and Matarishwan. (I–164–46)[29]

The differences between Hinduism and Christianity are only in the cultural veneer, and in doctrines of each which are not properly based on their Scriptures. Beneath this, at the level of the real meaning of the Scriptures, there is a close identity. And although the Christian Scriptures may not be quite so close to the Scriptures of religions other than Hinduism, there still are many areas of overlap, and it still is clear that all the main religions of the world are sincerely worshipping the same God, and in much the same way. There may be substantial differences between religions on the worldly level, but finally, in God, all religions meet.

It is going to take a lot of goodwill and energy to resolve the differences between religions, and for men and women of different religions to learn to respect and honor each other. It is important this happen, though, for, on an increasingly small planet, it is no longer possible for us to properly love our neighbor without doing so. It is the inevitable way of the future, and the sooner the faithful of all religions embark on the spiritual voyage of learning to respect, honor and love those of other faiths, the sooner they will convince the non-religious of the world that knowing God is something worth striving for. We are, after all, known by our fruits, and the spectacle of religions fighting each other reflects poorly on religion in general. Christian exclusivism is certainly one of the main objections discerning people in the West have to Christianity.

Rudyard Kipling's oft-quoted poem, "The Ballad of East and West," points out what is, at the core, the only real difference between Christianity and other religions, and the importance of dialogue in resolving it:

> Oh, East is East and West is West, and never the
>   twain shall meet,
> Till Earth and Sky stand presently at God's great
>   judgment seat;
> But there is neither East nor West, Border nor
>   Breed nor Birth,
> When two strong men stand face to face,
>   though they come from the ends of the earth.

Are we strong enough to "stand face to face" with Eastern religions and befriend them? Can Christians be involved in what the Benedictine Father Bede Griffiths called "The Marriage of East and West?"[30] I hope we can, for this marriage is inevitable, and the future strength of the Christian church may well depend on it being a willing partner in it.

Chapter 19

The End of Worldliness, and the Return of Jesus

Many Christians have the attitude that the world is going to rack and ruin. It's no longer safe to walk the streets. Crime is ten times as bad as it was in the good old days. The world is destined to terrible destruction in the next few years. Even apparently good trends like communism's retreat from Europe are just the devil deceiving us into thinking things are going well so he can complete his final death blow to the world. Only God-fearing Christians will be plucked from the flames in the last days. Most of the world's people are about to die agonizing deaths, then go to hell for an eternity of torment. This will happen very soon now, when Jesus returns to "rapture" Christians who believe in the literal truth of the Bible, and cast the rest of the world into "tribulation." All this is predicted in the Bible books of Matthew and Revelation. And they're telling you all this so you can turn to Jesus and be saved.

The evangelical film industry strongly pushes this line, using fear to convert people. The executive producer of one of its films, *A Thief in the Night*, estimated that this film which cost only $68,000 to make led to a harvest of over four million conversions, and made many millions of dollars in revenues. The film is a graphic portrayal of the world in tribulation after true Christians have been "raptured" (taken from the planet), and centers on the anguish of a woman called Patty who considers herself a Christian, but goes to a church whose minister is a theological liberal who refuses to interpret the Bible literally. Because of this she is left behind at the rapture while her husband, a "true" Christian, is taken by Jesus. The makers of this film have said that it works best when followed by an "altar call" or an invitation to conversion.[1]

The attitude exemplified by this movie, which has many variations, is a direct result of Christian exclusiveness combined with an "eschatology," or "end-time teaching," based on a particular, very literal, interpretation of chapter 24 of Matthew and the book of Revelation. In every century, from a few years after Jesus died to the present, there have been Christians who have thought this way, and were convinced that Jesus was coming back in their lifetime, and the world was about to end. Some admitted they didn't know the day or the hour, just that it would be soon. Others confidently predicted the year of Jesus' return, and some even the exact day. But on thousands of occasions, over twenty centuries, these predictions have been wrong. Yet, despite this, many Christians still believe the end of the world is coming soon. A few years ago, a book was published with a title along the lines of, "1,988 Reasons Why Jesus is Coming Back in 1988." When Jesus failed to come back in that year, a rather cruel cartoon proposed a new edition of the book to be called, "1,989 Reasons Why Jesus is coming back in 1989," with the 1,989th reason being that he didn't come back in 1988.[2] This is a fairly accurate reflection of the state of end-time teaching.

The belief that the world is ending soon is particularly prevalent among Pentecostal and evangelical Christians. Yet not all evangelicals and Pentecostals subscribe to this end-time teaching, and some have even pointed out its dangers. Arden Burrell, a prominent pastor and administrator in the Pentecostal Assemblies of God church in Australia, has pointed out one of the main problems with such teachings. His warning to the church was, "Your eschatology is defeating you." He explained this by saying that the belief that Jesus is coming back within a few years was causing people to put both their temporal and spiritual lives on hold. They were not making proper plans and provision for their future, or their children's future, nor were they making an effort in their spiritual lives to do the will of God, and grow in God's strength. Instead they were using the supposed imminent return of Jesus as an excuse for carelessness and laziness. I remember the ambivalent feelings of one intelligent teenager in that church regarding the return of Jesus: of course she looked forward to Jesus coming, but she hoped he would come later rather that sooner, so she and the children she hoped to have could enjoy their lives first. I felt this was a very healthy attitude, nevertheless, it highlighted one of the chief problems with end-time teachings, which is that only one generation of human beings can both be present at its fulfillment, and not miss out on the chance of a reasonably full life on earth. And this, of course, explains why some people in each generation of Christians think Jesus will return in their lifetime, and usually toward the middle or end of it. There is the rather selfish wish that they be privileged over all generations, quite in addition to being a part of the small elect which is saved, while the vast masses of humanity are sent to burn forever in hell.

This selfish and exclusive attitude doesn't impress discriminating people, and only helps bring the church into disrepute. The damage being caused to the church, combined with the repeated failures of end-time predictions to eventuate, must surely lead many Christians to look at the books of Matthew and Revelation again, in an objective way, to see whether there is not a more universal significance to these so called "end-time" teachings, which every generation of Christians could participate in. Martin Luther dismissed the book of Revelation as irrelevant to Christian life and theology, and urged that it be excluded from the canon of Scripture.[3] While I agree with Luther about the need for relevance, I disagree, of course, with his proposal to remove the book of Revelation from the Bible. We can't just exclude books from the Bible because we don't like them, or can't make sense of them. In any event, I believe Revelation can, and should, be interpreted in a way which is relevant to Christian life. Indeed, I believe it can be read as an allegory of the joys, struggles and triumphs of living the spiritual life. In this chapter I am going to look into and discuss this interpretation. I am not claiming it is the only true interpretation, the last word on the subject. Rather, I hope it will suggest some new directions which can be followed up by others. Discovering a universal symbolic significance in writings of such vision as these does not necessarily deny the eventual literal truth of what certain parts of them are saying, but if it allows each generation of Christians to see its relevance to themselves, even though they are not living in the literal end-times, then I believe it is worthwhile. I believe all the New Testament teachings were meant to be universally significant to all Christians, and, indeed, to all seekers after God, whatever their religion, even though certain parts of them need to be interpreted in the light of their historical context and purpose.

The book of Revelation was written in about 90-95 A.D., for the edification of Christians who had been waiting sixty years in eager anticipation of Jesus' return to earth, and whose faith, in many cases, must have been beginning to wane. It was an encouragement for them to stand firm, and an inspiration for their faith — a book of eternal, timeless realities. Pat Alexander points out in *The Lion Handbook to the Bible* that the book of Revelation is apocalyptic literature, visionary and poetic, making frequent use of imagery and symbols, and that to take it literally is to go against its whole spirit.[4]

A knowledge of the numerology of the time is also important in understanding Revelation. A part of the reason for ascribing symbolic importance to certain numbers was that the ancient languages of the Bible had no separate numerals, and letters of the alphabet doubled as numerals. These letters themselves had meanings, so to ascribe meanings to the numbers represented by them was a natural progression. Revelation's author (traditionally considered to be John the Evangelist) makes much use of the number seven, which often stands for completeness and perfection. So the "seven spirits" (Rev 1:4) refers to the Holy Spirit, with seven meaning "holy," quite apart from its meaning as a number.[5] Later I will show how "4," "6," "12," "666" and "1000" also have meanings as adjectives, rather than, or in addition to, their meanings as numbers.

Before we can even start to interpret Revelation, though, we have to understand why many early Christians believed Jesus was coming back within their lifetime. The reason lies in what Jesus himself said, in Chapter 24 of Matthew's Gospel.

On leaving the temple one day, Jesus was approached by his disciples, who called his attention to its buildings. This prompted Jesus to remark, in prediction of the destruction of Jerusalem in 70 A.D., that "not one stone here will be left on another; every one will be thrown down." (Matt 24:2) Later, on the Mount of Olives, the disciples came to him privately and asked him to elaborate on his prediction:

"Tell us," they said, "when will this happen, and what will be the sign of your coming and of the end of the age."   (Matt 24:3)

In reply Jesus gave his disciples some detailed predictions of the future, and the difficulties they would face in it, before he came back to them. Some of his predictions of travail could apply to just about any time in the earth's history, so people from all centuries have thought it applied to their own times. These include:

"Nation will rise against nation, and kingdom against kingdom. There will be famines and earthquakes..."   (Matt 24:7)

"Then you will be handed over to be persecuted and put to death, and you will be hated by all nations because of me." (Matt 24:9)

and,

"Because of the increase of wickedness, the love of most will grow cold, but he who stands firm to the end will be saved. And this gospel of the kingdom will be preached in the whole world as a testimony to all nations, and then the end will come."   (Matt 24:12–14)

It must, however, be remembered that Jesus was being asked to elaborate on his prediction of the destruction of the temple, and that he was addressing his disciples with predictions of what they, personally, would experience during their lifetimes, and warning them against being deceived by certain events. To make doubly sure he was not misunderstood, Jesus completed his prophecy with these words:

"I tell you the truth, this generation will certainly not pass away until all these things have happened."   (Matt 24:34)

Despite the clarity of this statement, some Bibles footnote the word "generation" with "Or race," presumably to leave open the interpretation that all these things Jesus saw could be applied to much later times, even our own. The reason why Christians want to interpret the word "generation" as "race" is that one of the predictions Jesus made of this time, that would "certainly" happen before "this generation" passed away, was that he would return "with power and great glory." (Matt 24:30) Since Jesus apparently did not come back in that generation, it is presumed that by "generation" Jesus must have meant "race." It is, however, a big step, fraught with danger, to assume Jesus meant something different from what he actually said. Nor could this be a translation problem, as the Greek word used, *genea*, properly means generation, is derived from a word meaning "kin," and is the root of the English words "generation" and "genealogy." By implication it can also mean an "age," a "nation" or a "time," but a "race" is not mentioned by Greek dictionaries as an implied meaning.[6] This is, presumably, why translators feel constrained to retain the translation of "generation," even though they would like it to mean "race." Another reason is that Jesus said the same thing in a slightly different way on another occasion:

> "...the Son of Man is going to come in his Father's glory with his angels, and then he will reward each person according to what he has done. I tell you the truth, some who are standing here will not taste death before they see the Son of Man coming in his kingdom."   (Matt 16:27–28)

This confirms Jesus really was predicting he would come back while at least some of the current generation of people were still alive. And this is, of course, why the early Christians, to whom the book of Revelation was addressed, were so convinced Jesus would return in their lifetime. Do we have to admit, then, that this prediction of Jesus' was wrong? I don't think so. I believe Jesus really did come back in that generation, and has been coming back to every generation since then, but that most people did not, and do not, recognize his presence. Most people were expecting Jesus to return in a physical body, albeit a glorious one, which could be seen with their everyday eyes, but it was not to be like that. When Jesus explained that the kingdom of God is not a physical place somewhere out there, but is intuitively perceived and experienced "within" ourselves, he put it in these words:

> "The kingdom of God does not come visibly, nor will people
> say, 'Here it is,' or 'There it is,' because the kingdom of God
> is within you."   (Luke 17: 20–21)

Speaking of his return, in Matthew 24, Jesus made a similar use of the words "Here" and "There," suggesting a like meaning:

> "So if anyone tells you, 'There he is, out in the desert,' do not
> go out; or, 'Here he is, in the inner rooms,' do not believe it.
> For as the lightning comes from the east and flashes to the west,
> so will be the coming of the Son of Man."   (Matt 24:26–27)

The image of the lightning flashing from the east to the west speaks of omnipresence, of being all places at once: it is symbolic of a powerful spiritual presence. It is like Jesus' image of those born of the Spirit:

> "The wind blows wherever it pleases. You hear its sound, but
> you cannot tell where it comes from or where it is going. So
> it is with everyone born of the Spirit."   (John 3:8)

And, indeed, this is the key to what Jesus meant by his return. He meant he would be born again in the hearts and consciousness of those who have been born of the Spirit, and that his powerful and glorious presence would be with them. Seeing something "in the clouds of the sky" is an image of spiritual perception, and the "trumpet call" is an image of the interiorly heard sound of the "Amen" (or the "Om," of Hinduism), the "sound of rushing waters" (Rev 1:15), the roar of the universe, heard by those who have been born again of the Spirit. This is why Jesus said,

> "They will see the Son of Man coming on the clouds of the sky,
> with power and great glory. And he will send his angels with a loud
> trumpet call, and they will gather his elect from the four winds,

from one end of the heavens to the other."   (Matt 24:30–31)

So when Jesus said, "some who are standing here will not taste death before they see the Son of Man coming in his kingdom," (Matt 16:28) he meant that in their current lifetime, some of those in his presence would be born again in Spirit, and would see him come "IN HIS KINGDOM." And which kingdom is this? It is the kingdom of God, for, as is explained many times in the Bible, Jesus is heir to this kingdom, and we are co-heirs with him (e.g. Romans 8:17). And where is the kingdom of God? It is "WITHIN YOU"—and that is precisely where Jesus returns. All these references to the kingdom of God and Jesus' return are consistent with each other, and within themselves, when seen in this light. When people are born again of the Spirit, they become God's elect, those who have chosen Him rather than the worldly egotistical way of living, and so Jesus said that when he comes with his angels, they will gather his elect from "the four winds," that is from all corners of the earth, and from "one end of the heavens to the other"—from all planets in the universe where there is sentient life. And Jesus and his angels will continue to gather his elect in every generation, when people come to God, and are born again of the Spirit.

Jesus was asked two questions by his disciples: one was about the destruction of the temple, and the other was about the sign of his coming and the end of the age. So he talked about the destruction and anguish which was in store for Jerusalem, and the spreading of his gospel around the world (which was probably referring to just the known, or "civilized," world, the Greek *oikoumene*, extending from the Mediterranean area through to India[7]). Both of these things did, in fact, happen within the lifetime of his disciples. And he also talked about how he would come again into the lives of many of them. What is more, his two answers are associated, for the destruction of Jerusalem was a fitting image for the destruction of worldliness which must occur in people's lives before they can be born again of the Spirit. So the "end of the world" means two things in Matthew and Revelation: the destruction of Jerusalem and

Israel, the end of their nation and world as they knew it, and
the end of worldliness in those born again of the Spirit. Jesus
predicted the anguish would be great leading up to both of
these great endings. Certainly the sacking of Jerusalem was to
be devastating, but also, as those who have been born again
spiritually know, there is no greater anguish than the falling
apart of our little worldly empires — our realization that we
cannot cope on our own — which precedes giving our lives to
God.

This is a profoundly different way of looking at "end-time"
teachings, but it is one which makes sense of it all, explains
why the world hasn't physically come to an end, and involves
every generation of people equally, as the "end-time" of the
worldliness of those ready to surrender to God approaches,
and they are born again of the Spirit and become a part of
God's elite. This is not to say the world will not end one day; it
must end at some time, and if not before, it will happen in
about seven billion years time when the sun heats up to the
point where life on earth cannot be sustained. Seeing the basic
meaning of these Scriptures, though, and understanding its
symbolism, enables us to focus on the true end of this world for
us, as we give our life to God: the end times of our lives here
on earth, and the end of our association with the world's ways.

The Book of Revelation can be much better understood if
we approach it with this view of the "end times." It was written
to inspire the lagging faith of those who were patiently waiting
for Jesus to return, by giving them a vision of just how Jesus
comes back to those who truly give their lives to God, and
showing them some of the wonderful things that are in store
for them. John was a man who meditated deeply on God, and
was given a vision to pass on to the early churches:

> On the Lord's day I was in the Spirit, and I heard behind me a
> loud voice like a trumpet, which said: "Write on a scroll what
> you see and send it to the seven churches..."   (Rev 1:10–11)

The Lord's day may have been Sunday, but it could have been
any day devoted to waiting on God in silent prayer and medi-

tation. As in Matthew's Gospel, the "loud voice like a trumpet" is the intuitively heard voice of God, a part of the inner spiritual vision, not any externally heard sound. John hearing the voice "behind" him means he heard it behind his physical senses, in an intuitive way. Anyone who wants to know God, and is prepared to spend time meditating on Him, will, in time, be able to hear this voice of God. It may be as the ever-comforting "Om" or "Amen" sound, which John, in accord with many others, describes as being "like the sound of rushing waters" (Rev 1:15), or it may be through the voice of intuition or conscience, bringing specific guidance or information. John describes how he reacted to this voice:

> I turned round to see the voice that was speaking to me. And
> when I turned I saw seven golden lampstands... (Rev 1:12)

In the Greek the word "round" isn't there; the literal translation is, "I turned to see the voice which spoke with me." As a key to interpreting Revelation, I am advocating the suggestion that John didn't turn round, but turned within, and what he saw was his astral body, the body of light which survives physical death, centered around the seven cerebro-spinal centers (or chakras), glowing like "seven golden lamp-stands." These are the brain center, called in the Vedas the "thousand petalled lotus of light," and the six spinal centers. They correspond to the brain, the medulla oblongata, and the five main nerve centers, or plexuses, along the spinal cord, which feed nerves to the various parts of the body: the cervical (neck), thoracic (heart), lumbar (solar plexus), sacral (hara), and coccygeal centers. The significance of these spinal centers to spiritual perception is that if we are to withdraw our consciousness and life energy from the outer world of the senses into the kingdom of heaven within, so we can really love the Lord our God with all our "mind" and all our "strength," we need to reverse the flow of nervous energy, which normally flows out into the world, and re-direct it so it circulates around the "temple of the Holy Spirit" within. In practice, this involves reversing the flow of perception at these main nerve centers. These nerve centers are the "gates" through which we move out into identification with the world, or withdraw into the kingdom of God within. There are Yoga techniques, designed to give control over these nerve centers, which greatly hasten the process of finding the "kingdom of God" within. Some of these Yoga techniques involve circulating "life energy" around the seven cerebro-spinal centers, often through *prana-yama* methods, whereby the "life force" is controlled through breathing techniques. The techniques I am best acquainted with are the Kriya Yoga techniques, brought to the West by Parama-hansa Yogananda, and taught by the organization he started, Self-Realization Fellowship.[8] People from all religions can apply to learn these techniques. The fact that John reveals his use of such techniques in the verses of Revelation we have just looked at establishes an excellent precedent for their use by Christians. That John really did practice and advocate a life-force control technique similar to some Yoga techniques, can be further confirmed by analyzing this explanation of his:

> The mystery of the seven stars that you saw in my right hand and of the seven golden lampstands is this: The seven stars are the angels of the seven churches, and the seven lampstands are the seven churches.   (Rev 1:20)

Churches are always, in one way or another, meant to be links between this physical world and the spiritual world, routes of salvation, ways of escaping from the suffering of this world. John is here explaining that this is what the seven golden lampstands, the seven cerebro-spinal centers (or chakras) are: they are the way in and out from the physical realm to the heavenly realm — the route of our salvation, our escape to heaven — so he calls them churches. The seven stars were earlier said to be held in the "right hand" of the astral body (verse 16), and this is reiterated in this verse. The right hand is an image of control and power. What this means is that we can have control and power over these stars, not outwardly, in a physical way, but inwardly through the grace of God, as the astral body is holding them in the power of the Spirit. In verse

16 the stars are left unexplained, but in verse 20 John says, "The seven stars are the seven angels of the seven churches, and the seven lampstands are the seven churches." In other words, the stars are the power and light (angels) of each of the seven lampstands or cerebro-spinal centers (churches).[9] John is saying we can manipulate and control the energy in these centers (their stars, or angels) so as to use them as "churches"— links to the kingdom of God within. Yoga techniques such as Kriya Yoga are designed to do exactly this. Such a Yoga, and the spiritual blessing by which it is effective, is the outworking of God's grace, a priceless gift offered to all who really want to know God enough to go to the trouble of seeking it out.

With this knowledge it is easy to see who it is, "who holds the seven stars in his right hand and walks among the seven golden lampstands" (Rev 2:1). It is the divine power of Christ we each have access to within us, there to tap into if we choose to identify with it rather than with the world.

In talking about the problems and strengths of the seven church congregations, John is talking about the various problems individuals typically face, the strengths they have been blessed with, and the warnings they need to heed if they are to "overcome," and receive the rewards from God he so beautifully describes:

> To him who overcomes and does my will to the end, I will give authority over the nations…I will also give him the morning star. He who has an ear, let him hear what the Spirit says to the churches.   (Rev 2:26,28–29)

The morning star is an image of Christ's presence and power— the way, as we have seen, Jesus comes back to those who have overcome the world, and been born of the Spirit. The image is explained in the last chapter of Revelation, where Jesus talks of his coming back:

> "I, Jesus, have sent my angel to give you this testimony for the churches. I am the Root and the Offspring of David, and the bright morning star."   (Rev 22:16)

The Sanskrit word "Om" (pronounced "Aum") refers to the Holy Spirit, and is named after his voice, "like the sound of rushing waters," which can be heard within by those who are in tune with God. The word "Amen" has a similar sound (when pronounced "Ah-men," as it should be), and that it is also a name for the Holy Spirit is shown by this verse:

> These are the words of the Amen, the faithful and true witness,
> the ruler of God's creation.   (Rev 3:14)

In Chapter 4 John again refers to the cerebro-spinal centers, or chakras, as gates to the kingdom of heaven, and to the astral body of light, formed around these seven glowing centers ("seven lamps... blazing"), which together contain the seven-fold spirit of God. This truly describes how the body is the temple of the Holy Spirit:

> After this I looked, and there before me was a door standing
> open in heaven, And the voice I had first heard speaking to me
> like a trumpet said, "Come up here, and I will show you what
> must take place after this." At once I was in the Spirit, and there
> before me was a throne in heaven with someone sitting on it...
> From the throne came flashes of lightning, rumblings and peals
> of thunder. Before the throne, seven lamps were blazing. These
> are the seven spirits of God. Also before the throne there was
> what looked like a sea of glass, clear as crystal. (Rev 4:1–2,5–6)

The "sea of glass, clear as crystal" is an image of the perfect intuitive perception that is possible when all thoughts are calmed, and the mind is withdrawn from the senses and reverently concentrated on God alone. Thoughts are ripples on the lake of the mind, which break up and distort the image of God which is shining there always. But through meditation the mind becomes calm, the waves of thought gradually subside, and before long the presence of God is felt, just as the image of the moon appears in a still lake.

In this sea of glass, John saw the truth about the two ways of living: the worldly way, which the masses in each generation choose, and the way of following God, which only a few people, the "elect" in each generation, choose. The "seven seals" (Rev 6–8) maintain the secrecy about the power of the seven chakras, known only to the elect: each is a two-way gate, and the power residing in them is a two-edged sword. By withdrawing the life force up into the spine and brain through each of these nerve centers, the kingdom of God within can be realized, but by allowing the life force to go down the spine and out through these nerve centers into the physical world of sense attachment, worldliness, with all its troubles, results. These are the two choices. John symbolically pictures the results of each. First there are these preliminary verses:

> After this I saw four angels standing at the four corners of the earth, holding back the four winds...Then I saw another angel coming up from the east, having the seal of the living God. He called out in a loud voice to the four angels...: "Do not harm the land or the sea or the trees until we put a seal on the foreheads of the servants of our God." Then I heard the numbers of those who were sealed: 144,000 from all the tribes of Israel.
> (Rev 7:1–4)

"Four" stands for the earth, and the four angels are the laws of nature which govern the way the material world works. Nature will have no power to harm the servants of God, as they are living under God's law, and are not bound by natural law. The "144,000" represent all the people who have chosen God, and the twelve tribes of Israel represent all the nations of the world. "Twelve" symbolizes the full extent of something. That 12,000 of the elect come from each of the twelve tribes, shows that no nation or people or religion is favoured over any other. The elect is:

> a great multitude that no-one could count, from every nation, tribe, people and language...   (Rev 7:9)

They are people who have been in the "great tribulation" of worldliness, but have come out of it by following the way of purity and perfection Jesus taught. In the picturesque language of the vision, "they have washed their robes and made them white in the blood of the lamb." (Rev: 7:14) Their reward, in living in the kingdom of God, is that:

"they are before the throne of God and serve him day and night
in his temple; and he who sits on the throne will spread his tent
over them. Never again will they hunger; never again will they
thirst. The sun will not beat upon them, nor any scorching heat.
For the lamb at the center of the throne will be their shepherd;
he will lead them to springs of living water. And God will wipe
away every tear from their eyes."   (Rev 7:15–17)

By contrast, those who turn their back on God, and reach out
into worldliness through their senses, wreak a terrible havoc on
the world. The image of the "angels" (life energy), of the
golden lampstands (chakras) being sent downward to the earth,
rather than upward to God, is vividly portrayed:

The first angel sounded his trumpet, and there came hail and
fire mixed with blood, and it was hurled down upon the earth.
A third of the earth was burned up, a third of the trees were
burned up, and all the green grass was burned up. (Rev 8:7)

With all of the first six angels, havoc is brought to earth, and
one third of everything is destroyed. The seventh angel, however, is the energy of the "thousand-petalled lotus" of the
brain. It is the highest and most important nerve center, and
even when its energy is directed toward the world, it calls
human beings to see the holy in life, and begin to think of God.
So it is that thinking, reflective people are most likely to realize
the folly of living in a worldly way, become sick of its alter-
nating joys and troubles, and look for permanent happiness.
When the seventh angel sounded his trumpet, there were loud
voices in heaven, which said:

"The kingdom of the world has become the kingdom of our Lord,
and of his Christ and he will reign for ever and ever." (Rev 11:15)

This is a change within an individual: a conversion. Once this
genuinely happens, a person will never look back—Christ "will
reign for ever and ever" with that person. This brings great
rejoicing in heaven, where the twenty-four elders, who were
seated on their thrones before God, fell on their faces and
worshipped God, saying:

> "We give thanks to you, Lord God Almighty, who is and who was,
> because you have taken your great power and have begun to
> reign."   (Rev 11:16–17)

But God has only just "begun to reign" in such a person's life,
and a gigantic battle between good and evil must take place, as
the person's bad habits and selfish tendencies, built up over incarnations, are painfully weeded out. The new spiritual seeker,
determined to find God, is given a lovely image in Revelation:

> ...a woman clothed with the sun, with the moon under her feet
> and a crown of twelve stars on her head. She was pregnant and
> cried out in pain as she was about to give birth.   (Rev 12:1–2)

This shows how much God values every new person who
comes to Him: he dresses them in the glory of the universe,
and is there to help them do battle with their old worldly
nature and defeat it. Before this battle with the devil, in the
form of the "dragon," the woman gives birth to "a male child,
who will rule all the nations with an iron scepter," and who is
"snatched up to God and to his throne." (Rev 12:5) The child
is clearly Jesus, and the woman giving birth is the spiritual
seeker being born again of the Spirit, and giving birth to Christ
in his heart—a beautiful image of the way Jesus comes again.

Two further aspects of evil in the world are then discussed:
the two beasts. The first represents the obviously blasphemous
and egotistical works of some human beings, the second, a
more subtle and insidious form of worldliness, which is
sophisticated, deceptive, and pretends to be doing good. This is
the infamous and widely discussed beast who:

> ...forced everyone, small and great, rich and poor, free and
> slave, to receive a mark on his right hand or on his forehead,
> so that no-one could buy or sell unless he had the mark, which
> is the name of the beast or the number of his name. This calls
> for wisdom. If anyone has insight, let him calculate the number
> of the beast, for it is man's number. His number is 666.
>   (Rev 13:16–18)

People do either display the mark of the world or show their
freedom in God. But this passage also has a deeper meaning. It

refers to the world being organized in such a way that it makes it very difficult for people not to be worldly, where it is almost impossible to do business (buying or selling) without becoming tied up with its unscrupulousness. It is very easy for worldliness to rub off on those who have recently decided to seek God, and for it to drag them back into its clutches. Wisdom and insight are needed to find the way out of this problem, for even Godly people need to buy and sell, and in other ways deal with the world. The answer lies in the fact that the mark of the beast is "man's number." The essence of worldliness lies in people being egotistical and wanting to do things in their own human way, rather than through seeking God's way. With this insight, God's people can deal with the world safely, and not become corrupted by it: what they have to do is remain centered in the thought of God, avoid putting themselves first, and always ask God what He wants them to do, rather than doing things their own way. "I did it my way" is the way of the world, which gratifies the ego, but leads to inevitable pain and sorrow. "I did it God's way" is the way to eternal happiness.

In the symbolism of numbers, "6" was considered a human number, and no matter how many times it is repeated, it always falls short of "7," God's number.[10] The number 666 is also almost exactly two-thirds of 1,000, which is, in this symbolism, a perfect, complete number, as in the number of the elect, which is 12x12x1000, and the millennium, which is "1,000" years of peace. Man's number being two-thirds of perfection is significant. When the first six angels hurled their strength down to earth (Rev 8 and 9), which, as we saw, is an image of people's sense identification with the world, "a third" of everything that was touched was destroyed, leaving just two-thirds intact. This is the way of the world: even at its best, for every two things that go right, there will be something that will go wrong, progress is always "two steps forward and one step backwards," and for every two days of happiness there will be a day of sadness somewhere down the line. This duality of the world can't be avoided; it is its very nature. Only in the kingdom of heaven can perfection be found. And this is why living in the kingdom of heaven is described as a "thousand" years. Once people have overcome their worldly habits and tendencies (won the battle with the dragon), avoided the deception of the beast (worldliness tempting them back), then, in the language of Revelation, their "Babylon" has fallen, there is great rejoicing, and they live in the millennium, the "thousand" or perfect years of living in the kingdom of heaven, during which the worldliness and duality of the earth they live on does not affect them, and temptation does not assail them. They are in the world still, but not of the world. Though, literally, the word "thousand" is used as a number, its real meaning is only apparent when its numerology is understood.

After being strengthened by living with God during these perfect years or "millennium," the elect are again tempted by Satan (Rev 20:7). The devil loves to test the saints, and even, as we know, took a delight in tempting Jesus in the wilderness. But with the strength of God they now have, the saintly have no trouble in defeating the devil. And this really is the end of temptation, worldliness and deception for such saints: these evils are then defeated forever. In the language of Revelation,

> the devil...was thrown into the lake of burning sulfur, where the beast and the false prophet had been thrown. They will be tormented day and night for ever and ever. (Rev 20:10)

There is one more aspect of this drama of salvation to be covered — what happens at the death of the physical body — and John goes on to shed light on this. As it is a time of transition, a judgment must be made about where each soul is to go next. What John saw was that "each person was judged according to what he had done." (Rev 20:13) This is the end of physical death for the Godly who have overcome worldliness: death belongs to material existence, "the lake of fire," so whatever impression of the realness of physical death these graduating souls have brought with them must be cast off, and returned to earth, along with all the worldly souls who still hanker after a material existence. As Revelation puts it:

...death and Hades were thrown into the lake of fire. The lake
of fire is the second death. If anyone's name was not found
written in the book of life, he was thrown into the lake of fire.
                                    (Rev 20:14)

An earlier passage showed that this lake of fire, or burning
sulfur, is the permanent home of temptation (the devil), worldliness (the beast) and deceptiveness and false teaching (the false
prophet). Now it is also shown to be the place where death,
Hades and worldly people reside. This certainly sounds like
earth, or some other material planet. And, indeed, the lake of
fire is the material plane of existence.

   Those whose names are written in "the book of life" do not
return to a material existence. For them the "first earth" has
"passed away," and they graduate to a totally new existence:

   Then I saw a new heaven and a new earth, for the first heaven
   and the first earth had passed away, and there was no longer any
   sea. I saw the Holy City, the new Jerusalem, coming down out of
   heaven from God, prepared as a bride beautifully dressed for her
   husband.   (Rev 21:1–2)

This heavenly city:

   ...shone with the glory of God, and its brilliance was like that of
   a very precious jewel, like jasper, clear as crystal...The street of
   the city was of pure gold, like transparent glass... The city does
   not need the sun or the moon to shine on it, for the glory of
   God gives it light, and the Lamb is its lamp... Nothing impure
   will ever enter it, nor will anyone who does what is shameful or
   deceitful, but only those whose names are written in the Lamb's
   book of life.   (Rev 21:11,21,23,27)

The Hindus would call this an astral world, and it is the reward
for those who have overcome worldliness. Compare its description with that of the astral world Hiranyaloka, described by Sri
Yukteswar in the chapter "The Resurrection of Sri Yukteswar"
in Paramahansa Yogananda's *Autobiography of a Yogi* Here are
some snippets of a description which runs for some pages:

   "The astral world is infinitely beautiful, clean, pure, and orderly
   There are no dead planets or barren lands. The terrestrial ble-

mishes — weeds, bacteria, insects, snakes — are absent. Unlike the variable climates and seasons of the earth, the astral planets maintain the even temperature of an eternal spring, with occasional luminous white snow and rain of many-colored lights. Astral planets abound in opal lakes and bright seas and rainbow rivers...

"The earth is dark with warfare and murder in the sea, land, and air...but the astral realms know a happy harmony and equality."[11]

John's vision, and the book of Revelation, end here, with Jesus saying,

"Behold, I am coming soon! Blessed is he who keeps the words of the prophecy in this book."

If this coming again of Jesus is understood in the personal, spiritual context I have been proposing, rather than the traditional context of an end to world history, the book of Revelation becomes much more joyous, coherent and understandable, and a lot more relevant to Christians of all times. It describes the actual process of salvation which all Christians, indeed all seekers after God, must go through.

A great advantage of this interpretation is its power to reconcile evangelical Christianity with the more liberal social gospel. The "postmillennialism" of the nineteenth century led to the church being involved in social reform, in an attempt to help establish the paradise on earth of the millennium, and so hasten the return of Jesus. Much of the impetus for the social gospel came from this. Under "premillennialism," which came into fashion among evangelicals after the turn of the twentieth century, Christ was seen as returning before the millennium, and establishing it himself. In this situation, striving to improve the world seemed pointless. Evangelicals abandoned the social gospel, leaving it to liberal Christians, who continued to espouse it. My analysis in this chapter confirms the premillennialist sequence of events:

1/ Jesus returning (being born in our hearts),

2/ the tribulation (as we struggle with bad habits, etc.), and

3/ the millennium (perfect years of peace, living in the
   kingdom of heaven within, while still on earth).

This analysis does not, however, suggest social reform is futile,
for the world is not seen as being about to end. Indeed, the
contrary can be shown, for if we wish to have Jesus return to us
we need to heed what he said, that, "...he will reward each
person according to what he has done." (Matt 16:27; Rev 20:
13) This makes the social gospel very relevant and necessary.

Chapter 20

Meditation — Coming to Personally Know God

God is not just a far-off, impersonal creator of the universe. He can be known, and He wants to know us. This is the good news, the "gospel," the world is waiting for. God continually reaches out into the lives of non-believers, often in little ways, yet those who have started to see the inadequacy of living in a worldly way, and are open to a new approach, will often be receptive to Him. A brush with God will be a life-changing experience for them, and they will be drawn to seek Him. Their search will often begin at a church. Although new seekers usually just come and quietly assess a church, what they are hoping is that there will be people there who know God, and will be able to introduce them to Him. If a church can't actually introduce these seekers to God, or show them how to find Him, they will leave the church and search elsewhere. It is not enough for a church to just teach about God, and for its members to admire and worship Him from a distance. Such a church is merely a God fan club, and will not satisfy a person who really wants to know God. The inability of churches to actually introduce people to God is the main reason so many spiritual seekers leave the church and look elsewhere for a spiritual path. There is a true story of a teen-age girl who went along to a church and thought it was obvious from the way the congregation were singing and chanting that they were on very friendly terms with God. When she said she wanted to know God, they told her that you have to be baptized to be pure in heart, and that until you are pure in heart you cannot see God. She received her baptism, but still wasn't able see God, even after giving the baptism "time to take." This profoundly disappointed her, and she left the church, disillusioned, deciding the only reality she could believe in was a rational, logical one.[1]

Some seekers who leave the church end up in New Age organizations, others find their way to one of the other main religions of the world, but still others become disillusioned with the search altogether, and fall back on the relative peace they can find in being caring and compassionate friends to those around them, responsible citizens of the world they live in, and in seeking the truth through intellect and learning. Eventually this will lead them to the truth, and on to a real path to God, so they are not lost. Nevertheless, the Christian church has let them down, and the path they eventually find is unlikely to be conventional Christianity—evangelical, mainline Protestant or Catholic. This is particularly lamentable, considering Christianity is the religious tradition of their society, and should, if it were functioning properly, be the best spiritual path for them. As the Hindu saint Sri Ramakrishna said,

> God has made different religions to suit different aspirants, times, and countries. All doctrines are only so many paths; but a path is by no means God Himself. Indeed, one can reach God if one follows any of the paths with whole hearted devotion... Every man should follow his own religion. A Christian should follow Christianity, a Mohammedan should follow Mohammedanism and so on. For the Hindus the ancient path, the path of the Aryan sages, is best.[2]

Joseph Campbell quoted Carl Jung's view that "religion is a defence against religious experience," and that the "concepts and ideas" of a religion "short-circuit transcendent experience—the experience of deep mystery..."[3] And this is what usually happens. What a change it would be if a person seeking God could walk into a church and hear the leader of the service say that their church believed the whole point of religion is to help people achieve actual personal communion with God, and that to this end they were going to teach all those present a simple way to meditate on God, so they could spend half an hour together in silent meditation, seeking the "kingdom of God" within themselves. A true seeker after God would be likely to stay with that church! Most churches will be like that one day; most will have the peace of God around them that the Quaker meeting-house in Easton, New York, had, one summer morning in 1775, when an Indian chief wanted to attack it:

> "Indian come white man house," he said, pointing to the village, "Indian want kill white man, one, two, three, six, all!" He reached for the tomahawk in his belt with a fierce gesture: "Indian come, see white man sit in house. No gun, no arrow, no knife. All quiet, all still, worshipping Great Spirit. *Great Spirit inside Indian, too.*" He touched his breast. "Then Great Spirit say: 'Indian! no kill them.'"

It is one thing for churches to say people should spend time each day silently waiting on God, as a few do, but until they actually practice this in their services, people will not take the call to wait on God seriously. Nor will they even know how to do it. By silently meditating on God together, as Quakers and some other groups already do, people learn something about how to meditate which cannot be conveyed through words, and is much harder to learn alone. As Jesus said,

> "...where two or three are gathered together in my name, there am I in the midst of them."   (Matt 18:20 AV)

In a group, the vibrations of peace and joy from experienced meditators help those who are new to it tune in to God. Yet, in essence, meditation and prayer is a solitary activity, quality time spent together by a person and God, in deep communion. The Gospels tell us Jesus spent long hours in communion with God. Mark recounts that:

> Very early in the morning, while it was still dark, Jesus got up, left the house and went off to a solitary place, where he prayed.
>   (Mark 1:35)

Luke says, "Jesus often withdrew to lonely places and prayed," (Luke 5:16) and that,

> One of those days Jesus went out into the hills to pray, and spent the night praying to God.   (Luke 6:12)

In Psalms it says, "Be still, and know that I am God," (Psalm 46:10) and "when on your beds, search your hearts and be silent." (Psalm 4:4)

To some Christians the word "meditation" smacks of the "New Age," and is rejected. This is probably because meditation is so often a part of the spiritual practice of Hindus and Buddhists. The word is not, however, of Indian origin; Eastern religious paths use the word because it is the English word for what they do. Teachers from these Eastern paths realized there was a tradition in the Catholic church of still silent communion with God, which went under the name of "meditation," so they used this word to describe in English the same practice in their paths. To abandon a practice which has long been part of the Christian tradition, or even just the word for it, just because another religion also practices it, and uses the same word, would be the height of exclusive silliness. Hindus do a lot of praying, and, when communicating in English, use the word "prayer" for it, yet I don't suppose any Christians are going to stop praying as a result! Although the word "meditation" is not used in the New Testament for this prolonged, still, silent communion with God, it being referred to simply as "prayer," in the Old Testament the word is used. Genesis says that Isaac:

...went out into the field one evening to meditate. (Gen 24:63)

David ends one of his psalms with this lovely plea:

Let the words of my mouth,
and the meditation of my heart,
be acceptable in thy sight,
O Lord, my strength, and my redeemer. (Psalm 19:14 AV)

In a later psalm, David speaks to God from the depths of his heart:

O God, you are my God; early will I seek you:
my soul thirsts for you,
my flesh longs for you,
in a dry and thirsty land, where no water is.
I have seen you in the sanctuary,
and seen your power and glory.

Because your loving kindness is better than life,
my lips shall praise you;

all my life I shall bless you,
and lift up my hands in your name.
My soul will be satisfied, as with the richest foods,
and my mouth will praise you with joyful lips.

On my bed I remember you;
And meditate on you through the watches of the night.
Because you have always helped me,
I rejoice in the shadow of your wings.
I stay close to you,
and your right hand upholds me.
                    (Psalm 63:1–8 AT)[4]

David meditating on God "through the watches of the night" is
reminiscent of how Jesus "spent the night praying to God."
Clearly this is a thing which those who want to be close to God
do. It is not, however, necessary to meditate all night long to
come to know God, though to do so even once would bring
great blessings. Even Jesus often just rose very early in the
morning to meditate (Mark 1:35), and I don't suppose David
meditated right through the night all that often. Five minutes
or so of prayer each day is not enough, though. At least half an
hour, morning and night is what most teachers recommend,
although the depth of meditation (the oneness with God made
possible by freedom from distracting thoughts) is more important than the time spent, and a shorter time is certainly better
than none at all.

The ancient tradition of meditation in the Catholic church
was largely confined to its monastic orders, but it has, in recent
years, been revived for the use of the laity by the Benedictine
monk John Main. He established the "World Community for
Christian Meditation," an ecumenical organization with members from many denominations. Father Laurence Freeman is
now the spiritual head of this organization which is made up of
over five hundred meditation groups and centers around the
world.[5] The World Community for Christian Meditation advocates a "mantra" form of meditation, and suggests two half-
hour periods of meditation each day, as well as meeting for
group meditations on a regular basis. Laurence Freeman says,

> All meditation aims to bring the person, mind and body, to
> silence, stillness and simplicity of spirit by the means of an
> inner "object of attention."[6]

In mantra forms of meditation, this inner object of attention is
a "mantra," a word or short phrase which is mentally repeated
again and again until the attention is drawn away from the
outer world of the senses, and focused on the kingdom of God
within. Holy words like "Amen" or "Om" are often used, but
the method is effective with any word which doesn't have
strong worldly connotations. The ancient Indian sage, Patanjali,
said, "Meditate on Om to actually contact God." In our times,
Laurence Freeman said,

> Meditation is a universal spiritual path. It leads us deeper than
> thought and imagination to the silent center of our spirit which
> is our point of communion with God in love.[7]

And this just about sums up meditation. It is a path to God for
all people, of all religions. It is well known that there is a
strong tradition of meditation within Hinduism and Buddhism,
and now we can see there is also such a tradition within
Judaism and Christianity. Islam is not without a concept of
meditation, either, as shown by this passage from the Qur'an:

> Arise in the midst of the night and commune with thy God…
> things will be revealed to thee thou didst not know before and
> thy path will be made smooth.[8]

The Romantic poets even displayed a knowledge of meditation.
Tennyson practiced a form of mantra meditation, and said he
often entered a state where "individuality dissolved into boundless being," giving him an intense awareness of:

> …transcendent wonder, associated with absolute clearness of
> mind, and where death was an almost laughable impossibility.[9]

Coleridge, in his poem "The Eolian Harp," likens people to
this instrument, which when the wind plays on it, produces
"Such a soft floating witchery of sound." He asks:

And what if all of animated nature,
Be but organic Harps diversely fram'd,
That tremble into thought, as o'er them sweeps
Plastic and vast, one intellectual breeze,
At once the Soul of each and God of all?[10]

Both Tennyson and Coleridge have captured something of the nature and experience of meditation. Yet it may take time for the meditator to develop such a transcendental awareness as Tennyson's, and the most common fruit of meditation for most people will be a feeling of closeness to God, and a wonderful peace, which, if it is dwelt on and consciously retained when emerging from meditation, can last long into the day. Wordsworth was closer to this, when he spoke of "that inward eye which is the bliss of solitude," in his poem "The Daffodils." Paul talked of it as:

...the peace of God, which passeth all understanding. (Phil 4:7 AV)

Meditation loses much of what it has to offer if it is not directed toward knowing God. Yet in the beginning you don't have to love Him. Love for God will soon come to a person who is determined to know Him, and is willing to try doing things His way, for, at this point Christ is born again within such a person to show him or her God. And to know God is to love Him — He is the source of all love. And to love God is to want to spend time with Him in the kingdom of heaven within, at His feet, surrendered to Him, soaking up His very goodness through being near Him, and being gradually transformed by it. This is what meditation becomes, and those who persevere with it will soon be able to say, with Paul:

"No eye has seen, no ear has heard, no mind has conceived,
what God has prepared for those who love him" — but God
has revealed it to us by his Spirit. The Spirit searches all
things, even the deep things of God.   (1 Cor 2:9–10)

When people's love for God grows, through meditation, it reaches the stage where, if they are out in the world too long, they just long to sink deep into meditation, and escape into His arms. Sri Yukteswar used to say to his disciple, the young Yoga-nanda:

"The darkness of *maya* is silently approaching. Let us hie homeward within."[11]

And Kahlil Gibran, in his poem "Jesus, the Son of Man" said,

When love becomes vast, love becomes wordless.
And when memory is overladen, it seeks the silent deep.[12]

There are many spiritual paths which teach meditation, and it can be hard for the new seeker to choose from among them. One guide is to find out how much it is going to cost you. Jesus said, "You cannot serve both God and Money." (Matt 6:24) A spiritual organization which makes a handsome profit from teaching you is serving its own desire to make money, not God, and is unlikely to be able to introduce you to God. Another pointer is to beware of the easy path. Organizations which say you can live exactly as you wish to, and that you will be saved just by virtue of belonging to them, and subscribing to their beliefs, are not there to show you God: they have some other agenda. Discipline, dedication and perseverance are required on the spiritual path. God wants to know that you really are serious about finding Him, and following Him, before he will reveal Himself to you. As Jesus put it,

...small is the gate, and narrow the road that leads to life, and only a few find it.   (Matt 7:14)

Only a few in any one generation, that is; eventually all will find it. Also beware the exclusive path. Some spiritual organiz-ations from both East and West say their way is the only way to salvation, or that we haven't the free will to choose God, and only certain people God chooses will be saved. This is the ego speaking, with all its desire to win at other people's expense. God wants all people to be saved, and has given everyone the free will to choose between the world and Himself. Exclusive-ness is rampant in Christianity, but is certainly not confined to it. An example of exclusiveness in an Eastern path is when one of them claims that liberation from the world can only come through a guru or master who is in the flesh. This is tantamount to saying Jesus' saving power died with him on the cross, so excludes all of Christianity for a start. It also excludes most of the other religious groups of the world. Finally, you should be able to try a path out for a while before pledging yourself to it, and you should try out as many as you need, to find the one which really suits you. Then, once you have found your path, stay with it, and give it all your loyalty—that is the way to God. As Jesus said,

> "If you hold to my teaching, you are really my disciples. Then
> you will know the truth, and the truth will set you free."
>   (John 8:31–32)

My own path is Self-Realization Fellowship, founded by Paramahansa Yogananda, who wrote the celebrated and widely-read *Autobiography of a Yogi*. Members of all religions can subscribe to its lessons, and learn its techniques, including the life-force control techniques of Kriya Yoga. Students don't need to renounce their current religion, though they can make Self-Realization Fellowship their church if they wish to. There is a trial period of a year, during which students subscribe to a series of lessons and are taught a number of effective meditation techniques. After one year of lessons, students can decide to make Self-Realization Fellowship their path if they wish to, and apply for the first Kriya Yoga technique. Jesus is revered as a divine incarnation by this path, and his teachings are highly regarded. In its many Meditation Groups and Centers around the world, the main weekly service includes a Bible reading and commentary. One of its aims is to show the fundamental oneness of original Christianity and original Yoga (the Hindu science of union with God), and to show that the true foundation of all religious practice is meditation on God. If you are interested in finding out more about this path, you could read *Autobiography of a Yogi*, which many libraries hold copies of, or write to or phone Self-Realization Fellowship for more information.[13]

Although I recommend belonging to a religious organization which teaches meditation, such as the World Community for Christian Meditation, mentioned earlier, or Self-Realization Fellowship, some seekers may wish to try meditation first, to see whether it appeals to them. For their benefit, I am ending this chapter, and the book, with a simple meditation technique all can use, and a few pointers on its use. It is a variation of a widely known technique I first learned from Paul Brunton's *The Secret Path*,[14] a book which is well worth reading.

The technique is a *pranayama* or breathing, technique, so, although it is not absolutely necessary, it would be very beneficial for those who wish to practice it to first learn how to breathe properly. Most people take short quick breaths by expanding their chests. Yogis, opera singers and cats all breathe slowly and deeply down into their abdomens without moving their chests much at all — a technique called abdominal (or diaphragmatic) breathing. Deep, slow breathing has a naturally calming effect, very helpful to meditation. Most courses and books on Hatha Yoga teach abdominal breathing (and other beneficial variants such as alternate-nostril breathing), so you could learn how to breathe this way, and at the same time do the sort of exercises which would help you to be able to sit still comfortably, if you learned Hatha Yoga. The tensions and restlessness which interfere with meditation can also be greatly reduced by aerobic exercise, so it is a good idea to regularly do some vigorous sport you enjoy, especially after a stressful day at work. Living a balanced, healthy life makes it easier to meditate successfully.

To enable you to start meditating as soon as possible, I am going to briefly explain how to learn to breathe abdominally. It is not hard. Initially, practice it while lying on your back, on a rug on the floor, or on a firm bed, with a thin pillow or cushion under your head, so you are comfortable. Put your hands by your side, tense and relax your whole body a couple of times, then completely relax. Wherever you feel any tension, consciously relax the muscles in the area. Once relaxed, rest your hands on your abdomen, so you can feel it move as you breathe. Breathe right out, as far as you can without straining, then slowly breathe in by expanding the abdomen, rather than the chest. With your hands, feel your stomach move up, and the bottom of your rib cage move out sideways a little. Your chest will automatically expand slightly, as your lungs fill up with air, but you are not sucking the air in by expanding your chest, you are sucking it in by lowering and flattening the arched diaphragm below the lungs down into the abdomen. When you have breathed in as much as you can without straining, hold the breath for a moment, close your eyes, and feel the peace of relaxation. Then slowly breath out, first by letting the slightly expanded chest contract, then by contracting the abdomen. Feel the stomach drop, and the sides of the rib cage contract inward. Keep breathing this way for a few minutes, as slowly and deeply as you comfortably can. You will find that as you keep doing it, you can breath more and more slowly and deeply, and that as you do so a peaceful calm will descend on you. Once you have been practicing for a while, the breath in and the breath out should each take about ten seconds, with a pause of a few seconds between the inward and outward breaths. Once you have mastered this, try to breathe this way all the time, whenever you are conscious of your breathing. Eventually you will find you are doing it automatically, and it has become your normal way of breathing. It will both benefit your health, and make it easier to meditate.

Now for the meditation technique. After doing your yoga or other exercises, bathing, and practicing relaxation and abdominal breathing exercises for a few minutes, sit down in a quiet place, where there is fresh air. It doesn't matter whether you sit on a firm chair, such as a dining chair, or cross-legged on the floor. What is important is that your back is held straight and upright, and you are comfortable. Put your hands on your lap (or on your knees if you are sitting cross-legged) and keep your head level. Gently close your eyes, and focus your mental gaze slightly upward through the point between the eyebrows, the so-called "third eye." Jesus referred to this when he said,

> The light of the body is the eye: if therefore thine eye be single,
> thy whole body shall be full of light.   (Matt 6:22 AV)

Breathe naturally, but otherwise keep still. If you wish, say a short prayer to God, in the language of your heart, asking Him to guide you, and to bless you with his presence. Then, while you are slowly breathing in, calmly concentrate on the incoming breath. Soak up the peace and stillness of the moment between the breaths, then, while slowly breathing out, concentrate on the outgoing breath. Continue doing this for about ten minutes, just watching the breath, without making any attempt to control it. Feel the peace steal over you as you do this; it is the radiance of God's love. You will probably feel just a little of this lovely peace to start with, but as you continue meditating, you will feel it more and more. As you sink into the bliss of God's presence your breath will naturally become very slow, and the periods between breaths will, without strain, naturally increase in duration up to a few seconds or more, and in this stillness you will go even deeper into the presence of God. This "breathless" state, involving a temporary lack of desire to breathe, is nothing to be alarmed by. It is the joy of communing with God literally "taking your breath away." It may be a while before you experience this, but eventually, when the time is right, the breathless state will come. Don't actively strive for it, though; it is like chasing a butterfly — the more you chase it the more it will elude you, but when you sit quietly and still, it will come and sit on you. Just concentrate on the techniques you know, and on loving God, and the various levels of bliss will come of their own accord, when God sends them, for they are the gifts of His gradually unfolding presence.

The aim of concentrating on observing the in-going and out-going breath is to divert the mind from thinking of outward things, so it can turn inward to the kingdom of God. To start with, most people find their minds are seething with thoughts, which come between them and God during meditation, ruffling the lake of peace, so the image of God can't be seen in it. This is probably the greatest obstacle you will have to face. But don't despair. By persevering you show God how much you want Him. And the technique of watching the breath is very effective in gradually stilling the mind. While practicing this technique, don't fight any worldly thoughts which cross your mind — you will just spawn a whole lot more thoughts by doing so — just acknowledge them and let them pass by, and return to being with God. The more you meditate, the easier this will become, and you will find you are making progress toward loving God with "all your mind," rather than with just a small part of it — by being totally with Him, and not being distracted by thoughts of other things.

Meditation does take time to master, but it is not difficult. As Carole King says in her song, "I Think I Can Hear You," all you have to do is "be."[15] You will find that the less you "try" while meditating, the more you will succeed. Just "be" and let go of your worries and cares. You won't fall into oblivion if you let go of your anxieties for a few minutes, but you may well slip into a blissful state where you will be absolutely safe in the loving arms of God. It can take some time and patience, though, to learn to fully let go and just "be." To just be with God, and not think about a-thousand-and-one other things, also requires perseverance, and some humility in accepting the need for a few helpful techniques.

Once you have mastered the basic technique, adding a "mantra" to it during a part of your meditation may help you to further still your mind. If you wish to try this, choose a simple one-syllable word such as "Om" (pronounced more like "Aum") or "God," or a two-syllable word like "Ah-men," "Yah-weh," "Je-sus" or "So Hum," and mentally say it while you are breathing in and out and observing the breath. With a two-syllable word, mentally say the first syllable, with a long, drawn-out, vowel sound, as you slowly breathe in, and the second, in the same way, as you breathe out. Repeating a mantra again and again provides yet another inward focus of attention, along with the breath, which is not going to generate any thought patterns.

The reason for sitting with the back straight and upright is to ensure the life force can withdraw into the spine as you meditate, away from identification with the sensory nerves at the surfaces of your body. Feel your awareness at the nerve centers along the spine turn around from reaching down and out into the world, to withdrawing inward to the spinal chord and upward to the brain. After a while you can start to feel like a disembodied heart and mind (spinal chord and brain) living in the sea of God's love, which is why Paul said,

> ...the peace of God, which passeth all understanding, shall keep your hearts and minds, through Christ Jesus.   (Phil 4:7 AV)

And it is why the third century philosopher Plotinus, who influenced early Christianity so much, said true prayer is nothing more or less than "lifting up the heart and mind to God" in unbroken contemplation.[16]

To start with, practice this technique for about ten minutes, twice a day, then gradually increase it to about twenty minutes. Early morning, sunset, and before going to bed, are good times to meditate. Try to keep meditating for five to ten minutes after you have finished doing the technique, and just be aware of your peace and closeness to God, and cherish it. And when you get up, hold on to the peace and joy you have found, and consciously take it with you into the rush and hurry of your day. Whenever you have a moment to spare during the day, think of God, and practice being aware of His presence.[17] It will be a great blessing to you. Paramahansa Yogananda said,

> Although I am planning and doing things in the world, it is only to please the Lord. I test myself: even when I am working I whisper within, "Where are You, Lord?" and the whole world changes. There is nothing but a great Light, and I am a little bubble in that Ocean of Light. Such is the joy of existence in God.[18]

If you have shown God you love Him, by meditating on Him regularly, He will respond to an appeal like this, at any time of the night or day, even if you only have a few seconds to give Him.

There is a change beginning to happen in the church which will be looked back on as a great spiritual reformation, dwarfing that of the sixteenth century, and, along with reform of the church, it will be driven by large numbers of Christians learning to meditate, and really coming to know God. Then the church will surely be blessed, and its sincere practicing members will become "as numerous as the stars in the sky and as the sand on the seashore." (Gen 22:17)

May peace be with you, and God bless you.

Notes and Citations

Publication details of books cited are noted in the Bibilography.

Chapter 1
1. Arnold Toynbee, "The Historical Anticedents," in *The Crucible of Christianity*, p. 37.

Chapter 2
1. Toynbee, op. cit., pp. 26, 42.
2. See Dothan, T. *The Philistines and their Material Culture.*
3. All the quotes from the Bible in this book, unless otherwise specified, are from the elegant English of the New International Version (Hodder and Stoughton, London, 1978). Quotes have also been taken from the Authorized (King James) Version (AV), the Jerusalem Bible (JB, as in this case), or are my own translation (AT). When this is the case, the Bible reference is followed by "AV," "JB" or "AT" to indicate the source.
4. Ofer Bar-Yosef, "From Hunter to Herder in Southern Sinai," in *Temples and High Places in Biblical times*, pp. 156–157.
5. Roland de Vaux, *Ancient Israel*, pp. 65–67. Vaux here confirms the impossibility of the Biblical figures on the size of the Exodus, and proposes from a number of lines of inquiry that the total population of Judaea and Israel never exceeded about one million, which was the population of modern Palestine in 1931, before Zionist immigration began.
6. Vermes, G. *The Dead Sea Scrolls in English*, p. 262. Eight generations is assumed as an historical possibility on the basis of an alternate tradition of a stay of 210 years in Egypt, rather than the 430 years claimed in Exodus 7:40. Vermes here refers to this tradition, and some evidence for it from the Dead Sea Scrolls.

7. Youngman, B.R. *The Lands and Peoples of the Living Bible*, p.56.
8. Some researchers have proposed that only a small portion of the ancient Israelites were slaves in Egypt, perhaps just the Levites, who often had Egyptian names, and who had no territory of their own after they returned. See Richard Elliot Friedman, *Who Wrote the Bible?*, p. 82.
9. Vaux, op. cit., p. 65.
10. Ibid., pp. 438, 441.
11. *Encyclopedia of World Mythology*, p.107.
12. Some other references to El include: Gen 21:33; 24:3; 28:10–19; 33:20; 35:6–7; 46:3; Ps 18:14; 47:3; 97:9.
13. Vaux, op. cit., p. 47. The following discussion draws on this too.
14. Ibid., pp. 47–48.
15. Ibid., p. 445.
16. See 1 Kings 18.
17. Vaux, op. cit. pp. 6, 92.
18. Ibid., p. 9.
19. Ibid., p. 50.
20. Ibid., p. 99. Vaux here supports this view.
21. Richard Elliot Friedman, *Who Wrote the Bible?*, pp. 10, 40 41.
22. Ibid., pp. 43–45., following the work of Baruch Halpern.
23. Ibid., p. 49.
24. Pfeiffer, C.F. *The Biblical World* pp. 347–348. Also see Jeremiah 34:7.
25. A parallel passage in the ancient sacred texts of Ugarit shows that this passage should probably read "wither" rather than "forget [its skill]," as it is usually translated. See John Romer, *Testament*, p. 79.
26. H. G. Wells, *A Short History of the World*, pp. 81–82.
27. Toynbee, op. cit., p. 43.
28. Abraham Schalit, "Palestine Under the Seleucids and Romans," in *The Crucible of Christianity*, p. 70. And Kurt Schbert, "Jewish Religious Parties and Sects," in the same book, p. 87.

29. Arnold Toynbee, in the Introduction to *The Crucible of Christianity*, pp. 12–13.
30. Roland de Vaux, *Ancient Israel*, pp. 510–514.

Chapter 3

1. Josephus, *The Jewish War*, (Leob Vol II) II:119 (p. 369).
2. Ian Wilson, *Jesus: the evidence*, pp. 82–83, 87, 89.
3. Gaalyah Cornfield, Editor, *The Historical Jesus*, p. 147.
4. Kurt Schubert, "Jewish Religious Parties and Sects," in *The Crucible of Christianity*, p. 94.
5. Ibid., p 90.
6. H. G. Wells, *A Short History of the World* p. 136; *Mythological Encyclopedia*, pp. 88, 96–97, 91; M.J. Vermaseren, "Religions in Competition with Christianity," in *The Crucible of Christianity*, p. 258; Kurt Schubert, "A Faith Divided, Jewish religious parties and sects," in *The Crucible of Christianity*, p. 93.
7. David Flusser, "The Son of Man" in *The Crucible of Christianity*, p. 226.
8. A. Daniel Frankforter, *A History of the Christian Movement*, pp. 5–6.
9. Kurt Schubert, op. cit., p. 87.
10. Ibid., pp. 88–89.
11. Ibid., p. 94. Schubert records this story being according to Aboth de'Rabbi Nathan 4. The teacher was Johanan ben Zakdai, and his student was Joshua ben Hanonia.
12. G. Vermes, *The Dead Sea Scrolls in English*, p. 37.
13. Ibid., pp. 43, 84–5, 90, 105 — just a few of the many.
14. Gaalyah Cornfield, op. cit., p. 35.
15. Josephus, op. cit., II:130–132 (p. 373); Vermes, op. cit., pp. 6–7, 51, 69, 102.
16. Vermes, op. cit., pp. 49–50, 64, 94.
17. Ibid., pp. 15–16; Josephus, op. cit., II:122–127 (pp. 369–371)
18. Vermes, op. cit., pp. 52–55
19. Ibid., pp. 75, 77.
20. Ibid., p. 43.

21. Ibid., pp. 37–38, 42, 81, 90.
22. Ibid., pp. 51, 69, 82, 85, 97, 101, 102; Josephus, op. cit.
    II:120–121 (p. 369), II:161 (p. 385).
23. Vermes, op. cit., pp. 42–43, 65, 69, 79, 80, 84.
24. Ibid., p. 44.
25. Ibid., pp. 63, 66, 83.
26. Ibid., p. 82
27. Ibid., pp. 3–4, 48, 63, 68, 69.
28. Ibid., pp. 3–4. Vermes refers to the Horayoth iii: 8.
29. Ibid., p. 5.
30. Ibid., p. 56.
31. Ibid., p. 98.
32. Ibid., p. 43, for instance. And the War Rule, pp. 103–127.
33. Gaalyah Cornfield, op. cit., p. 121.
34. Ibid., p. 39.
35. Ibid., p. 74.
36. *Cambridge Ancient History* (1971), Vol X, p. 878.
37. Emil Schurer, *The History of the Jewish People in the Age of
    Jesus Christ*, Vol I, pp. 413–420. Many of the points I have
    raised about the deficiency of Luke's Nativity account, and
    more, are convincingly argued by Schurer in a detailed 28
    page discussion of the matter, in Vol I, pp. 400–428.
38. Ian Wilson, op. cit., pp. 55, 60.
39. Ibid., pp. 32–50; A.N. Wilson, *Jesus*, whole book but esp.
    Ch 3.
40. Robert M. Grant, "Rival Theologies, Gnosticism, Marcion,
    Origen" in *The Crucible of Christianity*, p. 328; A.N.
    Wilson., Ch 3.
41. Gaalyah Cornfield, op. cit., p. 41.
42. Robert M. Grant, op. cit., p. 329. Here Grant relates that
    Origen took the same view as I do on this matter. Origen
    concluded that God planned it this way in order to
    encourage thought. If everything were clear, he said, we
    might assume the only meaning is the literal one, whereas
    in fact there is a strong spiritual meaning as well, which is
    much more important.

Chapter 4

1. Vaux, op. cit., p. 29. Vaux states the minimum ages for marriage in the later days of ancient Israel, that is around Jesus' time, were set by Rabbis as 12 for girls and 13 for boys.

2. Alan Watts in his introduction to *A Pilgrim's Guide to Planet Earth.*, p. 5.

3. H. G. Wells, *A Short History of the World* p. 104.

4. Romilar Thapar, *A History of India 1*, pp. 73–74. The Third Buddhist Council was held at Patiliputra.

5. Ibid., p. 109.

6. Huston Smith, *The Religions of Man*, p. 38.

7. Holger Kersten, *Jesus Lived in India*, p. 78.

8. Nicolas Notovitch, *The Unknown Life of Jesus Christ*, pp. 31–32.

9. Ibid. pp. 32–43. This condensed version of the "Issa Scriptures" was made by me from the scriptures presented by Notovitch in his book. All the details of Issa's travels and encounters have been included, along with some of his quoted teachings. Some suspect statements and teachings, which could be interpolations by Buddhist scribes, Gnostics, or Notovitch himself, along with some repetitive material, have been omitted. Some less striking teachings have also been omitted, though they may well be genuine, in the interests of brevity. One addition (of three words in square brackets) was made as a result of comparison with Roerich's translation (see note 15).

10. Ibid. pp. 10, 21, 31.

11. Ian Wilson, *Jesus: the evidence*, pp. 152–154. Also pp. 46–48, 177, 121–122, 124–126, 170–172, 181.

12. Vol II, p. 136. Mrs Harvey wrote about this in 1854, 33 years before Notovitch visited Hemis.

13. Swami Abhedananda, *In Kashmir and Tibet*, translated into English by Prasun Kumar De, Per Sinclair and Jayasri Majumdar, part of which is included in Elizabeth Clare Prophet, *The Lost Years of Jesus*, a book which is largely an anthology of source materials concerning Jesus' supposed

visit to India. p. 255.
14. Ibid. pp. 251–261.
15. Elizabeth Clare Prophet, *The Lost Years of Jesus*, pp. 283–309. She presents a selection of Roerich's writings, including his translation of parts of the Issa Scriptures.
16. Ibid., p 68. Further details are given on pp. 347–348. The photograph referred to is reproduced in the book.
17. William O. Douglas, *Beyond the High Himalayas*, p. 152.
18. Prophet, op. cit., pp. 70–72.
19. Ibid., p. 72.
20. Sri Daya Mata, in *Self-Realization* magazine, Winter 1992, p. 16.
21. Prophet, op. cit., p. 15.
22. Roberts, A, and Donaldson, J. *The Ante-Nicene Fathers*, Vol I, containing Irenaeus' "Against Heresies." pp. 391–392. Also see Chapter 6, note 7.
23. Kersten, op. cit., p. 176.
24. Ibid., p. 184.
25. Ibid., p. 187.
26. Ibid., p. 206.
27. Penelope Chetwode, *Kulu: the End of the Habitable World*, p. 154.

Chapter 5

1. Paramahansa Yogananda explained that the reason why it was right for John to baptize Jesus is that in previous lives they were Elijah and Elisha respectively, master and disciple, and that Jesus was honoring his Master, or Guru. Elisha surpassed his master Elijah, though, when he observed Elijah being taken up to heaven in a chariot of fire, and received a double portion of his spirit (2 Kings 2), and so when they returned as John the Baptist and Jesus, John acknowledged Jesus' superiority.
2. More than likely, considering:
1/ the Zealots wanted the Messiah to lead the Jews to military victory over the Romans, and would almost certainly have tried to recruit Jesus to their cause; 2/ Satan

is usually considered to be a physical embodiment of the devil, which is a spirit (eg: Fulop-Miller, in *Saints that Moved the World* in the chapter about St Anthony, p. 27); 3/ Jesus said similar words, "Get thee behind me Satan" (Matt 16:23) to a man on another occasion—the apostle Peter, when Peter suggested out of a worldly kindness that Jesus take the easy way out, and not be killed. A Zealot may have been present in person, or it may have been the memory of what Zealots had previously offered him, that assailed Jesus in the desert.

There is some interpretation in the next few paragraphs as well. The rather condensed record of Jesus' teachings often requires some interpretation. I have given an interpretation here which sees the teachings as a practical guide to living, and is consistent both with what is said in other parts of the Bible and with the spiritual teachings of other religions. It owes a lot to Swami Prabhavandanda's *Sermon on the Mount according to Vedanta*.

3. Matt 5:22. I will explain in chapter 15 how I've derived this interpretation from this passage.
4. Holger Kersten, *Jesus Lived in India*, p. 28.
5. Swami Kriyananda, *The Path, Autobiography of a Western Yogi* p. 447.
6. See Chapter 3.
7. Tom Harpur, *For Christ's Sake*, pp. 48–53. Harpur has an excellent discussion of how priests have perverted the beautiful and spiritually important symbolism of the communion.
8. This point is also made by David Flusser in "Jesus in the Context of History," in *The Crucible of Christianity*, p. 227.

Chapter 6

1. M.J. Vermaseren, "Religions in competition with Christianity," in *The Crucible of Christianity*, p. 254.
2. H.G. Wells, *A Short History of the World*, p. 146.
3. Encyclopedia of Religion, Vol. 4, p. 156.

4. H.G. Wells, op. cit., p. 145.
5. Elaine Pagels, *The Gnostic Gospels*, pp. 44, 48, 49.
6. Ibid., pp. 45, 47.
7. Irenaeus, "Against Heresies" in *The Ante-Nicene Fathers*, Vol I. Also see Chapter 4, note 22.
8. *Cambridge Ancient History*, Vol. XII, pp. 450, 474–475; Pagels, op. cit., p. 55.
9. My own free translation into modern idiom. For a word-for-word translation, giving a feel for Irenaeus' pompous, long-winded style, see Irenaeus, op. cit., pp. 334–335.
10. H. G. Wells, op. cit., p. 147.
11. Eusebius, *The History of the Church*, pp. 141, 145.
12. Ibid., p. 144.
13. My own translation. For another translation, see Eusebius, op. cit., pp. 146–147.
14. Eusebius, op. cit., p. 145.
15. Martin E. Marty, *A Short History of Christianity*, p. 63.
16. *The Encyclopedia of Religion*, Vol 11, p. 111.
17. *New Catholic Encyclopedia* Vol 10, p. 770.
18. Ibid., p. 771; *The Encyclopedia of Religion*, Vol 11, p. 110.
19. *New Catholic Encyclopedia*, Vol 10, p. 771.
20. *The Encyclopedia of Religion*, Vol 13, p. 457.
21. Ibid., Vol 12, p. 256; A. Hilary Armstrong, "Greek philosophy from the age of Cicero to Plotinus," in *The Crucible of Christianity*, p. 212.
22. *New Catholic Encyclopedia*, Vol 10, p. 772.
23. Martin E. Marty, op. cit., p. 66.
24. Ibid., p. 76.

Chapter 7

1. *Cambridge Ancient History*, Vol XI, p. 12. A translation of the Latin "Vae, puto, deus fio." I am indebted to John Romer for the idea of starting a chapter this way.
2. *Cambridge Ancient History*, Vol XII, pp. 329–339.
3. Ibid., pp. 365–367; Romer, op. cit., pp. 207–208.
4. *Cambridge Ancient History*, Vol XII, p. 340. His country palace was at Salonae.

5. John Romer, *Testament*, pp. 208–209.
6. Halsberghe, Gaston H. *The Cult of Sol Invictus*, pp. 49–50.
7. Ibid., pp.54–67.
8. Ibid., pp. 70, 83, 90–91, 100–102.
9. Ibid., pp. 130, 137, 141–144.
10. Ibid., p. 136.
11. Ibid., pp. 152–153, 145, 154–155, 167.
12. *Cambridge Ancient History*, Vol XII, pp. 343–344.
13. Ian Wilson, *Jesus: the evidence*, pp. 158–160.
14. Ibid., p. 160; *Cambridge Medieval History*, Vol I, pp. 9–15.
15. Romer, op. cit., pp. 212–213. Romer mentions this letter and discusses its impact.
16. Ibid., p. 212.
17. Martin E. Marty, *A Short History of Christianity* p. 75.
18. Ian Wilson, op. cit., p. 168.
19. Halsberghe, op. cit. pp. 174–175.

Chapter 8

1. Martin E. Marty, *A Short History of Christianity* p. 99.
2. Ibid., p. 99.
3. Ian Wilson, *Jesus: the evidence*, p. 170.
4. *The Encyclopedia of Religion* Vol 4, p. 126.
5. *Cambridge Medieval History* Vol II, p. 9.
6. *The Encyclopedia of Religion* Vol 11, p. 111.
7. Holger Kersten, *Jesus Lived in India*, p. 215.
8. *New Catholic Encyclopedia* Article on Justinian; Procopius, *The Secret History* — This whole book is full of the worst type of gossip, and imputes the basest of motives to the people discussed, in particular Theodora. Its author's prurience doesn't speak well for his objectivity, but it is likely that much of the book is based on fact. This author's other books of history are highly regarded.
9. John Scott, *The Authentic Jesus*, pp. 23–25.
10. Alfred Guillaume, *Islam*, pp. 16–19.
11. Ibid. pp. 18–19. Alfred Guillaume devoted much of his life to living in Muslim countries and studying Islam.

Chapter 9

1. Martin E. Marty, *A Short History of Christianity*, pp. 72–75.
2. G.P. Fisher, *The History of the Church*, p. 126.
3. Saint Augustine, *Confessions* VIII.12. The passage he read from Paul's letters was Romans 13:13–14.
4. G.P. Fisher, op. cit., pp. 135–140.
5. Saint Augustine, quoted by Martin E. Marty, op. cit., p. 103.
6. Ibid., p. 103.
7. G.P. Fisher, op. cit., p. 141.
8. Martin E. Marty, op. cit., p. 103.
9. Charles Edward Russell, *Charlemagne, First of the Moderns*, pp. 53–54, v.
10. Ibid., pp. 114–118.
11. Timothy O'Neill, *The Irish Hand*, p. 18.
12. Russell, op. cit., pp. 115–116.
13. Ibid., pp. 81–85. Gives an excellent description of the illiteracy, squalor, barbarity, and outright filth of the dark ages.
14. John Romer, *Testament*, pp. 280, 283–384.
15. G.P. Fisher, op. cit., p. 223.
16. H. G. Wells, *A Short History of the World* pp. 184–185.
17. Ibid., p. 185.
18. Martin E. Marty, op. cit., pp. 110–111.
19. Tim Dowley, Ed, *A Lion Handbook, The History of Christianity*, pp. 321, 324.
20. Ibid., pp. 322–323.
21. Ibid., pp. 327–329.
22. Jeanne Achterberg, *Woman As Healer*, p. 85,
23. Quaife, G.R., *Godly Zeal and Furious Rage*, p. 79.
24. Ibid.
25. Jeanne Achterberg.op. cit., p. 85.
26. Ibid., pp. 85, 98.
27. Trevor-Roper, H.R. *The European Witch Craze of the 16th and 17th Centuries*, p. 64.
28. Ibid., p. 65.

29. Ibid., p. 13.
30. Ibid., pp. 24–25; Tim Dowley, op. cit., p. 326.
31. Trevor-Roper, op. cit. pp. 66–67.
32. Ibid., p. 101.
33. Jeanne Achterberg, op. cit., p. 12.
34. *The Burning Times*, documentary. Directed by Donna Read. (National Film Board of Canada, 1990); Quaife, op. cit. pp. 10–11.
35. Quaife, op. cit. p. 12.
36. Jeanne Achterberg, op. cit., p. 90.
37. Trevor-Roper, op. cit. pp. 34–35.
38. Jeanne Achterberg, op. cit., p. 85; Trevor-Roper, op. cit. p. 79.
39. Jeanne Achterberg, op. cit., p. 86.
40. Ibid., p. 88.
41. Ibid., pp. 90–91; Quaife, op. cit., p. 29, which shows that Johann Weyer and Thomas Ady (1656) made the same point. Ady showed the word translated as "witch" in fact had multiple meanings.
42. Quaife, op. cit., p. 15.
43. Ibid., p. 31.
44. Quoted in *The Burning Times*, op. cit.
45. Ibid.,
46. Ibid.,
47. Trevor-Roper, op. cit., p. 27.
48. *The Burning Times*, op. cit.
49. Trevor-Roper, op. cit., pp. 7–14.
50. Jeanne Achterberg, op. cit., p. 98.

Chapter 10

1. H.G. Wells, *A Short History of the World* p. 187; *Cambridge Medieval History*, Vol VI, pp. 131–133, 701; Alfred Guillaume, *Islam*. This whole book is very useful in understanding Islam, but chapters 4 to 7 are particularly relevant.
2. H.G. Wells, op. cit., pp. 187–188; *Cambridge Medieval History*, Vol VI, p. 146.

3. H.G. Wells., op. cit., pp. 188–189; *Cambridge Medieval History*, Vol VI, p. 700.
4. H.G. Wells, op.cit., pp. 191–192; Tim Dowley, Ed, *A Lion Handbook, The History of Christianity* p. 344.
5. John. H. Yoder and Alan Kreider, "The Anabaptists," in *A Lion Handbook, The History of Christianity* (Ed. Tim Dowley) pp. 402–405.
6. Trevor-Roper, H.R. *The European Witch Craze of the 16th and 17th Centuries*, pp. 66–67. Also see chapter 9.
7. A. Lindt., "John Calvin" in *A Lion Handbook*, op. cit., p. 381.
8. Colin Brown, "Reason and Unreason" in *A Lion Handbook*, op cit., pp. 494–495.
9. Robert D. Linder, "The Catholic Reformation" in *A Lion Handbook*, op. cit., pp. 421–423.
10. Anthony C. Thiselton, "An Age of Anxiety" in *A Lion Handbook*, op. cit., p. 623.
11. Matthew Fox, *The Coming of the Cosmic Christ*—Part I outlines the ideas.
12. Bede Griffiths, *The Marriage of East and West*.
13. John Briggs, "Present and Future" in *A Lion Handbook*, op. cit., p. 669.
14. Sri Yukteswar, quoted by Paramahansa Yogananda, *Autobiography of a Yogi*, p. 116.

Chapter 11

1. Vermes, G. *The Dead Sea Scrolls in English*, p. 19. Also see the discussion at the end of chapter 3.
2. Richard Elliot Friedman, *Who Wrote the Bible?*, pp. 17–28.
3. Ibid., pp. 161–216.
4. Ibid, pp. 15–32, 130, 136–149, 246–255; *The Jerusalem Bible*, Popular Edition, Introduction to the Pentateuch, p. 3. Scholars agree that the Deuteronomic source is from the time of King Josiah, just before the fall of Jerusalem (in 587 B.C.), but the dating of the Priestly source is controversial. It was once thought it was written during the exile, but it now seems likely that the author was a Jerusalem priest

during King Hezekiah's reign, just after the fall of the northern kingdom of Israel (in 722 B.C.). The two other date from the time of the two kingdoms, after the reign of King Solomon (about 800 B.C.). It seems the "J" source was written in Judah, and the "E" source in Israel, from the two somewhat different points of view of the priesthoods of each nation. One way of distinguishing between these two older sources is by their use of different names for God. One of these authors calls God Yahweh (or Jehovah) right from the start, so was called "J." The other calls God Elohim up until the time God tells Moses to call Him Yahweh, so has been referred to as "E."

5. Bloom, Harold. *The Book of J*, Translated by David Rosenberg, with comments by Harold Bloom.
6. Robert M. Grant, "Rival Theologies, Gnosticism, Marcion, Origen" in *The Crucible of Christianity*, p. 328.
7. Jeanette Winterson, "God the Sod," *New Statesman*, May 10, 1991.
8. Roland de Vaux, *Ancient Israel*, p. 10. Certainly hospitality was important to nomadic peoples. Vaux discusses this here. But we would have to see a morality which put hospitality way above protecting one's own daughters, as is the case with Lot, as being very primitive.
9. Robert M. Grant, "Rival Theologies, Gnosticism, Marcion, Origen" in *The Crucible of Christianity*, p. 329.
10. Vermes, op. cit., pp. 251–256.
11. Bloom, op. cit., pp. 7, 9; Friedman, op. cit., pp. 87, 50–88.
12. Bloom, op. cit., p. 9.; Friedman, op. cit., p.86. Bloom thinks J was probably a woman. Friedman considers J could have been a woman, both because of J's sympathetic treatment of women such as Tamar, and because women held influential positions in the court of Judah.
13. John Romer, *Testament*, pp. 294–295.
14. Ian Wilson, *Are these the Words of Jesus?* pp. 14–15.
15. Ibid. Ch. 7 in particular.
16. Ibid., p. 139.
17. Ibid., p. 15.

18. Elaine Pagels, *The Gnostic Gospels*, pp. xviii–xix.
19. Ibid., p. 17.
20. Ibid., pp. 17–18, 43. Pagels refers to R. Bultmann *Theology of the New Testament*, trans. by K. Grobel (London, 1965), I, 327; R. Scroggs, "Paul: Sophos and Pneumatikos." *New Testament Studies* 14, 33–55; E. Pagels, *The Gnostic Paul* (Philadelphia, 1975),1–10,55–58, 157-164.
21. Ibid., pp. xix–xx.
22. Ian Wilson, op. cit., pp. 74, 41.
23. Robert M. Grant, "Rival Theologies, Gnosticism, Marcion, Origen" in *The Crucible of Christianity*, p. 326.
24. Elaine Pagels, op. cit., p. 21.
25. Ian Wilson, op. cit., p. 75.
26. Ibid., pp. 74, 41.
27. Ibid., Chapter 5.
28. Elaine Pagels, op. cit., p. xxxv.
29. Ian Wilson, op. cit., Chapter 3.
30. Ibid., p. 10. Note the *Decretum Gelasianum* does list a Gospel of Thomas, but from its content and date it obviously is a totally different book from the Gospel of Thomas found at Nag Hammadi.
31. Bertrand Russell, *Why I Am Not a Christian*, Reprinted from a 1927 lecture, pp. 2, 12.
32. See, for instance, the definition in James Strong, *A Concise Dictionary of the words in the Greek New Testament*, included in *STRONG'S Comprehensive Concordance of The Bible*. p. 17, definition 863.

Chapter 12

1. Steve Bruce, *The Rise and Fall of the New Christian Right*, pp. 29–30.
2. Ibid., p. 68.
3. Ibid., pp. 81–82.
4. Balmer, Randall, *Mine Eyes Have Seen the Glory*, p. 161.
5. For instance, see E. Royston Pike, "Lord Shaftesbury" in *100 Great Modern Lives*, p. 25.

Chapter 13

1. By which, in terms of Christianity, I mean ultra conservative evangelical Christians in general, not only, or even particularly, those who call themselves fundamentalists.
2. It is worth noting that the church of the time of the witch craze had a marked interest in millenarian ideas, in common with modern fundamentalism. See Trevor-Roper, H.R. *The European Witch Craze of the 16th and 17th Centuries*, p. 101.
3. Steve Bruce, *The Rise and Fall of the New Christian Right*, p. 53.
4. Ibid., p. 82.
5. Report on Satanic Abuse of Children, Australian Broadcasting Commission's "7.30 Report," National Edition. 1st Jan., 1993.
6. Jackie Pullinger, *Crack in the Wall*, p. 30.
7. Ibid.
8. Ibid.
9. Some versions say, "If your eyes are good" and "if your eyes are bad," but I have returned to the Greek, which clearly uses the singular "eye" and the word "single." The "eye" here is most probably not a physical eye, but either the spiritual "vision" a person has, or the spiritual "third eye" seen between the eyebrows by those who meditate. These two meanings are very close, and Jesus' single "eye" could even encompass both. Wordsworth was talking about something similar when he referred, in his poem "The Daffodils," to "that inward eye which is the bliss of solitude." Likewise, the "body" being full of light (in most versions), probably refers to the "whole being" being full of light, as the Greek "soma" is derived from a word meaning to be "whole," "well" or "saved," and this meaning ties in better with "eye" meaning "vision."

Chapter 14

1. Bertrand Russell, *What I Believe* (1925), reprinted in
   Why I Am Not a Christian, p. 66.
2. Ibid.
3. Peter Cameron, *Necessary Heresies*, p. 115. Peter Cameron
   talks about Christians he has met who more than just
   having an "unquestioning faith," in fact have an
   "unquestionable faith."
4. Steve Bruce, *The Rise and Fall of the New Christian Right*,
   p. 80.
5. Ibid., p. 183.

Chapter 15

1. Robert Skutch, *Journey Without Distance*, p. 19.
2. See, for instance, James Strong, *A Concise Dictionary of the
   Words in the Greek New Testament*, p. 20, definition 1067.
3. Sri Yukteswar, quoted by Paramahansa Yogananda,
   Autobiography of a Yogi, pp. 125–126.
4. The Bible references for those interested in looking these
   up are Matt 11:23,16:18; Luke 10:15; Acts 2:27,31; 2
   Peter 2:4; Rev 1:18,6:8,20:13,14. The numerous
   references to "Sheol" in the Old Testament can be looked
   up in a concordance under "hell" or "grave."
5. See, for instance, James Strong, op. cit., p. 9, def. 165 a
   p. 78, def. 5550.
6. For instance, the *Macquarie Dictionary's*, definitions of
   "aeon" and "aeonian," giving the Greek meanings of their
   respective roots "aion" and "aionios."
7. By Edith McNeill.

Chapter 16

1. Romans 2:6–8, and 1 Corinthians 3:8, that I know of.
2. John Romer, *Testament*, p. 300.
3. E.G. Rupp and Benjamin Drewery, *Martin Luther*, p.6.
4. One of God's provisions for quickly working through
   karma is the Kriya Yoga, referred to in chapters 19 and 20.

5. Liberal Catholic Church in Australia, 21 St John's Ave., Gordon. NSW 2072, AUSTRALIA (and in 30 other countries around the world), and Self-Realization Fellowship, 3880 San Rafael Avenue, LosAngeles, California 90065, U.S.A. (with centers around the world).

Chapter 17

1. *A Course in Miracles* can be purchased in many book shops.
2. Barbara Thiering, *Jesus the Man.* The "pesher" technique, about to be referred to, is explained in Ch 4, pp. 20–25.
3. Vermes, G. *The Dead Sea Scrolls in English*, pp. 7, 102.
4. Thiering, op. cit., pp. 23–24.
5. Ibid., p. 24.
6. Ibid., p. 21.
7. Ian Wilson, *Jesus: the evidence*, pp. 82–83.
8. Thiering, op. cit., p. 21.
9. Ibid., pp. 90–93.
10. Ibid., pp. 97–100.
11. Ibid., pp. 43–49.
12. Ian Wilson, op. cit., pp. 63–64. A statue of a Roman soldier from these times has been found in Europe, with an inscription below it giving his name as Pantera.
13. Joseph Campbell, *The Masks of God: Occidental Mythology*, pp. 260–261, 336–339.
14. Marianne Williamson, *A Return To Love*, pp. 254–255.
15. Ibid., p. 57.
16. Ibid., p. 21.
17. Ibid., p. xviii.
18. Ibid., p. 61.
19. From *A Course in Miracles*.

Chapter 18

1. John V. Taylor "The Theological Basis of Interfaith Dialogue," the first Lambeth Interfaith Lecture, November 1977, reprinted in *Christianity and Other Religions*, p. 215.

2. John Hick, "Whatever Path Men Choose is Mine," (1974), in *Christianity and Other Religions*, p. 178.

3. John V. Taylor, op. cit., p. 216.

4. John Hick, op. cit., p. 171.

5. Wilfred Cantwell Smith, "The Christian in a Religiously Plural World," (1976), in *Christianity and Other Religions*, p. 90.

6. Karl Rahner, "Christianity and the Non-Christian Religions," (1966), in *Christianity and Other Religions*, p. 54.

7. Wilfred Cantwell Smith, op. cit. p. 99.

8. Ibid., p. 98.

9. John Hick, op. cit., pp. 174–175.

10. Ibid., p. 175.

11. Ibid., p. 176.

12. Ibid.

13. Ibid., p. 174.

14. Ibid., p. 178.

15. Paul Tillich, "Christianity Judging Itself in the Light of its Encounter with the World Religions" (1963), in *Christianity and Other Religions*, p. 120.

16. Huston Smith, *The Religions of Man*, p. 16.

17. Ibid., pp. 4–5. Readers who wish to start their own dialogue with other religions could do no better than to read Huston Smith's book—it is an excellent point of departure.

18. John Hick, op. cit., p. 180.

19. Ibid., pp. 180–181.

20. Ibid., p. 182.

21. Pointed out by Swami Prabhavananda, *The Sermon on the Mount according to Vedanta*, p. 39.

22. *Bhagavad-Gita, The Song of God*, Translated by Swami Prabhavananda and Christopher Isherwood, with an introduction by Aldous Huxley. Chapter 4.

23. Swami Prabhavananda, *The Sermon on the Mount according to Vedanta* p. 41.

24. Paramahansa Yogananda, *Songs of the Soul*, pp. 174–175.

25. *Bhagavad-Gita, The Song of God,* op. cit., Chapter 4.
26. Paramahansa Yogananda, *The Divine Romance,* p. 449.
27. Swami Prabhavananda, *The Sermon on the Mount according to Vedanta* p. 38.
28. My own rendition, compiled from seven different translations from the Sanskrit. The sources of these are: Mahaul R. Copalacharya, *The Heart of the Rigveda,* pp. 409–418; Johnothan Star, *Two Suns Rising,* p. 4.
29. Mahaul R. Copalacharya, *The Heart of the Rigveda,* p. 90.
30. From the title of Bede Griffiths Book *The Marriage of East and West.* Bede Griffiths was a great apostle of the need for Christianity and Hinduism to cooperate and support each other.

Chapter 19

1. Balmer, Randall, *Mine Eyes Have Seen the Glory,* p. 62.
2. I have been unable to track down the exact name of the book, or the name of the cartoonist. I may have the year wrong, but the gist of the story is unforgettable.
3. Balmer, op. cit., p. 33.
4. David and Pat Alexander (Ed.), *The Lion Handbook to the Bible,* pp. 645–646.
5. Ibid., p. 651.
6. For instance, see James Strong, *A Concise Dictionary of the Words in the Greek New Testament,* op. cit., p. 20, definition 1074.
7. Arnold Toynbee, "The Historical Anticedents," in *The Crucible of Christianity,* p. 37.
8. Self-Realization Fellowship, 3880 San Rafael Avenue, Los Angeles, California 90065, U.S.A.
9. Paramahansa Yogananda says essentially this in his commentary on *The Rubaiyat of Omar Khayyam: Wine of the Mystic,* pp 87–88.
10 Alexander, op. cit., p. 654.
11. Sri Yukteswar, quoted by Paramahansa Yogananda, *Autobiography of a Yogi,* pp. 402–403.

Chapter 20

1. Robert Skutch, *Journey Without Distance*, pp. 19–20.
2. Huston Smith, *The Religions of Man*, p. 78.
3. Quoted by Joseph Campbell, in the Documentary series "Joseph Campbell and the Power of Myth," Part 5: "The Masks of Eternity." Apostrophe S Productions, Inc., 1988.
4. This is my own rendition of this part of Psalm 63, made as a result of a careful comparison of the Authorized Version, the NIV, and the Jerusalem Bible. I have tried to keep some of the poetic beauty of the Authorized Version, and keep the translation accurate, while modernizing the language.
5. This information is from a media release on 7th Sept., 1992, of the "Christian Meditation Network." The U.S. address is "John Main Institute, 7315 Brookville Road, Chevy Chase, MD 20815, USA, ph: 301 652 8635." The International Center is at "23 Kensington square, London W8 5HN U.K. ph: 0171 9374679." There are centers and groups in many other countries as well.
6. Laurence Freeman, "Path to the still centre," in *The Tablet*, 21st March 1992.
7. From the publicity for Freeman's talk in Bendigo, Australia, 15th September, 1992.
8. Quoted by Kamala, in *Priceless Precepts*, p. 101.
9. Ibid., p. 12.
10. John Colmer, ed., *Coleridge, Selected Poems*, pp. 67–68.
11. Sri Yukteswar, quoted by Paramahansa Yogananda, *Autobiography of a Yogi*, p. 116.
12. Kahlil Gibran, *Jesus, the Son of Man*, p. 156.
13. Self-Realization Fellowship, 3880 San Rafael Avenue, Los Angeles, California 90065, U.S.A. Ph: (213) 225-2471.
14. Paul Brunton, *The Secret Path*.
15. Carole King, "I Think I Can Hear You," from her album *Rhymes and Reasons* (A&M/Ode records, 1972).
16. A. Hilary Armstrong, "Greek philosophy from the age of Cicero to Plotinus," in *The Crucible of Christianity*, p. 214.
17. To help and inspire you to this, it is well worth reading Brother Lawrence's short book *The Practice of the Presence*

of God. It is one of the great spiritual classics of
Christianity.
18. Paramahansa Yogananda, *Spiritual Diary* entry for July 26.

Bibliography

General Reference:

Cambridge Ancient History. S.A. Cook (Ed). Cambridge At The
  University Press., 1971.
Cambridge Medieval History. Cambridge University Press,
  1924.
Encyclopedia of Religion. Macmillan, 1987.
Encyclopedia of World Mythology. Book Club Associates,
  London 1970.
Macquarie Dictionary. Macquarie Library, Sydney, 1981.
New Catholic Encyclopedia. McGraw Hill, New York, 1967.
Strong, James. *STRONG'S Comprehensive Concordance of The
  Bible*. World Bible Publishers, Iowa Falls.

Sources:

Augustine, Saint. *Confessions*. Penguin Classics,
  Harmondsworth, 1961.
Bhagavad-Gita, The Song of God. Translated by Swami
  Prabhavananda and Christopher Isherwood, with an
  introduction by Aldous Huxley. Vedanta Press, Hollywood,
  California, 1947.**
Copalacharya, Mahaul R. *Heart of the Rigveda*. Somaiyd
  Publications, Bombay, 1971.
Eusebius. *The History of the Church*. Penguin Classics.
  Harmondsworth, 1965. Translation by G.A. Williamson.
Holy Bible, King James Version. At the University Press,
  Cambridge, 1611.
Holy Bible, New International Version. Hodder and Stoughton,
  London, 1978.**
Jerusalem Bible, Popular Edition. Darton, Longman & Todd,
  London, 1974.

Josephus, F. *The Jewish War* Vol II. Translated by H. Thackeray. Leob Classical Library. Heinemann.

Procopius. *The Secret History*. Penguin Classics, Harmondsworth, 1966.*

Roberts, A, and Donaldson. J. *The Ante-Nicene Fathers*, Vol I, containing Irenaeus' "Against Heresies." WM. B Eerdmans Publishing Company, Grand Rapids, 1956.

Vermcs, G. *The Dead Sea Scrolls in English*. Penguin Books, Harmondsworth, 1987.*

Modern Books:

Achterberg, Jeanne. *Woman As Healer*. Rider, London, 1990.

Alexander, David and Pat (Ed.). *The Lion Handbook to the Bible*. Lion Publishing, Herts, England, 1973.

Balmer, Randall. *Mine Eyes Have Seen the Glory*. Oxford University Press, New York, 1993.**

Biran, A. *Temples and High Places in Biblical times*, Jerusalem, 1981.

Bloom, Harold, and Rosenberg, David. *The Book of J*. Grove Weidenfeld, New York, 1991.

Bruce, Steve. *The Rise and Fall of the New Christian Right*, Clarendon Press, Oxford, 1988.

Brunton, Paul. *The Secret Path*. Rider & Company, London, 1934.***

Cameron, Peter. *Necessary Heresies: Alternatives to Fundamentalism*. New South Wales University Press, Sydney, 1993.***

Campbell, Joseph. *The Masks of God: Occidental Mythology*. Souvenir Press, London, 1974.

Canning, John (Ed.). *100 Great Modern Lives*. Century Books, London, 1972.

Chetwode, Penelope. *Kulu: The End of the Habitable World*. John Murray, London, 1972.

Colmer, John, (Ed.). *Coleridge, Selected Poems*, Oxford University Press, 1965.

Cornfield, Gaalyah (Ed.). *The Historical Jesus*. Macmillan, New York, 1982.

Dothan, T. *The Philistines and their Material Culture*. Jerusalem, 1982.

Dowley, Tim, (Editor). *A Lion Handbook, The History of Christianity* Lion, Oxford, 1990.

Douglas, William O., *Beyond the High Himalayas*. Doubleday & Co., Garden City, N.Y., 1952.

Fisher, G.P. *The History of the Church*. Hodder & Stoughton, London, 1922.

Foundation for Inner Peace. *A Course in Miracles*. Foundation for Inner Peace, Inc., Mill Valley CA, 1975.*

Fox, Matthew. *The Coming of the Cosmic Christ*. Harper & Row, New York, 1988.

Frankforter, A. Daniel. *A History of the Christian Movement*. Nelson-Hall, Chicago, 1978.

Friedman, Richard Elliot. *Who Wrote the Bible?* Jonathan Cape, London, 1987.*

Gibran, Kahlil. *Jesus, the Son of Man*, Heineman, London, 1928.*

Griffiths, Bede. *The Marriage of East and West*. HarperCollins, London, 1983.

Guillaume, Alfred. *Islam*. Penguin Books, Harmondsworth, 1956.**

Halsberghe, Gaston H. *The Cult of Sol Invictus*. E.J Brill, Leiden, 1972.**

Harpur, Tom. *For Christ's Sake*. McClelland & Stewart, Toronto, 1986.**

Hick, John, and Hebblethwaite, Brian. (Editors and contributors) *Christianity and Other Religions*. Collins Fount, Glasgow, 1980.*

Kamala, *Priceless Precepts*. Private Printing. P.O. Box 11017 Piedmont Station, Oakland, California 94611, 1969.**

Kersten, Holger. *Jesus Lived in India*. Element books, Shaftesbury, U.K., 1986.*

Kriyananda, Swami. *The Path, Autobiography of a Western Yogi*. Ananda Publications, Nevada City, California, 1977.**

Lawrence, Brother. *The Practice of the Presence of God.* Hodder & Stoughton, London, 1981.

Marty, Martin E. *A Short History of Christianity.* Meridian, New American Library, New York, 1959.

Notovitch, Nicolas. *The Unknown Life of Jesus Christ,* translated from French into English by Alexina Loranger. Tree of Life Publications, Joshua Tree, CA, 1980.*

O'Neill, Timothy. *The Irish Hand,* Translated by James Carney. Dolmen Press, Montrath, Portlaoise, Ireland, 1984.

Pagels, Elaine. *The Gnostic Gospels.* Vintage (Random House), New York, 1979.**

Prabhavananda, Swami. *The Sermon on the Mount according to Vedanta.* Vedanta Press, Hollywood, California, 1963.***

Prophet, Elizabeth Clare. *The Lost Years of Jesus.* Summit University Press, Corwin Springs Montana, 406-848-9891 Web Site: http://www.tsl.org. 1984, 1987. Pocket book edition.

Pullinger, Jackie. *Crack in the Wall.* Hodder and Stoughton, London, 1989.

Quaife, G.R. *Godly Zeal and Furious Rage.* Croom Helm, London, 1987.

Romer, John. *Testament.* Collins Dove, Melbourne, 1989.

Rupp, E.G. and Drewery, Benjamin. *Martin Luther.* Edward Arnold, London, 1970.

Russell, Bertrand. *Why I Am Not a Christian.* George Allen & Unwin, London, 1957.*

Russell, Charles Edward. *Charlemagne, First of the Moderns.* Haughton Mifflin Company, Boston, 1930.

Schurer, Emil. *The History of the Jewish People in the Age of Jesus Christ.* T & T Clark LD, Edinburgh, 1973.

Scott, John. *The Authentic Jesus.* HarperCollins, London,1992.

Skutch, Robert. *Journey Without Distance.* Celestial Arts, Berkeley, CA, 1984.*

Smith, Huston. *The Religions of Man.* Harper & Row, New York, 1958.**

Star, Johnothan. *Two Suns Rising.* Bantam, New York, 1991.

Thapar, Romilar. *A History of India 1*. Penguin Books, Harmondsworth, 1966.

Thiering, Barbara. *Jesus the Man*. Doubleday, Sydney, 1992.

Toynbee, Arnold (Ed. & contributer), *The Crucible of Christianity*, Judaism, Hellenism and the historical background to the Christian Faith. Thames and Hudson, London, 1969.

Trevor-Roper, H.R. *The European Witch Craze of the 16th and 17th Centuries*. Penguin, Harmondsworth, 1969.

Vaux, Roland de. *Ancient Israel, Its Life and Institutions*. English translation by John McHugh. Darton, Longman & Todd, London, 1961.

Watts, Alan (Introduction by) *A Pilgrim's Guide to Planet Earth*. Spiritual Community Publications, San Rafael, California, 1974.

Wells, H.G., *A Short History of the World*. Watts & C0., London, 1948.***

Williamson, Marianne. *A Return To Love*. Aquarian, an imprint of HarperCollins, New York, 1992.***

Wilson, A.N. *Jesus*. Sinclair-Stevenson, London, 1992.

Wilson, Ian. *Are These the Words of Jesus?* Lennard Publishing, Oxford, 1990.*

Wilson, Ian. *Jesus: the evidence*. HarperCollins, N.Y., 1988.

Yogananda, Paramahansa. *The Divine Romance*. Self Realization Fellowship, Los Angeles, 1986.**

Yogananda, Paramahansa. *Songs of the Soul*. Self-Realization Fellowship, Los Angeles, 1983.**

Yogananda, Paramahansa. *Spiritual Diary*. Self-Realization Fellowship, Los Angeles, 1982.**

Yogananda, Paramahansa. *Autobiography of a Yogi*. Self-Realization Fellowship, Los Angeles, 1981 (Hard-cover edition)***

Yogananda, Paramahansa., *Wine of the Mystic*. Self-Realization Fellowship, Los Angeles, 1984.**

Youngman, Bernard R. *The Lands and Peoples of the Living Bible*. Bell Publishing, New York, 1959.

Note: asterisks indicate recommended reading.

Index

Order Form

☎ Telephone orders: Toll Free: 1(800) 460-6690

✉ Postal orders:
   Publication Services, Inc.
   8803 Tara Lane,
   Austin, Texas 78737

❑ Please send me a copy of *In Search of the Loving God*, at $16.95 + $1.00 shipping

❑ Please send me___copies of *In Search of the Loving God*, at $16.95 each + $1.00 total shipping. (free shipping on additional copies)

Please send my book(s) to:

Name:_____

Address:_____

City:_____ State:____ Zip:_____

Phone: (___)_____

Payment:

❑ Check or money order ❑ Visa ❑ Mastercard
Card Number:_____

Name on card:_____Exp. Date:___/___

Please make checks out to: Publication Services, Inc.

Call *toll free* and order now